Lifelines and Deadlines

Selected Nonfiction

Also by James Lovegrove

Novels
The Hope
Days
The Foreigners
Untied Kingdom
Worldstorm
Provender Gleed

With Peter Crowther
Escardy Gap

The Pantheon series
The Age Of Ra
The Age Of Zeus
The Age Of Odin
Age Of Aztec
Age Of Voodoo
Age Of Godpunk
Age Of Shiva

The Redlaw series
Redlaw
Redlaw: Red Eye

The Dev Harmer Missions
World Of Fire
World Of Water

Novellas
How The Other Half Lives
Gig
Age Of Anansi
Age Of Satan
Age Of Gaia

Sherlock Holmes
The Stuff Of Nightmares
Gods Of War
The Thinking Engine

Collections of Short Fiction
Imagined Slights
Diversifications

For Younger Readers
The Web: Computopia
Warsuit 1. 0
The Black Phone

For Reluctant Readers
Wings
The House of Lazarus
Ant God
Cold Keep
Dead Brigade
Kill Swap
Free Runner

The 5 Lords Of Pain series
The Lord Of The Mountain
The Lord Of The Void
The Lord Of Tears
The Lord Of The Typhoon
The Lord Of Fire

Writing as Jay Amory
The Clouded World series
The Fledging Of Az Gabrielson
Pirates Of The Relentless Desert
Darkening For A Fall
Empire Of Chaos

"As a survey of the field over the last few decades this collection really can't be bettered. Lovegrove knows how to temper his wide knowledge with wit, how to cut to the heart of a well-judged critical assessment, and he's simply incapable of filing dull copy. He's always fair, always readable, always wise. If there's a better reviewer of SF, Fantasy and Horror working today, then I'd like to meet them. Mind you, I'd like to meet anybody, really. I'm bitterly lonely."

— *Adam Roberts, author of Jack Glass, Saint Rebor, and Sibilant Fricative.*

Lifelines and Deadlines

Selected Nonfiction

James Lovegrove

Steel Quill Books
An Imprint of NewCon Press

First edition, published in the UK September 2015
by Steel Quill Books,
an Imprint of NewCon Press
41 Wheatsheaf Road, Alconbury Weston, Cambs, PE28 4LF

SQ002 (softback)

10 9 8 7 6 5 4 3 2 1

ISBN: 978-1-910935-00-2 (softback)

Cover art © 2014 by Adam Brockbank
Cover layout by Storm Constantine

Minor Editorial Interference by Ian Whates
Interior layout by Storm Constantine

Contents

Introduction

"James," I hear you scream (in a politely exasperated manner), "why *Lifelines And Deadlines*? Why that title? What does it mean?"

Well, this is a collection of journalism, so that ought to explain the deadlines part. Journalism is all about filing copy in time. If you're like me, someone who hates to be caught slacking and can't abide last-minute rush jobs, that means in *very* good time.

As for the lifelines part...

When you're a professional author, your income is irregular. It comes in the form of advances, which arrive whenever you sign a contract, deliver a manuscript and have a book published, and royalties, which crop up twice a year in spring and autumn. There's also the annual Public Lending Right payout – money accruing from library loans of your books – every February, and any foreign language rights sales that happen to turn up out of the blue.

So consistent paid work, which journalism can be, is a godsend. It can get you through the lean months. It's reliable. It supports you. A lifeline.

I first embarked on a parallel career as a reviewer in the mid-90s, contributing to the nonfiction section of esteemed SF semi-pro 'zine *Interzone*. Editor David Pringle very kindly allowed this twenty-something tyro author, with only one published novel under his belt, room to roam in his magazine's back pages (as well as accepting the occasional short story off me).

The arrangement continued even after I moved from the UK to the States for a couple of years. In that pre-internet age, getting my work to David entailed sending 3½-inch floppy disks across the Atlantic in special little cardboard packets. It was costly and labour-intensive, but that's how we rolled in the days before the World Wide Web was spun.

The early reviews in this book are culled from that era and mix big-name authors and trad SF with quirky first-timers and space oddities.

From there we segue into reviews I wrote during the early noughties for the Alien Online website, founded and curated by Darren Turpin (or Ariel, to use the *nom de keyboard* he went by back then). These include a vituperative vivisection of a novel called *Gene* by Stel Pavlou which caused such a kerfuffle it effectively killed the site. The piece was a hatchet job pure and simple, and Mr Pavlou objected strongly to it, and one thing led to another, and no more Alien Online. I don't regret a word I wrote – it's a truly wretched book – but I do regret the furore it caused and the unfortunate, unintended consequences.

The incident did, moreover, provoke one of the most vividly memorable descriptions I have ever read of the risks inherent in reviewing. Adam Roberts, defending my honour and integrity in a forum thread, wrote that, "Lovegrove is an author himself, so understands what it is to be criticised as well as to criticise. His balls are, as it were, swinging out there." A charming image, that. Thank you, Adam.

I graduated to writing for a broadsheet newspaper, the *Financial Times* no less, in 2007, after the then books pages editor Rosie Blau commissioned an essay from me tying together four recent SF novel releases. It's here in the Essays section of this book under the title "The Terrestrial Alien".

Rosie must have liked what I did, because I quickly became the Pink 'Un's go-to SF reviewer, and also for a time its teen fiction reviewer, and latterly its children's book reviewer. Her stringent editing – and that of her successors Rebecca Rose, Lorien Kite, Isabel Berwick and Neville Hawcock – has helped me hone my craft and taught me to weigh every sentence, every clause, carefully. The inflexible word counts which are part and parcel of newspaper journalism have also assisted in that regard.

That's the reviews. Then there are the forewords which, as with the entries in each section of the book, appear in chronological order. These intros were commissioned by my friend and erstwhile collaborator Pete Crowther for various of the books produced by his PS Publishing imprint. PS, in case you don't know, is a boutique outfit whose commitment to genre publishing is second to none. Whether it's a lavishly illustrated, slipcased, limited-print-run edition of a Stephen King novel or a simple, slender hardback chapbook showcasing short stories by some no less admired but perhaps more obscure writer, you can't really go wrong with a PS title.

Under the Essays heading you will find the following: incidental pieces I have composed for various blogs; more of those multi-book reviews for the *FT*; an appreciation of Colin Wilson, an author whose nonfiction exerted a profound influence on me in my twenties (the article appeared in an *SFX* special edition on the subject of the paranormal); and a lengthy thesis on apocalyptic SF, which formed part of an academic survey of the many genres of science fiction, *Strange Divisions And Alien Territories*, edited by Keith Brooke and published by Palgrave Macmillan.

Last but not least, we come to the Comics section. Comics have been my passion since I was little. You'll learn how I first discovered them in the piece entitled "Four-Colour Freak". You'll also encounter some blog pieces on the topic, some reviews of graphic novels (mostly for the Alien Online), and some themed essays. The entries in the last category were penned for the sadly now defunct magazine *Comic Heroes*, under the editorial aegises – aeges? aegii? – of Jes Bickham, Matt Bielby and Dave Golder.

If you're not a comics fan, I'd advise you to skip this section. Then again, I'd advise you not to. If I can somehow infect you with the comics bug through my enthusiasm for the medium, that would be deeply gratifying.

Finally, I have to thank Ian Whates of NewCon Press for agreeing to publish *Lifelines And Deadlines*. It may not be a dead cert for the bestseller lists but it is the work of an ardent, zealous reader trying his best to communicate what he loves – and in a few instances doesn't love – about these artefacts we call books and the worlds they can open up and the flights of imagination they can inspire.

In the lines that follow – written to order, written to fill column inches, written to pay bills – I hope there's life.

– J. M. H. L.
November 2014

Reviews

Fairyland by Paul J. McAuley (1995)

The possibilities that genetic engineering opens up for mankind are as awesome as they are terrifying. The thought of tampering with the very stuff of which we are made should fill any sane human being with a deep sense of unease, and yet at the same time who would not welcome gene-therapy cures for cancer, heart disease, AIDS? Who would not want the ageing process retarded or a serious deformity corrected? And yet what if it turns out that prolonged youth is available only to the very wealthy? And who defines the criteria for physical perfection? What is physical perfection anyway? Looking like Cher? Like Pamela Anderson? Like, for crying out loud, Michael Jackson?

Fertile soil, and in *Fairyland* Paul J. McAuley has harvested a barn-full. Here is a near future where genetic engineering has run amok, where altering your RNA with a twist of nanotechnology is as easy as altering your lager with a twist of lime, and where what was once the province of the men in white coats is now sold on the streets like crack-cocaine. In short, yet another mystery of science has become commonplace, just as the electricity that powers your home was once a mere spark in Faraday's laboratory.

Fairyland centres around Alex Sharkey, gene hacker and designer of exquisite viral drugs that tweak the double-helix and fuck the mind; an overweight mummy's boy with a Wildean sense of fashion and a well-developed sense of self-preservation. When a drug-deal goes bad, Alex is forced to ally himself with Milena, a hyper-intelligent nine-year-old who needs his help to pull off an audacious scheme. She wants to take 'dolls' – genetically-tailored baboons who do all the mindless, menial work, the Epsilons of this particular brave new world – and transform them into independently thinking creatures capable of reproducing and evolving.

Thanks to Alex's biotechnological know-how, she succeeds – in spades. Drawing on the mythologies of human culture, the newly invented subspecies refashion themselves as a superior race with talents and tastes that render them indistinguishable from fairies – not the fey, sprightly creatures that skip through Victorian literature and the Cottingley photographs but the full-on, grudge-toting, child-abducting, mighty morphin power strangers of *Tam Lin* and middle-European folklore. These guys have little regard or respect for humans. All they want is a place of their own where they can live and breed undisturbed – a fairyland – and woe betide whoever gets in the way of their ambition.

Unwittingly, or perhaps through the agencies of a higher power, Alex again and again finds himself on hand to experience the birth-pangs of successive fairy generations. Struggling to come to terms with the monsters he has created, he is at once Frankenstein and helpless onlooker, tragic hero and comic figure. During an unusually creepy battle in a darkened Albanian forest, as venom-spitting and stealth-cloaked fairies attack from the trees, he gladly leaves the fighting to his companions; his priorities are intellectual and more abstract. He is the classic passive protagonist, the done-to rather than the doer, a quality he shares with the central characters of other McAuley novels such as *Red Dust* and *Pasquale's Angel* – men caught up in circumstances beyond their control, simply trying to survive. But, though he would prefer to keep his distance, Alex has more in common with his creations than he might perhaps wish. Like the fairies, he is seeking a fairyland of his own, one engendered by his childhood memories of London and living with his mother, and like the fairies he shape-shifts – changing his identity, his name (for names have power), even his motives – in the name of self-preservation. Much of the 'father' is reflected in his 'children'.

Fairyland is a kaleidoscope of realities, some virtual, some drug-altered. Dozens of different characters flit through its pages, adding to the impressionistic vision of a planet in chaos. Even with Alex at its core (an unreliable lynchpin at best), events in the novel seem to fragment as they unfold. The distinctions between the fairies' self-perpetuating mythology and the harsh facts of a cyber-future become blurred. Nothing is certain. The reader is entering a fairyland of McAuley's creation, and the rules are... There are no rules. Make no mistake, *Fairyland*, despite its title, is hard SF – 'hard' as in techno-buff, but also as in difficult. The ideas and the prose are densely woven. Skipping a single sentence can also mean missing a major plot point. But the rewards for the concentration the novel demands are memorable images, brain-inverting concepts and flashes of arid humour (for instance, a viral drug that gives you a complete UFO abduction experience complete with "fuzzy false memories of rape" is called the

Strieber). If McAuley isn't on your reading-list already, *Fairyland* is as good an introduction as any to the work of this frighteningly intelligent and intelligently frightening SF author.

Rose Madder by Stephen King (1995)

Rose Madder might be regarded as the third in a trilogy of 'spousal abuse' novels by Stephen King, the first two being *Gerald's Game* and *Dolores Claiborne*. Shorter, more intimate and with a narrower focus than King's usual 600-page plus behemoths, these three books take the theme of men using their positions of authority and superior physical strength to belittle and harm their wives and then show how the wives fight back, using guile and cunning instead of brute force. Men are King's new monsters, not vampires, not rabid St. Bernards, not haunted cars, not mad axe-wielding ex-nurses; men who bully, torment, beat and despise the so-called weaker sex because they can do it and because, thanks to centuries of tacit approval of this kind of behaviour, they can get away with it.

Rosie Daniels is married to a beast of a human being called Norman. When we first see her she is crouched in the corner of their living room in the throes of a miscarriage brought on by her husband's fists. He is in the kitchen washing his hands and humming 'When a Man Loves a Woman'. It's a shocking, hideous moment, the proverbial punch in the gut that softens the reader up for what follows.

After fourteen years of this kind of treatment, Rosie finally snaps and, scarcely able to believe what she is doing, leaves home. She heads off to an unnamed city, starts a new life, stumbles into a well-paid job, finds a genuinely good man to love – the only problem is, Norman, as well as being a vicious bastard, is a cop. He's trained to track people down. So, no matter how well Rosie tries to hide her trail, sooner or later he's going to catch up with her, and then he's not going to plead with her to come back to him; he's going to make sure she never goes home to anyone ever again...

Unlike *Gerald's Game* and *Dolores Claiborne*, in which the supernatural events are pushed so far into the background as to be almost undetectable, in *Rose Madder* King embraces the story's fantastical elements with a total lack of inhibition. Shortly after arriving in the city Rosie comes across a painting in a pawn shop that, when hung on the wall in her apartment, transforms into a gateway into a mythical world of female power. There, she learns all that is magical and terrifying about womanhood, and there, too, resides her only hope of defeating

Norman. 'Rose Madder' is not just the name of an artist's pigment; it becomes the name of the goddess-like being depicted in the painting and also an emblem of the ascendance of Rosie's darker side.

Had this been a book written by a woman, it would be easy to dismiss it as a wish-fulfilment fantasy of female empowerment, *Thelma and Louise* meets *Alice Through the Looking-Glass*. Since it has been written by a man, his motives deserve scrutiny. King has been accused of an inability to flesh out believable female characters. With *Rose Madder* and its two thematic predecessors, did he set himself the challenge of responding to that criticism? Or perhaps, given the Pro-Choice sub-plot in *Insomnia*, women's issues have become his foremost concern, the way the secret machinations of government used to be. Each, in its way, concerns the abuse of power, after all.

The sad fact is that *Rose Madder*, for all its undoubted worthiness, is suspenseless and dull. The novel only really sings when we see things from Norman's point of view. His racist, profane interior monologue is filled with the King *bon mots* we know and love, and his savage misogyny is far more credible than the bitter-edged saintliness of the women at the refuge where Rosie first finds sanctuary after arriving in the city. Perhaps the awful truth is that we would prefer to read (and write) about monsters rather than saints, and that, as Milton discovered with Satan, an author can't help giving his devils all the best lines.

King must at least be admired for trying to push the envelope of his talent when it would be all too easy for an author in his exalted position to turn out one *Needful Things* after another.

The Lost World by Michael Crichton (1995)

It's hard to feel sorry for Michael Crichton – phenomenally successful author, film-maker and TV producer, with an annual income reported to be in the region of $40 million – but the pressures he was under while writing the sequel to *Jurassic Park* must have been awful. Thanks to Spielberg and some breathtaking computer animation and animatronic model-work, *Jurassic Park* is no longer Crichton's baby; it has grown and mutated into a multimillion-dollar monster, a Frankenstein franchise. So any chance that the sequel might expand on the premise of the original, might take off in new and unexpected directions, was doomed from the outset. Crichton has had to keep one eye on the fact that the book is inevitably going to be adapted into a movie, and movie sequels as a rule chew up, swallow and digest the elements that made the first movie successful then vomit them up in a less appetising mixture. In *The Lost World* the constraints Crichton was under show. Unless he is a man truly unafraid of compromise, even he must have felt, as he pounded the book out, that he was selling himself, and admirers of the first novel, short.

For a start there's that title. The Lost World theory is, apparently, a well-known hypothesis in palaeontological circles, referring to the possibility that somewhere on the planet there is a self-contained environment so isolated from human civilisation that dinosaurs still exist there, as postulated by Conan Doyle in his novel of that name. Back when Doyle was writing, that such a pocket of the past could have survived would have seemed plausible. Nowadays, in a world that has been charted by satellite to the smallest pixel, it's more of an intellectual conceit than anything. The theory has some relevance to Crichton's novel, in as much as most of the action takes place on a remote island where dinosaurs left over from the Jurassic Park breeding program have been allowed to roam free, and the word 'lost' carries echoes of the book's subtextual concern, which is the problem of extinction, but still, to use the title of one of the first and best-known dinosaur novels for your own dinosaur novel shows either perversity, hubris or a terrible lack of imagination.

As to the plot, it is virtually indistinguishable from that of *Jurassic Park*. Six years on, the park on Isla Nublar has been closed down and all the dinosaurs there destroyed. But it is rumoured that large lizard-like creatures are turning up on the coast of Costa Rica, dead from some inexplicable disease. Richard Levine, an independently wealthy and intellectually arrogant young palaeontologist, is putting together an expedition to investigate the rumours, and enlists the aid of chaos mathematician Ian Malcolm (the only character from the previous book to reappear in the sequel). Malcolm, who as we all know was badly injured on a similar expedition six years ago, is at first reluctant to go, but his scientific curiosity gradually gets the better of him, and when Levine disappears on a scouting mission to a second island where he believes the dinosaurs are located, Malcolm is obliged to mount a rescue mission. He is accompanied by his friend and not-quite-lover Sarah Harding, a ballsy biologist, and by two engineers, Thorne and Carr, who have built vehicles and weapons to Levine's specifications that should be able to cope with the sort of creatures they expect to encounter. Oh, and there are two kids, Kelly and Arby, who tag along for the ride as stowaways.

And it's the inclusion of the kids that clues us in as to what's going on here. The two children in *Jurassic Park*, the novel, were peripheral characters. In the movie, thanks to Spielberg, the action centred around them. In *The Lost World*, only by the most artificial of plot devices can Crichton get Kelly and Arby to the island, and it seems even he cannot believe he has been quite so cynical, because he is thereafter unable to justify their presence in the novel or make either of them credible as characters. Kelly and Arby are not ordinary children. They are geeky geniuses who are both, of course, fiendishly handy with computers. They talk like adults, but at the same time their sole function is to ask basic but pertinent questions whenever anything complicated needs explaining in terms simple enough that a genius kid, or the average adult, can understand.

Kelly and Arby are the shrillest harmonics in the strained note of contrivance that resounds through *The Lost World*. To manoeuvre his characters, with all their expensive, specially-designed equipment, into situations where they are in danger of being eaten, Crichton has to twist plot and motivation into pretzel shapes, and although there is the occasional palm-sweat moment, for the most part the T. rex chases and raptor attacks and all-terrain vehicle crashes are lacklustre and perfunctory, there not because they belong but because they are expected. It goes without saying that the dinosaurs act, as they did in the original book, as a kind of moral nemesis: all the 'bad' characters end up as dino-dinner, all the 'good' characters survive.

One of the 'bad' characters goes by the name of Lewis Dodgson, and if Crichton wants us to make the association with the author of *Alice in Wonderland*, we can only do so disparagingly. *Jurassic Park* was, indeed, a Wonderland, but *The Lost World* fails to take us through the looking-glass, merely holds up a dull, distorted mirror to its predecessor.

Raptor Red by Robert T. Bakker (1995)

Palaeontologist Robert T. Bakker claims to have been an 'unofficial consultant' to the special-effects artists involved in the making of the movie of *Jurassic Park*, by which one assumes he means they asked him for a lot of advice on dinosaurs but didn't pay him for it. Now he has decided, quite rightly, to grab a piece of the pie for himself with *Raptor Red*, the story of a female Utahraptor (the palaeontologically correct name for the velociraptor) and her struggle to survive in prehistoric America, find a mate and raise a family of little baby Utahraptors.

As plots go, it's hardly a bone fragment, but then Bakker has deliberately avoided anthropomorphisation, and without human-like dialogue and interaction there's not a lot that can be achieved in the way of dramatic tension or character arcs when your cast consists entirely of big lizards and small mammals. Evolutionary necessity and natural selection are the prime motivating factors in *Raptor Red*. The novel is a single strand in the vast ongoing story of Life, and yet in spite of the fact that she embodies all that is brutal, cunning and selfish in Nature, Raptor Red herself comes across as an admirable and indomitable figure. Reading the book, you find yourself growing fond of a vicious predator, a dinosaur no less.

Bakker writes in a chatty, informal style. Sometimes his datadumps are a little too long on detail, and he has a penchant for bizarre, ungainly sound effects – TTTTTWUNK! , Whoooph-whoooph, Zip-blb-blb-blb, Bffffffft – but his gift for getting you inside the head of, say, a turtle and seeing and hearing and smelling everything from a turtle's point of view is remarkable, and the whole lost world of a hundred and twenty million years ago is wonderfully realised. How much of what Bakker is offering us is fact and how much supposition is open to debate, but then the processes of palaeontology are not unlike those of fiction – the extrapolation of what you know into the larger context of what you don't know but feel to be true.

In short, *Raptor Red* is more than just an expanded footnote to *Jurassic Park*. It's a unique and thought-provoking work that takes a scaffold of science and builds imaginatively on it. Well worth a look.

The 6 Messiahs by Mark Frost (1995)

Sir Arthur Conan Doyle, author of the original *The Lost World*, appears as the hero of Mark Frost's *The 6 Messiahs*, as he did in its predecessor *The List of 7*. In that novel the young Doyle, still a struggling author, enjoyed a breathless adventure in the company of Jack Sparks, secret agent to Her Majesty the Queen, in which they fought reanimated mummies, giant slugs and a conspiracy to topple the throne masterminded by an evil genius who happened to be Sparks' older brother. *The 6 Messiahs* takes place a decade on, during which time Doyle's best-known literary creation has brought him unprecedented success and international fame. Already Doyle is beginning to tire of the adulation, and his mood of frustration and jaded enthusiasm sets the tone for the whole novel.

Doyle is on a publicity trip to the United States, accompanied by his younger brother Innes. While crossing the Atlantic, they stumble on a plot to steal the great texts of the world's main religions. Joined by a mysterious priest, they follow the trail through New York and Chicago to a place called the New City in the Arizona desert, where a weird cult have their headquarters. Several other people have been drawn to the New City by dream-visions of an ominous dark tower, and with their aid Doyle confronts a madman who has plans to unleash a momentous, apocalyptic evil on the world. You can guess the rest.

The identities of the mysterious priest and the madman are pretty obvious from the word go, and for some reason turn-of-the-century America offers a less amenable setting for this sort of Victorian hokum than dear old Blighty, but Frost has at least tried to make the sequel different from the original. *The 6 Messiahs* puts a dark, world-weary spin on the joyous absurdities of *The List of 7*, resulting in a leaner, gloomier and ultimately less riveting read, but it's fun all the same.

Blue Mars by Kim Stanley Robinson (1996)

With *Blue Mars* Kim Stanley Robinson brings to an end an impressive feat of science-based worldbuilding, a chronicle of over two hundred years of future history so immaculately realised that it has seemed, at times, to be the truth foretold. Of course they probably said much the same about *The Shape of Things To Come*, but Wells' speculations had more to do with his political inclinations and desires than with prescience. Robinson is not averse to utopian dreaming either, but his *Mars* trilogy grounds the utopian ideal in practical possibility and sets out a blueprint for achieving it, detailing the journey rather than the destination. This, combined with Robinson's depth of research in an awesome array of fields, his sinewy, allusive prose and his firm grasp of the flaws and foibles that add depth to character, works the miracle of making a dream appear not just worthy of pursuit but attainable.

For anyone who has read the preceding volumes in the trilogy, *Blue Mars* feels just like coming home. Michel the psychotherapist, Ann the geologist (as hard and as stratified with secrets as the rocks she studies), the scientifically brilliant but socially autistic Sax, Maya the irascible earth mother, dark horse Nadia, the peripatetic and possibly mad Coyote... meeting these characters again is like joining up with old friends after a long absence. The tie that binds them together as members of the fabled First Hundred who began the process of colonising and terraforming the Red Planet also binds them to us. We have been with them ever since they landed on Mars and took their first tentative toddling steps out onto the low-g surface. We have observed their squabbles and shifting alliances, we have endured with them the struggle for independence from Earth in both *Red Mars* and *Green Mars*, and in *Blue Mars* we see them enjoying the fruits of the peace and prosperity they have laboured so long and hard to engineer. Impossibly advanced in years, their lives artificially extended, they are coming to grips with the fact that they have done as much as any human beings can ever hope to, and also coming to grips with a condition arising as a result of their prolonged senescence, namely that while their physical faculties remain unimpaired, their mental faculties are, alarmingly, starting to fail. They are living legends, responsible for founding a new civilisation, one based on fairness, equality, justice, and care for the environment, one that is genuinely civilised, but what are they to do now when such a past is behind them, and what is the use of owning such a past if their memory cells, unable to cope with three times as much information as they were designed to hold, are failing, and it is becoming harder and harder to remember anything?

The Mars of *Blue Mars*, with its elegantly designed townships and ship-towns, its huge expanses of unspoilt territory, the freedom for everyone to do pretty much as he or she pleases, a communal sense of working together for a greater good, and the opportunity for spectacularly adventurous leisure activities, is a virtual Eden, and therein lies the problem for its inhabitants. To the twenty billion denizens of a flooded, teeming, full-to-bursting Earth, the next-door neighbour planet is the Promised Land, the new America, and naturally every Terran wants to move there. Solving that problem and helping draft a new constitution for this New World occupies the surviving members of the First Hundred for most of the novel, giving them a focus in their declining years, a pin around which to fasten the crumbling fragments of lives made redundant by success and the rise of younger, brighter generations. Regrettably, the minutiae of political wrangling and constitution-drafting make for some patience-testing chapters, Robinson so caught up in his knowledge of systems of government and his (admittedly inspired) synthesis of history's more successful modes of democracy that he often appears to be overlooking one fundamental point, namely that the reader is possibly marginally less obsessed with the nitty-gritty of the worldbuilding process than he is and wants to get back to the characters and the story. Impressive these passages may be, but a pleasure to peruse? Perhaps.

But one can forgive Robinson such longeurs for the effusive, exotic brilliance that abounds elsewhere in *Blue Mars*. The chapters dealing with the return to Earth of Sax, Maya and Michel – and the first visit of Nirgal, a native-born Martian, to the cradle of humanity – are vibrant with both the nostalgia and the strangeness of the experience. After so long away, for the Martian colonists Earth has become the alien planet, the 'Mars'. The gravity is crushing, the colours painfully vivid, the air thick to breathe – all of which reminds Sax, Maya and Michel that the world they have helped create can never be another Earth and that therefore it must always be somewhere new, different and hopefully better. Nirgal, meanwhile, seven foot tall, narrow-chested, bronze-skinned, is truly of another species, a human being who does not belong and cannot physiologically handle Earth – the paradox is reinforced when he contracts a potentially lethal pulmonary illness from an Earth virus and has to be hastily shuttled back to Mars. Going home has other drawbacks, as Michel discovers when a brief stay in his native Provence leaves him almost incurably homesick.

The question of home is one of the book's central themes – what constitutes home, whether a person defines his or her own sense of place or a sense of place defines the person – and the answer, Robinson suggests, is that home is not just where your memories tell you you belong but where the environment welcomes you and lets you be. It's another facet of the old nature/nurture debate. People are not simply the products of the commingling of their parents' genes but of where and how they were brought up. Thus when Sax attempts to restore the failing memories of the remaining members of the First Hundred, he isn't just trying to save them from disorientating mental blackouts and unwelcome peak experiences but, in effect, trying to recreate them anew, to remind them once again of who they are and what they have done and why they deserve to be proud of themselves and the society they have founded. If Sax can, with a few casual taps of a computer keyboard, bring about an ice age (as he does), or bring his friends, in effect, back to life, then science in Robinson's twenty-third century has given men the powers of gods, but *Blue Mars* is telling us that divinity is worthless unless it is tempered with a sense of self and its close cousin, a sense of place.

The Reality Dysfunction by Peter F. Hamilton (1996)

Peter F. Hamilton's *The Reality Dysfunction* projects us three hundred or so years into the future, to a time when the golden age is in full swing and far-flung corners of the galaxy have been colonised by humans whom genetic engineering has rendered long-lived and physically perfect, godlike if not quite true gods. Biotechnology has made possible quasi-telepathic communication across the gulfs of space, and sentient spaceships ply the spacelanes, empathically linked to their human captains. The distinction between artificial intelligence and the human mind, between inorganic and organic, has become so blurred as to be all but meaningless. Disease is nonexistent, sexual promiscuity is rife, safe and enthusiastically endorsed, and you can drink almost as much as you want to without serious ill-effect, which most SF convention attendees would indeed consider a blessing.

From the moment *The Reality Dysfunction* begins, it is clear that Hamilton's joy in science-tethered flights of fancy is going to be infectious. The first chapter is pure space opera, all exploding starships and (literally) bone-shattering g-forces. Hurrah! But it is also clear that everything is destined to go Horribly Wrong. After all, there is nothing intrinsically interesting about a golden age. Perfection is boring to write about. Without conflict, where is the story? The creation or destruction of a golden age, on the other hand, offers meatier material to work with, and once Hamilton gets going dismantling his twenty-sixth century status quo, *The Reality Dysfunction* really takes off. This happens about a third of the way into the book, which means there are three hundred pages of scene-setting to get through first. Those three hundred pages are vital, since you can't establish several different races and worlds and a huge cast of characters in just a handful of chapters, and they aren't dull – Hamilton knows better than most SF writers that a good, short, sharp shock of action can spice up even the plainest infodump – but they are there and they do have to be ingested and digested before the fireworks can commence, like the nutritious slices of bread and butter you used to have to eat at teatime as a child before you were allowed to start in on the jam tarts and cake.

Principally we are introduced to two main offshoots of the human race, the Adamists and the Edenists (the latter enjoying constant access to a consensual collective consciousness), and to two pivotal characters. The first is Joshua Calvert, who dreams of refitting and flying his father's ship, the *Lady Macbeth*, and whose space pilot's instincts are matched only by his arrant precociousness. The other is Ione Saldana, beautiful young empress of the artificial satellite habitat Tranquillity, with whom Joshua has lots of splendidly athletic sex (with Ione, that is, not with the artificial satellite habitat, although in Hamilton's twenty-sixth century anything is possible). The queen and the roguish hero are an odd couple as old as Malory, or perhaps as *Star Wars*, but in Hamilton's hands they are no mere cliché; they are more complex than that. Ione is in many ways reminiscent of Julia Evans, the multibillionaire heiress and philanthropic businesswoman from Hamilton's previous trio of novels, the Greg Mandel books, but her power exceeds even Julia's. Thanks to her mental affinity with Tranquillity, Ione sees and hears everything that goes on within her realm, although this gift is always underplayed and sometimes humorously glossed. Joshua, meanwhile, is the archetypal reluctant hero, inspired to heroic deeds either by self-interest or in spite of his best interests. Space opera has always been about traditions, and Joshua and Ione are perhaps *The Reality Dysfunction*'s only two stereotypes, but for all that Hamilton gives them engaging and credible personalities and handles well the uncertain pitch and yaw of their love affair.

Joshua and Ione are the book's emotional core, its Lancelot and Guinevere, its top-billed stars, but there are several other characters of equal importance and a host of supporting players, far too many to enumerate here. The action centres on a frontier planet, Lalonde, and follows a group of recently arrived colonists as they travel upriver to their new home and, inevitably, towards a heart of darkness. Initially the evil resides in the soul of Quinn Dexter, one of the group of convicts conscripted to serve as the colonists' workhorses, but it soon manifests itself physically in spectacular fashion. What is inadvertently unleashed on Lalonde by a complicated confluence of events is a force which, gradually at first but with increasing rapidity, makes it obvious that not only is the golden age at an end but there is every chance that a new dark age may be imminent. Hence the overall title for the trilogy, *Night's Dawn*.

It is hard to discuss *The Reality Dysfunction* without mentioning its size. At 950-odd pages, it is a behemoth; more accurately, it is one third of a behemoth which, when completed, will run to approximately one million words. Size, as we all know, isn't everything, and 950 pages without real substance and badly written are 950 pages which would better have been left blank or, preferably, as tree. Happily, *The Reality Dysfunction* has all the substance Hamilton's mighty imagination can give it. For evidence, look no further than the chapter describing the homeworld of the Ly-cilph, an alien race so bizarre that they simply *must* exist somewhere out there, or to the battle scene in the closing chapters where near-indestructible knights in armour duke it out with armed-to-the-teeth cyborg mercenaries who lob nuclear devices around like hand grenades. As for the writing, it is as dense and as detailed as we have come to expect from Hamilton, not to mention as rich in sesquipedalianism. Indeed, it seems as if the author is on a mission to employ every single word in the English lexicon at least once in this book, and no doubt the few recondite terms he has failed to include this time will turn up over the course of the next two volumes.

The Reality Dysfunction is an epic in the traditional sense of the word – big, brash, sweeping, hyperbolic, exuberant, thunderously enjoyable – the sort of book Tolstoy would have produced had he availed himself of a bucketload of LSD before settling down to write *War and Peace*.

Psychoville and *Flesh Wounds* by Christopher Fowler (1996)

Christopher Fowler, the Bard of London, ventures a few miles outside
the perimeter of his urban muse for his sixth novel, *Psychoville*, the
action of which mostly takes place in Invicta Cross, a generic Sussex
New Town (but then aren't all New Towns generic?) built to catch the
affluent overspill from the brimming city. Invicta Cross, we learn, is "a
wonderland of clipped jade lawns and brand-new three-bedroom, twin-
garage mock-Tudor houses, where husbands carefully waxed their cars
(in the garage, not at the kerb) while their wives overcooked the Sunday
roast and the children stared morosely at televisions." The streets all
have names with royal associations – Spencer Close, Boadicea Parade –
and the residents are uniformly, staunchly middle-class with upward
aspirations.

Into this community arrive young Billy March and his parents. It is
1985, the dog days of Thatcherism, and the Marches have been ousted
from their Greenwich home, which is to be flattened to make way for a
motorway. Billy is a bookish, cinema-loving, hyperimaginative fourteen-
year-old, and a city kid through and through. He hates Invicta Cross,
and the feeling is reciprocated. The Marches, coming from the lower
end of the social scale, do not fit the New Town profile, and the initial
cautious welcome by the neighbours in their street, Balmoral Close,
soon darkens to resentment and eventually to outright hostility. Billy
does make a couple of friends at school – including April, a misfit like
himself – but by and large the Marches are treated with suspicion and
disdain wherever they go. They are snubbed, inconvenienced, insulted,
until inevitably, and under tragic circumstances, forced to leave.

Thus ends the first and better half of the novel. Fowler tightens the
net of persecution around the Marches with a subtle, understated
savagery. The neighbours in Balmoral Close are not intrinsically bad
people. Their evil stems from the fact that they just don't want anyone
'not like us' cluttering up their town. They crave sameness, they want to
look across the road and see a mirror of their own perfect lives, and the
Marches, unfortunately, are letting the side down. For this kind of
mindless conformity a New Town provides the perfect venue. The
apparent egalitarianism of rows of identical houses with similar-sized
gardens is, in fact, a kind of municipal Maoism, antithetical to the need

of some human beings to be individuals.

The second half of the novel takes place ten years later, as Billy returns to Invicta Cross, no longer a weedy outcast but a tanned, gym-muscled, suit-wearing, cellphone-toting corporate professional. And, of course, he has revenge in mind. And so, sadly, the tautness of *Psychoville* unravels, as Billy – with the aid of April, who has grown up into a certifiable psychotic with a June Allyson fetish – sets about turning the inhabitants of Balmoral Close against one another in much the same way that Leland Gaunt did with the inhabitants of Castle Rock in *Needful Things*. Fowler pulls off an outrageous twist about three-quarters of the way through the book, but as old scores are settled and the bodies mount, *Psychoville* ceases to be a darkly ironic meditation on the blandness of planned lifestyles and degenerates into a violent black comedy with murder as the punchline to each gag. The dreadful social injustice of the first half has been so teeth-grindingly well conveyed that one finds oneself wishing for a more refined resolution than mere slaughter.

Much more satisfying is Fowler's new collection of short stories, *Flesh Wounds*. Here are tales of extreme cruelty and decadence and solipsist apocalypse and hilarious failure and odd obsession, crafted in a lighter, looser, more literary style than is to be found in *Psychoville*. And there are some real gems. "*Jouissance de la mort*" is a lovely *jeu d'esprit*, a comic *la ronde* of death, while "Mother of the City" – the city being London, naturally – is one of those supernatural tales that reveals a secret beneath the face of everyday life which cannot possibly be true but which feels true, in this case that certain people are avatars of the cities they inhabit and that if you cross one of them, expect to face the wrath not just of the individual but of the place itself. "Night After Night of the Living Dead" tiptoes across the quivering tightrope between illusion and reality with a delicate, humorous tread, while "The Young Executives" turns on its head the perception that old people can seem creepy to the young, as it shows how a middle-aged widow, having taken on a job as a typist, learns the deeply sinister flipside to the brash ambitiousness of her youthful office colleagues.

As usual with any short-story collection, there are a couple of duds, and the line-drawings that preface each tale are, let's be generous here, functional, but taken as a whole *Flesh Wounds* is as impressive an assemblage of short fiction as you'll find anywhere, and a significantly more accurate barometer of what Fowler is capable of than *Psychoville*.

Whit by Iain Banks (1996)

Bifurcated Iain Banks, in no-middle-initial mode, has produced *Whit*, the story of nineteen-year-old Isis Whit, possessor of faith-healing powers which may or may not be genuine, and the favoured daughter of the Luskentyrians, a slightly loopy religious sect based at a remote farm estate in Scotland. As the novel opens, Isis takes her leave of the sect's small, close-knit community and heads for London in search of her cousin Morag, whom she has been commanded to bring back for the four-yearly Festival of Love. Though Isis has led a cloistered childhood in the familial embrace of the Luskentyrians, she is not entirely ignorant of the ways of the modern world, and as she wanders among the Bland – that's you and me – and encounters marijuana, video pornography, police brutality, Essex Man, Rastafarians and skinheads, Banks happily avoids the fish-out-of-water clichés one might have expected. Isis is no Don Quixote; she is naïve, yes, but she is also smart, savvy, adaptable and resourceful, with a solid core of faith that protects her when her wits won't.

Of course, this core of faith is also her blind spot, so that as she narrates to us the origins and beliefs of the Luskentyrians, we detect hypocrisies to which she remains blissfully oblivious. The irony is played for laughs, but as the plot unfolds and the scales start to fall away from Isis' eyes, there is the sense that her sincere delusion is and always will be purer than the self-serving theology propounded by her grandfather, the sect's founder. The Luskentyrians, it is made clear early on, are basically a love-cult. The Festival of Love is, frankly, an orgy. But Isis, innately chaste and untethered by physical needs, is the religious impulse incarnate, and though she may at times be uptight and holier-than-thou, her priggishness is that of the genuinely innocent. She's a complex character to have at the centre of what is actually a rather light-hearted novel, and enjoyment of *Whit* will largely depend on whether you find her engaging or you find yourself wanting to shout, "For God's sake pull that cork *out* of your arse, girl!" at her.

There are some nice literary flourishes. The sophistications of modern living are anathema to the Luskentyrians – they 'clutter' the soul, preventing one from hearing the quiet voice of God inside – so that when Isis describes a hi-fi stack she calls is a 'dark machine' and draws attention to its 'black mass', double-imaging a straightforward observation with Luddite and Satanist undertones. The sinful English capital is referred to as 'Babylondon', and the Luskentyrian cuisine is a fusion of its founder's Scottish and his first two wives' Asian palates, resulting in such concoctions as porridge tarka and skink aloo. Familiar Banksian elements are also present and correct: recreational drugs; bad driving; incisive use of pop-culture references; what Shakespearian critics would term 'bawdiness'; people living in remote, decaying splendour; concurrent dual past/present narratives; and a defiant Scottishness (London, we are helpfully informed, is a city located in south-east England). *Whit*, however, lacks the searing in-yer-faceness that made *Complicity* or – how sick Banks must be of seeing these three words – *The Wasp Factory* such compelling reading. It lacks, too, the soaring imaginative bravado of *Feersum Endjinn*. It's fun, it's funny, but it's not fundamental reading.

The Unconsoled by Kazuo Ishiguro(1996)

Dream-sequences in fiction are notoriously difficult to pull off, but that hasn't stopped Kazuo Ishiguro, in *The Unconsoled*, from attempting to write nothing less than a novel-length dream-sequence during which the dreamer never once suspects that he is dreaming and at the end of which he doesn't wake up.

The plot, such as it is, involves an English concert pianist, Ryder, who arrives at an unnamed city in mainland Europe in order to perform a concert. What evolves from this opening is a string of loosely-connected events which sweep Ryder randomly this way and that about the city and offer hints of a much more significant reason for his presence there than mere music. Music, in fact, is somehow inextricably linked to the city's continued success and survival, though it remains unclear exactly how. Everything in *The Unconsoled* remains unclear. The novel, like its central character, rides the surface of an ocean of uncertainty and nuance. Nothing is explored in depth, everything is taken at face value. Ryder never questions what is happening to him and greets even the most apparently startling of revelations, for instance that he has a wife and son in the city, with passive acceptance. He is both subjective first-person and omniscient narrator at once. On one occasion, while another character enters a house to talk to the occupant, Ryder remains outside, yet, though physically absent, is nonetheless privy to the conversation indoors as though he were actually there. On another occasion, two journalists discuss him in insulting terms as if he were not standing right beside them, which he is, smiling benignly whenever one of them directs a scathing remark about him to him, seemingly oblivious to the fact that he is the one being referred to.

This is the novel's central conceit. It hinges on the logic – or lack of logic – of dreams. A building miles outside the city turns out to be connected by a short passageway to the hotel Ryder is staying at in the middle of the city. Friends from Ryder's past turn up suddenly and remind him of events he has forgotten ever happened, as if they are planting memories in his brain by the power of suggestion. Complete strangers approach him and unburden their souls to him in long monologues that go on sometimes for several pages. At one point he thinks, for no particular reason, of the rusted old car in the drive of his parents' house that he used to play in as a child, and lo and behold a moment later he stumbles across that selfsame car. And throughout it all runs a dark and nervy undercurrent of anxiety, as Ryder's responsibilities gradually pile up, as he misses appointment after appointment he didn't know he had, and as he blithely allows himself to be diverted by some distraction and then diverted from that distraction by another distraction.

It's enough to drive you to distraction. Ishiguro writes some of the sparsest, most elegant, most luminous prose around and has a neat line in wry humour, but his technical skills alone are not enough to sustain interest for the whole of what is essentially one long (535 pages) shaggy-dog story. Towards the end the instinct in all of us that demands that a narrative have a beginning, a middle and an end, or at least a reasonable approximation of same, is crying out for some kind of resolution. None comes, and one is left with the uncomfortable feeling that one has just been the butt of an elaborate literary joke.

Debutantes – *Whiteout* by Sage Walker,
Luck in the Shadows by Lynn Flewelling,
Shade and Shadow by Francine G. Woodbury,
Mainline by Deborah Christian (1996)

Whiteout, the first novel from Sage Walker, is an ecopunk thriller set, as the cover blurb somewhat uninspiredly informs us, '20 minutes into the future. ' A team of console-jockeys known collectively as Edges earn their livings finessing the way the public perceive the actions of megacorporations. When a Japanese company, Tanaka, hires them to help effect some changes in the Antarctic Treaty so that Tanaka will be able to exploit that continent's natural resources, it would at first appear to be just another job for Edges, albeit one that raises a few questions of conscience among the team. It isn't long, though, before the seemingly straightforward assignment has been complicated by sabotage, political intrigue and, perhaps inevitably, murder, as the members of Edges discover that they are pawns in a sinister executive game. The media manipulators are themselves being manipulated, and the successful completion of their brief, and perhaps their very survival, depend on unmasking the identity of the dangerous businesswoman known as Evergreen, who will stop at nothing to thwart them. Will a handful of human beings be able to stand up to the might of the multinationals? This is a work of fiction – what do *you* think?

Whiteout is, self-consciously, a 'global' novel. Not only are its principle thematic concerns environmental issues such as over-fishing, pollution, and the protection of wilderness areas, but it features a variety of international settings and a multicultural cast of characters. Edges itself is made up of men and women from different nations, united by permanent electronic links that allow them instant access to one another's thoughts and lives, in spite of the fact that they are strewn across the planet. Herein lie the novel's greatest strength and also its greatest flaw. These disparate yet intimately bound individuals find their electronic relationships, because conducted in virtual settings (artificial and therefore controllable), much easier to deal with than those they fumble through in the awkward physicality of 'Fleshtime'. However, having established this neat paradox, Walker then lets her characters – principally Signy Thomas, who is the main viewpoint of the book – fret endlessly about the friendships and sexual relationships at play within the loose structure of Edges. Page after page is frittered away on musings on the nature of love and trust which overload the plot, slowing its forward momentum. There are times, indeed, when *Whiteout* veers perilously close to becoming a kind of SF Aga saga, which is a shame, since Walker handles action sequences well. A few more of those to replace the hand-wringing soliloquies and the ungainly, slightly embarrassing sex scenes might have served the novel better, if that is not too churlishly masculine a criticism.

This is, when all is said and done, an enjoyable book, and Walker's zappy dialogue and descriptive eye suggest she is an author who knows what she is doing and is doing what she knows. If her subsequent novels can capitalise on the good qualities of her first, she ought to be around to entertain us for quite some time.

Lynn Flewelling's maiden effort, *Luck in the Shadows*, is a well-written piece of fiction containing sympathetic characters, believable dialogue and passages of artful description. It moves along at a fair lick and contains plenty of fights and escapes, close shaves and betrayals, turnabouts and twists. It is also, sad to say, desperately derivative, and as a result hard to like.

The plot goes like this. Unjustly imprisoned as a spy by the despot Asengai, young orphan goatherd Alec is sprung by a fellow prisoner, a foppish bard by the name of Rolan Silverleaf, who soon reveals himself to be a thief/spy/master-of-disguise called Serengil. Sensing latent greatness in the boy, Serengil takes him on as his apprentice. Consequently Alec gets caught up in the political skullduggery between two rival kingdoms, Skala and Plenimar, which are busy gearing themselves up for yet another war against each other. When Serengil is struck dangerously ill by a magic spell, Alec has to transport him to the port of Rhíminee, where lives a wizard, Nysander, who can cure him. In Rhíminee, Alec learns about the Lerans, a bloodline of long-lived, faerie-related royals who like nothing better than to sow civil discord and foment rebellion behind the scenes, as royals do. The rest of *Luck in the Shadows* is taken up with Alec's and Serengil's efforts to foil the Leran plot, but be warned: the novel ends on a suspended cadence, with a 'riveting sequel', *Stalking Darkness*, touted on the final page.

You will immediately be able to deduce from the foregoing précis that *Luck in the Shadows* contains little that is new in terms of setting, characterisation or structure. Alec is the archetypal Peasant Boy With An Important Destiny, Serengil is your average, general-purpose Rogue With A Heart Of Gold, and the two of them travel through a world where wizards cast enchantments and royals scheme and nearly everyone has an extremely silly name (Corruth í Glamien Yanari Meringil Bôkthersa takes the prize). Imagine a cocktail of Tolkien, Moorcock, Leiber and Howard from which all the intoxicating ingredients have been removed, and you will have some idea of the flavour of *Luck in the Shadows*: sweet, but lacking any kind of kick.

It is a pity that a writer as manifestly able as Flewelling should choose to recycle traditions rather than subvert them or establish new ones, but there you go. She can at least claim to be the third most famous novelist – after a certain moderately phenomenal Horror author and his wife – to reside in Bangor, Maine.

Unwisely Francine G. Woodbury appears to have ignored the advice traditionally offered to neophyte authors, namely write what you know. Her first novel, *Shade and Shadow*, is set in Oxford, but no Oxford you or I would recognise. Woodbury appears to have done little, if any, geographical research, and to anyone who has spent even a few hours in the City of Dreaming Spires her book's sense of place is shamefully poor. The ponderous antiquity, the eccentric streets and clammy climate, are all notable by their absence. The setting might as well be any university town; more precisely, given the British cast of characters' uniformly American habits and diction, any university town in the United States.

On the plus side, *Shade and Shadow*'s gimmick – that the practice of magic has become acceptable and widespread, a profession on a par with medicine or the law – is a relatively unusual one, and Woodbury has fun exploring the possibilities the premise offers, although one feels at times that she might have taken things a bit further. For example, her hero, Raoul Smythe, Professor of Magic, at one point goes out to a pub and, because he is in a self-destructive mood, picks a fight, which leaves him bloodied and bruised. It would have been more interesting, perhaps, had Smythe instead found himself some bar-room adept and challenged him or her to a magical duel.

And that is why *Shade and Shadow* disappoints. It doesn't matter too much that the plot is a bog-standard, by-the-numbers whodunit (the body in question belonging to Smythe's immediate superior in the

Faculty of Magic, and the finger of suspicion initially pointing at Smythe himself in order to give him a motive for becoming involved in the investigation). Woodbury's prose is fine, and the technical aspects of magic are well researched and presented. The problem is that the use of magic itself is infrequent and more often than not fails to thrill. Magic – certainly fictional magic – is exciting because of its dangerous strangeness, its unpredictable otherness, but in *Shade and Shadow* we are dealing not with earthy 'magick' of the Crowleyan variety but with its emasculated, 'k'-less inferior, a tamed version which, when reduced to a commonplace, is rendered doubly mundane.

This isn't quite an irredeemable flaw, and the novel contains sufficient wit and quirkiness to keep things bubbling along nicely, but one is left at the end with the sense of an opportunity squandered. Perhaps there will be a sequel. *Shade and Shadow* gives the impression of being the first in a series.

Last but not least, Deborah Christian's first outing, *Mainline*, comes bedecked with glittering testimonials from the likes of C. J. Cherryh, Nicola Griffith and Larry Niven, and for once the solicited praise is merited.

Thanks to an alien mutation in her genes, assassin-for-hire Reva has the ability to perceive all the divergent Lines of possibility which stem from any given moment. By entering a state of 'timetrance', she can see infinite alternate Nows spread out before her "like strobe-action figures overlaid one atop the other." Once she has selected the one she wants to follow, that then becomes her Mainline, her reality.

The talent serves her well in her chosen profession. By assessing a person's likely movements, she can sneak up on even the wariest target undetected, and should it appear that a situation isn't going to turn out her way, all she has to do is shift sideways into a Line where the outcome is in her favour. The downside of this is that she cannot allow herself to form any close personal attachments, since there is always the risk that someone she has grown close to in one Line may not exist in another.

All is fine until she meets Lish, a novice smuggler and arms dealer who, for all her spirited ambition, will probably not survive long without the help of someone like Reva. Between the two women there develops a strong mutual attraction to which Reva eventually succumbs against her better judgement, knowing that by tethering herself emotionally to one particular Mainline she is denying herself the escape route which has hitherto been essential to her survival. Bad timing, this, since Reva has just inadvertently brought extreme dishonour on an alien bodyguard called Yavobo by assassinating the employer he was sworn to protect. Yavobo belongs to the Aztrakhan, a race of eight-foot-tall warriors who abide by an aggressive code and take blows to their reputation very seriously indeed. The only way he can recover his dignity and restore his warrior pride is by tracking down and killing Reva, and this is what he attempts to do throughout the rest of the book, with increasing determination and relish.

It is a tribute to Christian's writing skills that she manages to make the reader concerned for the well-being of a central protagonist who is to all intents and purposes invulnerable. Reva's reasons for remaining with Lish, despite the fact that it compromises her safety, are plausibly developed and ring psychologically true. Both she and Yavobo are equally deadly, and both have tied themselves to intangible absolutes – he his samurai-like code, she her feelings for Lish – which bring them inner satisfaction, but at a price. The parallels and differences between the pair, hunter and hunted, are developed well.

An SF author is not constrained by a special-effects budget, and Christian, unfortunately, falls into the trap of making the alien races in *Mainline* uniformly humanoid. Some really *alien* aliens would not have gone amiss. And while she has a good ear for hard-boiled diction and a pleasing prose style, her reach occasionally exceeds her grasp. For instance, the phrase "a week's worth of heartbeats" is a meaningless redundancy which could have been better put as, simply, "a week", while "an incisor-revealing grin" is pure tautology: unless you have forgotten to put in your dentures, your grin is by definition going to expose teeth.

These minor quibbles aside, *Mainline* is taut, gripping and eventful, all the things a good SF thriller should be, and deserves wide success and, if it hasn't earned it already, the attention of a UK publisher.

The Neutronium Alchemist by Peter. F. Hamilton (1998)

There's no escaping it. No review of Peter F. Hamilton's *The Neutronium Alchemist* can possibly avoid mention of the book's size. It is, frankly, a big bugger, weighing in at 3lbs and nearly a thousand pages long. And when you consider that it is just the middle book of Hamilton's *Night's Dawn* trilogy, merely one of three similarly proportioned volumes, then the full extent of the author's ambition becomes apparent. No doubt about it: in terms of sheer length, this is a monumental work.

Physical dimensions aside, it's a work of vast scale as well. The sweep of the narrative spans virtually the entire universe, encompassing numerous different cultures, races and planets. Everything happens on a hyperbolic level. Nuclear weapons are tossed around as casually as firecrackers. People die in their droves. This is the space-opera equivalent of Wagner – grand, bombastic, and very, very long.

However, as every remotely insecure male knows, size isn't everything. Grandeur without substance rings hollow. *The Neutronium Alchemist* has the scope, but fortunately it also has the fine detail that puts its massively broad strokes into perspective.

As those who have read its predecessor, *The Reality Dysfunction*, will know, the denizens of Hamilton's hypertechnological twenty-sixth century have encountered a problem with which their science appears unable to cope. Dead souls have discovered a means of re-entering the realm of the living, by possessing the bodies of the recently deceased. When they do so, they find themselves capable of feats of 'energistic' power which are indistinguishable from – and probably identical to – magic. The 'beyond' from which they have escaped is an empty, hellish limbo, and so naturally they have no desire to return there, and equally naturally they want to rescue those who are still trapped there. And the only way to do this is, of course, to create more bodies to be possessed, which they achieve by torturing living victims till they submit to being taken over.

The Reality Dysfunction concluded with one world already entirely under the control of the possessed and several others heading that way. Without preface or preamble (new readers are not advised to start here), *The Neutronium Alchemist* picks up where the previous book left off. Quinn Dexter, member of a Satanic-style sect and the man who inadvertently triggered off the whole crisis in the first place, has moved to English-ethnic planet Norfolk, where he is in the process of furthering his nefarious scheme to bring about the onset of an apocalyptic Night. Meanwhile Dr Alkad Mzu, last seen escaping spectacularly from the artificial habitat Tranquillity, is on a quest to retrieve the doomsday weapon she invented, the titular Alchemist, a bomb capable of destroying a star. And, two hundred pages in, Hamilton finally reintroduces *The Reality Dysfunction*'s main protagonist, Joshua Calvert, a reluctantly heroic starship captain whose piloting skills saved the lives of several children at the end of the previous book and, in this book, make him the best candidate for going after Dr Mzu and preventing her from exacting her revenge on the planet Omuta, whose inhabitants were responsible for committing near-total genocide on her own race thirty years earlier.

For the most part, Hamilton marshals his cast of more than 150 characters with consummate control and skill as he takes them (and us) through a kaleidoscope of shifting allegiances, playing numerous variations on his basic theme of magic (limitless, lawless) versus science (governed by strict rules) and exploring to the full all the possibilities inherent in the situation. His worldbuilding is thorough and convincing, and where other authors might be content to let the central conceit of the dead coming back to life remain an unexplained MacGuffin ("They just do, all right?"), for Hamilton the whys and wherefores are essential to the plot. It would seem that divining the very nature of the 'beyond' will provide the key to resolving the crisis.

Of the dozens of concurrent sub-plots, the most interesting involves the reappearance of the soul of Al Capone, who, acclimatising quickly to the future, sets about building up his Organization anew, although this time he has his sights set on running an entire solar system rather than just one city. There is also the appearance of a mysterious, shadowy figure who would seem to be setting himself up as Quinn Dexter's nemesis, and whose identity Hamilton does not divulge.

Inevitably, however, with so much going on at once, at times the plot convolutions become a little confusing and the relentless pace and intermittent bursts of violence a little bewildering. On the whole Hamilton keeps the many balls he is juggling in the air, but occasionally one drops to the floor with a thud, for instance when Joshua discovers he has a half-brother. It's a plot-twist of the same order of magnitude of duffness as Luke and Leia in *Star Wars* finding out that they're siblings – the stuff of Victorian potboilers. Indeed, Joshua is the one character who, throughout both volumes of the trilogy so far, has consistently struck a false note. He is callow, shallow, for no obvious reason irresistible to women, profligate with his sexual favours (he has managed to impregnate not one but two of the principal female characters), and prone to major cock-ups and errors of judgement. He remains fundamentally noble, and we're meant to like him in spite of, and probably because of, his shortcomings, but basically he's a bit of a prat, a trad-SF spaceborne stud-bucket hero very much out of keeping with Hamilton's otherwise commendably nineties sensibilities. Imagine Captain Kirk, pre-paunch and pre-wig, turning up in an episode of *Next Generation*, and you will get the general idea.

These quibbles aside, *The Neutronium Alchemist* more than adequately fulfils its task of forming a bridge between *The Reality Dysfunction* and the finale of the trilogy, *The Naked God* (a title notably lacking in the polysyllabic portentousness of the other two). Word is, Hamilton's next series is going to run to at least five volumes, so catch him now, while he's still concise.

Area 7 by Matthew Reilly (2002)

When is a novel not a novel? When it's a thinly-disguised Hollywood blockbuster screenplay masquerading as a novel.

Matthew Reilly isn't interested in the possibilities of fiction – the limitless scope of the writer's imagination, narrative elision, experiments with form, texture and technique, development of credible and multi-layered characters. (In fact, he positively frowns on the last. "If developing characters slow down the action then developing characters get the chop!" he declares, proudly if somewhat ungrammatically.) What he is interested in is creating a book that reads and feels like a summer 'event' movie, one of those brain-dead action epics that regularly pack them in at the multiplexes. Logic and plausibility are not important. What matters is pace, spectacle, curled-lip one-liners, and a bomb countdown – preferably several bomb countdowns.

Actually, what Reilly is interested in most of all is becoming a movie director. This has been his stated aim in both of the self-promoting author interviews, of spurious provenance, that appear at the end of *Area 7* and its predecessor, *Temple*. He clearly perceives fiction as little more than a stepping stone to the greater prize of Hollywood moguldom. His avowed role models are George Lucas and Michael Crichton. This ought to give you some idea of the level of regard in which he holds the literary medium. Both Lucas and Crichton are very talented men, but neither's strength, it would be fair to say, lies in the ability to put words together well.

Thus we have a novel written by somebody who has not bothered to develop a facility for, or been born with a great love for, novel-writing. Reilly constantly has an eye on the silver screen as well as his computer screen, and the result, as you might expect, is an intelligence-insulting mess. Throughout *Area 7* one's jaw drops repeatedly, not in amazement, but in disbelief at the extremes of absurdity contained within.

The plot is suitably Hollywood high-concept. A white supremacist US Air Force general, Charles 'Caesar' Russell, takes control of the Air Force installation of the book's title. It so happens that the President is on a visit to Area 7 that day. It also so happens that Russell has somehow contrived to have had a microscopic transmitter attached to the President's heart during a surgical procedure a few years back. The transmitter is linked by satellite to fourteen nuclear-plasma warheads that have been deposited at airports all across America. If the President's heart stops, the warheads go off. What a scheme! You can imagine Michael Bay and Joel Silver wetting their pants at the pitch meeting, can't you.

Russell locks down the installation, then goes on TV to inform the American public that his team of crack troops will go after the President, guns blazing. If the President survives their assault, he will have shown himself to be a worthy leader of the nation. If not, then there won't be much of a nation left to lead.

The odds are stacked against the Prez, but fortunately there is among his bodyguard escort a Marine by the name of Shane Schofield. Schofield is the hero of a previous Reilly novel, *Ice Station*, and in that book proved himself to be everything that you could hope for in a hyped-up, ridiculous situation of this kind: cool-headed, phenomenally lucky, preternaturally indestructible. And so he is in *Area 7*. As the action unfolds, Schofield crashes an AWACS plane, engages in a high-speed powerboat chase, goes into space, swings across chasms, gets shot at, gets shot, is infected with a deadly virus, has a close encounter with a pair of komodo dragons, gets severely beaten up by a psychotic convict – and also manages to overcome his shyness with regard to a certain female colleague, *and* saves the life of a crucial-to-the-plot little boy.

It all sounds fun, right? Well, it might be if it were actually a movie, starring perhaps Tom Cruise, directed by John Woo, and you were at a loose end and it was a rainy day and there was nothing else on at the cinema. Even then, you would come out of the auditorium shaking your head and wondering just how stupid today's film-makers think their audiences are.

But you're a reader. You like books. Novels are the last redoubt of original thought, iconoclasm, idiosyncrasy, sedition, novelty, insight. You expect more from fiction than you ever do from mainstream cinema.

You expect, at the very least, that your author can do prose. Reilly cannot do prose, could not do prose if his life depended on it. He writes the way a breathless twelve-year-old writes when emulating the thrillers he's read. His pages are littered with italics and exclamation marks, just in case readers aren't getting the point that what's going on here is *exciting!* Frequently he uses one-sentence paragraphs like "And then it happened" or "And then he saw it". He isn't averse to playground hyperbole ("Python Willis was hit by about a million rounds."). He has no fear of clunking cliché – one quickly loses count of the number of "resounding booms" that reverberate through *Area 7* – and his grasp of character delineation is, to put it kindly, basic: bad guys are "evil-looking", scientists are bespectacled and geeky, kids are cute, spunky and well-behaved. To make his and our lives easier, most of *Area 7*'s cast have call-sign nicknames that handily encapsulate their personalities. We know to root for Scarecrow, Fox, Mother, Elvis, the smart soldier known as Brainiac, et al... just as we know we should boo the nasty soldiers named after snakes and the mad general who styles himself Caesar. It's comicbook in the very worst sense of the term. In fact, to call it comicbook is an insult to comicbooks.

Politically, Reilly affects the liberal-American stance which typifies most Hollywood output, i.e. it looks liberal but it's crypto-conservative, well to the right of liberalism as most of the rest of the world understands it. The white-supremacist baddie can justly be hated, but so too can some American turncoats who are prepared to betray their country to the (ugh!) Chinese. Meanwhile, the President is that kind of idealised movie president which America wishes it had and will never get. He's not a drooling senile nincompoop, nor a trouser-dropping Southern smoothie, nor a dead-eyed, empty-headed corporate stooge. He's noble, clean, decent, and not scared of rolling up his sleeves and getting his hands dirty. He's Harrison Ford in *Air Force One*, though without the dramatically-convenient military training.

Reilly himself is Australian, yet has entirely submerged his own cultural identity the better to write what he knows will sell well and be filmable. He has adopted an American vernacular style and plays shamelessly up to America's rose-tinted view of itself as a perfect country which not even the occasional bad apple can ruin. Furthermore he has targeted, with a brazen magpie abandon, all the movies that have done big box office recently and has incorporated them in various ways into the story. *Area 7* contains easily recognisable elements of the first two *Die Hard* films, *Aliens*, *Con Air*, the James Bond series, you name it. There's even a swipe from *Akira*. This would seem to indicate a clever, calculating mind, the mind at least of someone who's done his market research thoroughly. The convoluted plotting, likewise, and the depth of background research, show that Reilly has the ability to marshal ideas and assimilate information well. All that effort, though, all that brain-power, expended on such meaningless, derivative drivel. What a waste.

The fact that the plot of *Area 7* is almost identical to that of *Ice Station*, and shares fundamental structural similarities with that of *Temple*, only serves to emphasise that Reilly has no goal other than creating formulaic fodder for the masses. His graduation to the world of movie-making would therefore seem inevitable. Let's hope so, because that way the planet's woodpulp plantations will be spared from being turned into further examples of hackneyed post-literate pap like *Area 7*, and Reilly's gung-ho, immature worldview will have found its natural home.

Tropic of Night by Michael Gruber (2003)

Tropic of Night is a threefold tale. The first of its strands introduces us, in first-person present tense, to the main character, Jane Doe. This is, perhaps implausibly, her real name, accounted for by an excess of tradition and dearth of imagination on her family's part. It suits her, however, for when we meet Jane she is living in hiding, all but anonymous. She has faked suicide and assumed the name and identity of a deceased nun, Dolores Tuoey. An unprepossessing above-garage apartment in an unprepossessing quarter of unprepossessing Miami is now her home (and she the daughter of one of Long Island's premier dynasties). Why is she in hiding? This is not immediately made clear, but since Jane is a determined, redoubtable, fiercely intelligent young woman, not to mention lethally adept at aikido, we must assume that whatever menace she has taken flight from, it is significant and sinister.

The second strand takes the form of Jane's journal account of a trip to Africa with her husband, DeWitt Moore. All is not well with the marriage. Moore, a successful black (politically black) poet and playwright, has become a morose, boorish presence. The engine of their shared lives is misfiring. Ostensibly they're going to Africa on an anthropological expedition. Anthropology is Jane's field of expertise and her passion. Sorcery, in particular, fascinates her after her experiences a few years earlier with an obscure tribe of shamanistic Siberian nomads, the Chenka. Moore, for his part, is tagging along because he is interested in all permutations of black culture and regards Africa, naturally enough, as the *fons et origo*. But Jane also hopes the journey will help anneal the growing rift between the two of them. Not unexpectedly, things go Horribly Wrong.

The third strand centres on Detective Jimmy Paz of the Miami PD as he investigates the first of what turns out to be several gruesome slayings. A pregnant woman has been found in her apartment bedroom, neatly eviscerated. Her unborn foetus lies in the bathroom basin with certain organs missing, removed, excised. Paz is a second-generation Cuban immigrant, looked down on not only by his white colleagues, as one might perhaps expect, but also by his fellow Cubans (for having features that are too Negroid). Ironically, he is partnered with a none-more-Caucasian, Bible-bashing God-botherer by the name of Cletis

Barlow. The relationship between the two men, taut but affable, balanced on a cautiously attained mutual respect, a dance of opposites, is one of the novel's many delights.

The murder investigation turns up links to *santería*, the South American form of black magic. *Santería* is itself based on an older African form of witchcraft, *ndol*, practised by the Olo people of Mali, which happens to be where Jane Doe ended up on her African field trip. The disaster that befell the trip has consequences which are now making themselves felt in Miami in the shape of the ritual murders. Something big, apocalyptically big, is brewing.

Gruber weaves it all together calmly and tightly, past events echoing and resounding in the present. The concordances between the three strands aren't forced or overstated. For instance, a character we've encountered with Paz then crosses over into Jane's story, but anonymously and unobtrusively, even though, in retrospect, it was forehead-smackingly obvious that the two people are one and the same. Gruber also, through the journal and more so through an adroit use of flashback, establishes Jane's back-story in such a way that we are fed enough information to keep us intrigued but not so much that we can second-guess where the plot is going or how what happened in Mali dovetails with what is taking place now in Miami. His prose is pellucid, and his impersonation of Jane, in her journal entries, flawlessly convincing. He has a lovely, cynical eye – the liberal white couple who are Jane's husband's adoptive parents are depicted in middle age as "former peaceniks, marchers for civil rights, wracked, confused, failed by the gods of niceness and decency".

What's at the heart of *Tropic of Night*, however, and what elevates it above the rank of mere well-written page-turner, is its thoroughgoing, elegant exploration of the nature of magic. The novel not only discusses the relation of ancient magic to the modern world but investigates how and why magic might be applied, amassing a credible case for the existence of sorcery as a workable force, something with a sound scientific and psychological basis which also happens to ineffable and unquantifiable. Each supernatural occurrence is accorded a rational explanation. The power of invisibility, for example, is achieved by a sorcerer's ingesting psychoactive substances which, exuded as bodily secretions at the correct time, cause disorientation in the minds of everyone else in the vicinity. But in order to work, the power also relies on the sorcerer's unswerving belief in the ability to become invisible. Where you stand on the matter becomes, then, a question of faith, and Gruber leaves things ambiguous throughout. That in itself is one of the novel's strengths. Whether viewed subjectively, as by Jane, or objectively, as by Paz, black magic is seen to exist.

And with it, praise be to Wheatley, comes horror. *Tropic of Night* is not short of good scares. There are zombies, known to the Olo as *paarolawats*, although in Miami they look an awful lot like shuffling hoboes. There is spirit possession (one scene involving a small girl knowingly evokes *The Exorcist* but is no less spine-icing for that). There are demons and delusions and prophecies and gods-from-beyond. The so-called real world is shown to be altogether more pliable and less reliable than one might wish. Because Gruber maintains the tension between subjective and objective throughout, it would be hard to describe his book as a horror novel – the horror genre implicitly accepts the existence of the supernatural – yet the appellation sits on it as comfortably as any. By the same token, *Tropic of Night* isn't a serial-killer novel – it steadfastly refuses to recycle the clichés of the format, unlike so many other post-Harris thrillers – but then again, it is.

What it is, above all, is a superlative piece of pop-lit fiction. Rigorously researched and expertly executed, satisfying on every level, it carries the same combined intellectual and visceral charge as Jean-Christophe Grangé's *Blood Red Rivers* and George Dawes Green's *The Juror*. In common with both those novels, *Tropic of Night* will make a perfectly dreadful movie. There can be no higher recommendation than that.

McSweeney's Mammoth Treasury of Thrilling Tales, edited by Michael Chabon (2003)

As if the title weren't enough of a giveaway, or the cover image swiped from an old issue of *Red Star Mystery Magazine*, editor Michael Chabon puts the matter entirely beyond doubt in his prefatory note: this is a modern tribute to the glories of the pulp era. He puts a fancy gloss on the project, bemoaning the demise in popularity of short stories and wondering what the modern literary scene would be like had this not occurred, but what it comes down to is that he wanted to produce a publication "that would revive the lost genres of short fiction ... carrying the tradition all the way back to the days of *The Strand* and *Argosy*". Dave Eggers, publisher of literary quarterly *McSweeney's*, gave Chabon an issue of that magazine in which to fulfil his nostalgic dream, and Chabon has managed to gather together a roster of contributors to make other anthology editors wet their pants with envy – a mouth-watering assemblage of big, big names like Stephen King, Michael Crichton, Elmore Leonard, Neil Gaiman, Harlan Ellison, Michael Moorcock, and Nick Hornby, with legendary comics artist Howard Chaykin providing a black-and-white illustration to accompany each story.

And before we go any further, let us pause for a loud, resounding *AHEM!* Is Chabon wilfully ignorant, one wonders, or has he just not ventured very far into his local bookshop lately? Has he not explored past the front tables to find, in the benighted, cobwebby genre sections tucked away at the rear, that short fiction is alive and, if not well, then at least surviving? Is he unaware that numerous small-press publishers have been assiduously compiling and publishing short-fiction anthologies these past few years? Okay, so it's not exactly a return to the pulp magazine heyday, but the form has far from expired. How patronising of Chabon to believe he is single-handedly reviving a defunct tradition. And, more to the point, how surprising that the author of the wonderful *The Amazing Adventures of Kavalier and Clay* – which centres on, let's not forget, a pair of Golden Age comics creators – should be oblivious to the continuing hard work of others in the genre field.

There, rant over. But it can't be denied that around *McSweeney's Mammoth Treasury of Thrilling Tales* there does hang the familiar incense-like odour of mainstream condescension, not only in its editorial approach but in its content. We have here a number of mainstream, or at any rate non-genre authors, turning their hands to genre material and faring badly. We also – hurrah! – have a smaller number of established genre authors showing how it ought to be done.

Foremost among the latter is Michael Moorcock, whose "The Case of the Nazi Canary" is quite the best thing on offer in these pages. Which isn't surprising, since Moorcock is a past master of the pulp pastiche, able both to celebrate and at the same time slyly subvert pulp conventions. His tale features right-wing Metatemporal Detective, Seaton Begg, and his loyal cohort John 'Taffy' Sinclair as they investigate a murder in pre-war Berlin and come into conflict with the (even more right-wing) Nazi party and its (none more right-wing) top brass, namely Hess, Himmler, Hitler et al. The setting is one of Moorcock's multifarious slipstream Earths, only slightly removed from our own. Begg is distantly related to the Von Beks and his arch-nemesis is the albino Count Zodiac, so we have a few familiar landmarks to navigate by. The story is, however, nothing other than pure, unadulterated fun. Well plotted, ironically reactionary, wry-wink witty – if all of …*Thrilling Tales* had been of this quality, it would truly be an anthology to reckon with.

Coming a close second to Moorcock is Laurie King, whose Mary Russell novels are skilled and affectionate Sherlock Holmes homages, dovetailing the heroine's exploits neatly with those of the Great Detective. In this volume King contributes an engaging tale about a former globe-trotting adventuress who is losing her sight, her girlfriend, and possibly her sanity, for she has started to hear strange nocturnal digging sounds outside her remote backwoods cabin. Somewhat overwritten, with more information about looms and the craft of weaving than is really necessary, "Weaving the Dark" is nonetheless well wrought and clever, with a neat, smile-inducing payoff.

Equal second best is "Tedford and the Megalodon" by Jim Shepard, an author new to me. Ostensibly a straightforward man-versus-ruddy-great-fish tale, it is – like *Moby-Dick*, *The Old Man and the Sea*, and even *Jaws* – about so much more than that. As the hero pursues his (possibly mythical) giant prehistoric shark through the gelid seas of the Antarctic, he is also pursuing lost hopes and beliefs. A lone human in a canoe, armed with just a rifle, is hardly a worthy foe for a toothsome fifty-foot leviathan – but then there's no amount of protection any of us can take to guard against our inevitable ends.

Honourable mentions go to Glen David Gold's marvellously titled "The Tears of Squonk, and What Happened Thereafter" (a circus tale), Elmore Leonard's equally marvellously titled "How Carlos Webster Changed His Name to Carl and Became a Famous Oklahoma Lawman" (an enjoyable 1920s-set revenge yarn), Carol Emshwiller's "The General" (a broken-future, *Rogue Male*–style story), and Neil Gaiman's "Closing Time" (a ghost story that's also another of Gaiman's haunting meditations on his own boyhood and boyhood in general). All the above amply meet Chabon's stated criterion that his anthology should contain proper stories, not modernist 'moment-of-truth' tone-poems – stories with character and purpose and plot.

Together, however, they constitute less than half of ...*Thrilling Tales*, and the remainder of the book is nowhere near as good. Crichton's and Ellison's contributions aren't bad, just disappointing. The former stumbles around in the fringes of *noir* and seems lost, while the latter, though as ornery and eloquent as ever, delivers a one-joke skit that doesn't quite come off (but never mind, because with the furiously prolific Ellison there'll always be another story along in a moment).

Then there's Hornby's "Otherwise Pandemonium", which finds this most grossly overrated of writers playing a Stephen King riff, adopting middle-American teen vernacular and twice name-checking Stephen King, the narrator dismissing his own story as emphatically not a Stephen King story, which is of course a very Stephen King thing to do. Hornby has strayed from his very limited patch of turf. It's not a mistake he should repeat.

As for King himself, his "The Tale of Gray Dick" (stop sniggering at the back!) is tied into his Dark Tower/Gunslinger universe. I have to confess here that I find the Dark Tower cycle unreadable. I'm second to none in my admiration for King's 'proper' works but this rambling, multi-part fantasy effort, whose fictional universe has encroached more and more on the shared universe of his other novels in recent years, leaves me cold. It strikes me as a lumberingly self-conscious piece of myth-making and a bid for literary immortality that is surely unnecessary, King's literary immortality having already been secured by the rest of his oeuvre. "The Tale of Gray Dick" (and I mean it, stop sniggering, or the whole class will be staying in after school) does nothing to change that view.

There are further let downs and damp squibs. Rick Moody's "The Albertine Notes" isn't so much a story as an exploration of one solitary SF-ish concept, which goes on at such arse-aching length and with such interminable verbosity that you'd almost think Moody intended it as a test of readers' patience. Dave Eggers is guilty of much the same crime. "Up the Mountain Coming Down Slowly" is an over-long, glorified travel article about Kilimanjaro, which Eggers has obviously visited and climbed. Well done, sir! Now go away and phone *National Geographic*.

And although it's an unwritten law of anthology reviewing that Thou Shalt Not Single Out A Worst Contribution, there's one offering here that is so egregiously, so jaw-droppingly, so apocalyptically bad that I couldn't in all conscience not draw attention to it. "Chuck's Bucket" by Chris Offutt may look like a time-travel jape but in fact is one of the most narcissistic, ill-thought-through, cack-handed specimens of short fiction it has ever been my misfortune to peruse. Oh, and it's a story about not being able to write a story. Nobody has ever done *that* before.

Chabon himself breaks another unwritten law, that which decrees that An Editor Shall Not Contribute To The Anthology He Is Editing. He offers up "The Martian Agent, a Planetary Romance", a veritable *Boy's Own* romp set in an alternative-universe America which is still under the boot-heel of British colonialism and featuring, among other things, a big old airship. It would be unfair to comment on it further, since it's the first part of a serial, subsequent parts to appear in later issues of *McSweeney's*. It's fun as far as it goes but might work better, one feels, when completed and collected.

All in all, it would be nice to be able to recommend ...*Thrilling Tales* unreservedly. Apart from anything else, when are you going to see another stellar line-up like this one? And if the book, being such a high-profile project, does somehow re-ignite the craze for genre-fiction anthologies as Chabon hopes, then we will all benefit in the long run. It's doubtful, however, that it will, because in and of itself...*Thrilling Tales* proves that the mainstream does not understand, nor has the wherewithal, to generate good genre fiction. That arcane, highly evolved art-form is – for better or worse – best left to specialist practitioners with greater knowledge, tighter budgets and nimbler fingers.

Gene by Stel Pavlou (2005)

I must have committed some heinous misdeed in a previous life, because in this life my karmic punishment has been to have to read Stel Pavlou's *Gene*.

Let me up-front. This is a terrible book. It's not even terrible in a fun way. It's not enjoyable, well-executed hokum, for which I'm as much a sucker as the next person. It's just crap. From start to finish – pure, unmitigated, unadulterated crap.

It is also the worst-written novel I think I have ever come across. The prose is so atrocious that, while reading, by page 50 I wanted to tear my own eyes out and by page 100 I was seriously entertaining thoughts of suicide.

Any page chosen at random would yield countless specimens of appalling wordsmithery, but let me spare your sanity and offer just a couple of examples, from pages 21 and 22 respectively:

North aimed off as the venom of disgorged relief and guilty panic percolated through his every nerve.

The thundering dervish of hooves collapsed the distance between them with little ceremony.

Let us pause to parse the problems with these two sentences.

"North aimed off…" – Well, 'aim off' is a technical term that any pistol user will recognise, but in context it needs to be read a couple of times for its meaning to become clear.

"…the venom of disgorged relief…" – Is relief venomous? And is venom ever disgorged? Or relief, for that matter?

"…percolated through his every nerve" – I question whether emotions 'percolate' even metaphorically, and I'm certain they don't do so through the nervous system. Perhaps through the bloodstream…?

And having chewed through that lumpy stew of mixed metaphors and superfluous adjectives, let's turn to sentence two:

"The thundering dervish of hooves…" – A dervish is a Muslim mystic or, at a pinch, a frantic dance executed by same. Taking it one step further to convey the idea of beating horse hooves is an extrapolation too far.

"...collapsed the distance..." – A case of thesaurusitis here, because surely 'shrank' or 'reduced' would serve just as well, if not better. Also, 'collapse' used transitively has a very specific nuance, in the sense of causing a solid object to fall in on itself. It cannot be applied spatially.

"...with little ceremony" – Again Pavlou's *Roget's* has come into play, resulting in a hugely clumsy cadence. To me, 'with little ceremony' implies human agency. I don't believe it works when describing a sound, not even when that sound is a 'thundering dervish'.

Phew! Now, neither of these sentences is plain English, or even good English. And *Gene* contains 377 pages of this sort of stuff. The over-all impression one gets is of a creative-writing assignment produced by school kid who has read too many thrillers and is desperately trying to, but can't, replicate the idiom. It's the work of someone who doesn't understand that the hallmark of good prose is clarity. Using impactful words doesn't axiomatically result in impact, particularly if you keep piling them on till syntax groans beneath the weight and gives way.

I could try to justify the badness of Pavlou's prose as being some wry postmodern exercise, the novel's very existence positing a universe in such chaos that the only sensible response is to write chaotically. But it just won't wash, and anyway I lack the academic credentials and deconstructionist expertise to make the case with any success.

So instead I shall turn to Pavlou's dialogue. Here, again, he displays a tin ear. I'll forgo the for-instances and just say that generally, in *Gene*, the characters either regurgitate facts at one another or lob tough-guy jargon at one another, sometimes both at once. The result goes beyond stilted and into the realm of autistic. It's as if, eschewing naturalism altogether, Pavlou has decided that we live in a world where everyone declaims chunks of the *New Scientist* as though it were Tarantino, or vice versa.

Of course, all said and done, an inability to string a sentence together has not been a hindrance to the careers of many an author, and those who fall into this category are commonly fig-leafed with the title 'storyteller', or 'master storyteller' if the person concerned is unusually successful. (Step forward one Lord Archer, about whom Stephen King once brilliantly said that he writes "like old people fuck".) The implication is that such authors may not be great stylists but they sure can plot.

Pavlou is not even a storyteller. *Gene* has neither narrative sweep nor skilful, engaging, page-turner plot construction. It lollops along like a three-legged dog, sniffing at Big Ideas as it goes and occasionally widdling on them.

What's the book about?

I thought, and feared, you would ask.

It's about reincarnation and genetics and how the one might be linked to the other. It's about two men, a policeman called James North and an apparent psychopath called Eugene Dybbuk, one of whom is the reincarnation of a Babylonian magus called Athanatos and the other of whom is the reincarnation of an Ancient Greek warrior called Cyclades, although the twist is that neither knows which is which. It's about their recurring, *Highlander*-style struggle across the centuries, in different times and climes. It's about the culmination of their conflict in the present day. And it's about how much Google research Pavlou has done into various topics – the New York Police Department, the Trojan War, gene sequencing, classical civilisations – and how desperately he wants a Stateside bestseller and a movie deal (to this end he has set the book in America, not itself a crime, but he has also elected to use American spellings, which for a British author is a capital offence).

An incident at the Metropolitan Museum of Modern Art is what first pits North against Dybbuk, who is familiarly known as Gene (see what Pavlou did there?). Gradually North comes to realise that his and the other man's destinies are linked. He begins experiencing flashbacks into past lives, and is gentled through the self-discovery process by an Englishman called Porter, who is on hand to play Basil Exposition whenever necessary and is summarily killed off once he has outlived his usefulness.

Meanwhile an evil scientific research corporation called A-Gen has its hooks into Gene, wanting to experiment on his reincarnative physiology and exploit it as the key for unlocking the door to immortality. A-Gen is run by a pair of men called Savage and Lawless. That, in case there were still any doubt about the matter, means it really is an Evil Scientific Research Corporation.

Into this creaking, sub-Crichton setup Pavlou injects plenty of violence and copious quantities of gore. The object is to make the novel fast-paced and "grip the reader". The net effect, though, is more reminiscent of the relentless succession of events in a shoot-'em-up computer game. And nobody but an idiot would cite *Grand Theft Auto* or *Doom* as models of narrative planning. Cumulatively in this book the action scenes become tiresome. In tandem with the lugubrious infodump-interludes, they create a sense of enervation that is nothing short of nauseating.

Pavlou's previous novel, *Decipher*, which I had to misfortune to read too, on the recommendation of an ex-friend, had the virtue of being so camply overblown it was almost tolerable. Pavlou, as the press release accompanying *Gene* trumpets, is also responsible for the script for *The 51st State*, a movie which turns on a preposterous twist and which is so pants-soilingly poor that it will forever besmirch the CVs of its stars, Samuel L. Jackson and Robert Carlyle. With *Gene*, the former Threshers assistant whose 'rags to riches' literary success made him a tabloid nine days' wonder and a publicist's wet dream, has plumbed hitherto undreamed-of depths of crassness and inanity.

I've atoned for past sins by reading the novel from cover to cover, dutifully. Unless you used to be Genghis Khan or Adolf Hitler (or indeed both), I wholeheartedly urge you to avoid it if you can.

The Steep Approach To Garbadale by **Iain Banks (2007)**

Dead Air, Iain Banks' previous mainstream novel, was peppered with images of descent and plummeting. It described one man's fall from grace, set against the iconic, era-defining fall from grace that was 9/11.

Banks' new offering, *The Steep Approach To Garbadale*, likewise uses a modern headline-hitting disaster as its touchstone metaphor: the Boxing Day tsunami. Here, the event is recalled in flashback by the hero's girlfriend, who experienced it first-hand and has the scars to show. The motif of water and of tidal forces that cannot be fought, only ridden out and endured, runs through this energetic, satisfying novel.

Alban McGill belongs to a sprawling and vastly wealthy family, the Wopulds. Their fortune is derived from the proceeds of a *Risk*-like board game, *Empire!*, but Alban prefers to live apart from them, in self-imposed exile on a sink estate in Perth, because he finds his high principles at odds with his relatives' greed and closed-ranks clannishness. Alban is, though his forename suggests paleness, a dyed-in-the-wool black sheep.

Also, he is unable to forgive his family, and in particular ultra-matriarch Grandma Win, for a shaming incident that occurred twenty years earlier. A brief, passionate teenage affair with his first cousin Sophie resulted in ignominy and enforced separation for them both. They were thrown out of Lydcombe, the Wopulds' stately pile in Somerset – cast out of their lovers' Eden – and since then have been able to meet up again only intermittently. Alban is still seething about this, even though he is repeatedly told it was for his own good and deep down knows this to be true. Meanwhile, the suicide-by-drowning of his mother when he was very young hangs over him like a rain cloud.

The Wopulds are planning to sell the family business to an American multinational, Spraint (it's safe to assume that any corporation named after otter dung doesn't hail from the friendly end of the capitalist spectrum). For this reason an Extraordinary General Meeting has been called at another of the Wopuld stately piles, Garbadale, in the north of Scotland. Alban's journey there is paralleled with a voyage of introspection, as he attempts to discover how he truly feels about his kin, his past, and his desires for his own future.

Typically for the author, the narrative coils around itself, flashback twisting in on flashback, organic and achronological. Sections flit between present and past tenses, sometimes seemingly at random. Viewpoints shift away from Alban, so that we see him from the outside as well as from within (one of the alternative narrators is a druggie friend whose 'voice' is broad dialect and whose cavalier attitude to punctuation would send Lynne Truss into apostrophe apoplexy). The tone throughout, though, is consistently measured and wry, and Alban, for all his lapses into remorse, remains buoyant and likeably free from self-pity.

Many of the themes in *The Steep Approach To Garbadale* are ones Banks has explored before. There's the rich man living anonymously among 'ordinary' folk, as in *Espedair Street*. There's the family saga, complete with dark secrets, as in *The Crow Road*. There's the corrosive effect of big money on individuals, as in *The Business*. There's a whiff of incest, as in *A Song Of Stone*.

Here they're all brought together and re-examined entertainingly, new light through old windows. The jokes are good, too. At one point Alban's ageing uncle, Blake, quips, "I used to have a hearty dick... Now I've got a dicky heart." And a pair of sozzled, cohabiting aunts, Beryl and Doris, make for an engaging comedy double act.

Banks' own fondness for a tipple, whisky to be precise, has made itself known in a nonfiction book, *Raw Spirit*, and in his victory on *Celebrity Mastermind* in 2005 (specialist subject: malt whisky and the distilleries of Scotland).

On the evidence of this novel, he himself has mellowed and matured rather nicely. His work has grown smoother, perhaps less fiery going down than before, but still packing a subtle, intoxicating kick.

Dalek I Loved You by Nick Griffiths (2007)

This memoir follows the 'geek confessional' template established by Nick Hornby's *Fever Pitch* and emulated by books such as John O'Farrell's *Things Can Only Get Better*. In a nutshell: nice, affable middle-class bloke develops childhood obsession with sociocultural phenomenon, pursues it through thick and thin into adulthood, measures his own growth and development against the fortunes of the object of his mania, and in the closing pages sees his private passion gain public triumph and experiences sense of vindication as a result.

Where Hornby has Arsenal FC and O'Farrell Labour party politics, Griffiths is in thrall to *Dr Who*, or, to be precise, the Jon Pertwee/Tom Baker era of *Dr Who*. This will immediately tell you his age (he's just past 40). It will also tell you the readership *Dalek I Loved You* is primarily aimed at – not the new generation of *Who* fans won over by the show's recent, all-conquering renaissance but the fortysomethings who fondly remember the men-in-rubber-suit monsters and the quarry-near-Pinewood alien planets of the 1970s.

In one sense Griffiths is absolutely right to focus on the Pertwee/Baker period. The two actors' tenures as the Doctor represent, inarguably, the original series' Golden Age. Some might claim the Patrick Troughton years had merit, but only a raving lunatic would try to make a case for *Who* being any good while, say, Peter Davison or Sylvester McCoy were at the helm of the Tardis. If you're going to wax nostalgic about a TV show, for God's sake wax nostalgic about it when it was actually worth watching.

Griffiths writes well when evoking his early youth and the exhilaration of seeing foppish Pertwee and bonkers Baker prance through episodes such as *Spearhead From Space*, *The Green Death* and *Genesis Of The Daleks*. Those titles alone should spark a frisson of recognition, and perhaps remembered fear, in certain people of a certain age, and the book is at its strongest as Griffiths conjures up just how mind-blowing it was for an ordinary suburban kid to be transported, through *Who*, to a realm of danger and rampant SF imagination. Back then, what the show lacked in budgetary generosity was more than compensated for by the sheer inventiveness of its creators.

Lest we succumb to nerd overload, Griffiths makes sure to use the filter of hindsight to create an ironic distance between his grown-up self and the breathless fan he once was. Viewing beloved old episodes on dodgy VHS tapes and considerably better-quality DVDs, he's frank and funny about their plot holes and occasional bizarrity and rubbishness. Here, for instance, is his accurate description of a lesser-known *Who* alien, a Zygon:

Imagine a flame-coloured foetus that got up and walked, and grew to eight feet tall, while fighting with an octopus. You're pretty much there.

Equally witty is an account of a visit to a *Who* exhibition at Longleat with a reluctant girlfriend in tow. Griffiths' enthusiasm wilts as he discovers they're the only two people there and the so-called exhibition is just a few tatty old props shoved into a room.

The inherent problem with *Dalek I Loved You* is that, as Griffiths' life progresses and his veneration for *Dr Who* wanes, so does his book's *raison d'être*. The author himself seems to acknowledge as much. Having listed his favourite *Who* stories, Hornby-style, he then has to fill space by listing his favourite songs and books as well. Later chapters are taken up largely with his life at university and his faltering steps towards a career in journalism. During these pages the Doctor scarcely features, except in fleeting, flash-forward mentions of the noughties revival version, with which Griffiths, as a TV critic, has a professional but not so personal connection.

Dalek I Loved You offers little in the way of analysis of *Dr Who*'s success and longevity. It does, however, reveal a great deal about Nick Griffiths. He's as honest about himself, warts and all, as he is about the TV programme which, in one particular incarnation, he adored, wobbly sets and all.

The Pagan House by David Flusfeder (2007)

David Flusfeder's *The Pagan House* is topped and tailed with a framing sequence in which a narrator, who teaches creative writing, as Flusfeder himself has in the past, is handed a manuscript by one of his pupils, Edgar. Having thus placed a cordon of ironic quotation marks around what follows, Flusfeder lets Edgar's novel unfurl. It's the tale of a twelve-year-old who travels from London to upstate New York, to visit his grandmother Fay in her large rambling house. The place is populated by several rather unlovable family members, including coarse, caustic Uncle Frank, and also by Warren, Fay's Irish-born carer, who offers his services for free and is therefore viewed with suspicion by all.

When Fay's cat goes missing, presumed murdered, Edgar embarks on a desultory investigation. He also pursues, with a pubescent boy's typical romantic haplessness, a couple of the local girls. His main preoccupation, though, is masturbation. He discovers this 'capacity', as he calls it, during a near-fatal nosedive on the plane crossing the Atlantic. Thereafter, he's at it whenever and wherever he can manage.

Which is appropriate, because figuratively as well as literally Edgar is a bit of a wanker. He's priggish, prickly, precocious, prolix, and not exactly the most congenial of company in which to spend 400 pages of close-printed text. Even during the final segment of the book, when he revisits America as an adult, he's too dour and depressive to be engaging. Flusfeder seems to have intended him as a character whose sheer unattractiveness is meant to command our sympathies; we should like Edgar in spite of himself and ourselves. But it's so damn hard to.

Not least because Edgar over-writes horribly. He wants to show us every word in his vocabulary and strives for the kind of verbose literary effects that come easily to masters such as Updike, DeLillo and (when on form) Martin Amis. He'll write lines like "Later, he would encounter the ferocity of her temper, which […] was the ashamed subject of her largest self-reproach" – part of a lengthy sentence that needs careful re-reading to be deciphered. He'll conjure up descriptive images that simply don't work, e.g. "Edgar brushed his grandmother's hair as moon- and starlight made warring patterns on the coverlet" (oh yeah? And what does that look like?). He'll happily spend a long paragraph or two telling us what it's like to eat pizza or scrambled eggs.

So no wonder it takes him 150 pages to unearth what happened to the cat, and the rest of the novel to... well, mope around not achieving much, actually.

Interspersed with Edgar's solipsistic maunderings is a subplot involving the history of the family homestead. Originally it was built by a Victorian-era religious sect, the Perfectionists, who attempted to create an earthly Eden based on Communism, Christianity and free love. Edgar himself plays a game with his mother in which they try to diffuse the unsatisfactoriness of their lives by building and refurbishing an imaginary mansion, a paradisal dream home.

It's a nice touch, and there are enough of these, along with the odd line of witty dialogue and amusing incident, to sustain one's interest. But still the underlying theme of doomed domestic utopia strives to be heard amid the relentless fumblings of Edgar's self-exploration, just as the plot of *The Pagan House* struggles to breathe under the suffocating weight of his prose.

Matter by Iain M. Banks (2008)

When Iain Banks slots the middle initial between his forename and surname, you can expect science fiction on a grand scale, replete with brain-busting concepts and laced with a dry wit – elements perhaps most fully realised in his 1994 novel *Feersum Endjinn*.

That superb book was a stand-alone work. *Matter* is set in Banks' Culture universe, which he has previously explored in six novels, a novella and a couple of short stories. The Culture, in essence, are a galaxy-spanning mega-race whose mastery of technology has freed them from strife and want. Their 'post-scarcity' existence allows them to devote themselves to learning and pleasure, and their society is run along left-wing libertarian lines, so that they are reluctant to interfere with or impose their ethics on other races.

Occasionally, though, they have to, which is where their foreign policy department, Contact, comes in, along with the organisation that is Contact's iron fist in a velvet glove, Special Circumstances.

Matter's heroine, Djan Seriy Anaplian, is an SC agent and also the estranged daughter of King Hausk, ruler of Sarl, one of several concentric worlds embedded within a Shellworld, Sursamen. In the wake of a battle with Sarl's enemies, the Deldeyn, Hausk is murdered by his treacherous right-hand man Mertis tyl Loesp, who has designs on the throne and further ambitions besides.

The act is secretly witnessed by Hausk's eldest son Ferbin, who immediately goes on the run. Together with his manservant Choubris Holse he heads off in search of Anaplian for help. Meanwhile Oramen, Ferbin's younger brother, finds himself on the way to becoming prince regent and slowly realises the danger this puts him in, courtesy of tyl Loesp and his co-conspirators.

Partly, *Matter* is concerned with hierarchy, whether it be that of a feudal civilisation like Sarl, or that of the multiplicity of star-spanning races who fill the cosmos, with the Culture among those ranked at the very top. The arthropodal species the Oct, for instance, have ambitions to rise up the ladder and see a mysterious, powerful artefact buried deep within Sursamen as the means of achieving this feat. Their ruthless, devious pursuit of the object proves to have deadly consequences for lesser and higher beings alike.

Which isn't, however, intended as a moral lesson to prove that such stratification is necessary and should be rigidly adhered to. Rather, Banks' point is that the system works as long as there is trust and reasoned understanding between the different levels. This is epitomised in the relationship between Ferbin and Holse, which over the course of the novel develops from that of feckless royal and worldly-wise underling into something deeper and more mature, an equalisation from which both men benefit.

Banks' SF is superior stuff, mercifully free of the self-important solemnity that makes most space opera so stodgy and hard to digest. As with his mainstream work, you're never far from a scene of raucous intoxicant abuse or a gritty one-liner. There's the added thrill, though, of cool future-tech weaponry, not to mention sentient spaceships with silly names.

Does *Matter* matter? Matter of fact, it does, and its linear, action-propelled narrative means that any newcomer to Banks' deeply imagined universe could do worse than start here, while the already initiated will be anything but disappointed.

Kéthani by Eric Brown (2008)

Eric Brown's Kéthani tales were written over the course of nine years and first appeared in various magazines and anthologies. This book assembles them between two covers, with additional linking passages, a prologue and a coda, and what's immediately striking is how of a piece they are. Each story progressively describes a larger plot arc while remaining self-contained, in the manner of Ray Bradbury's *The Martian Chronicles*, and like that book *Kéthani*, although its component parts were created disparately and out of sequence, coheres into a seamless whole, a novel.

The spirit of Bradbury is detectable, too, in *Kéthani's* overall tone – its logical positivism, its sense of the transcendent, its willingness to admit to wonder. The central premise is that a race of aliens, the titular Kéthani, have established a presence on Earth overnight, erecting thousands of vast crystalline towers called Onward Stations which permit access to the stars. Humans are given the choice of having tiny implants inserted into their foreheads. When an implanted person dies, his or her body is taken to the nearest Onward Station and beamed into space by some process of matter transfer. Six months later the person returns, altered. Younger, wiser, kinder, resurrected in a body uncorruptible, with the option of spending eternity exploring the universe as a Kéthani ambassador.

Naturally this process raises all sorts of ethical, social and religious issues, which are explored in the course of the book. What if, for instance, your religious faith is such that you refuse an implant because you prefer the idea of a spiritual hereafter to a material one? What if you find yourself unable to trust the Kéthani's gift, fearing that they must have some unknowably alien hidden agenda? What if, with your marriage disintegrating or your relationship still tentatively new, the prospect of an eternity with your partner is too much to bear? Does someone brain-damaged from infancy return from the Kéthani treatment the same or different? Is murder still a crime in a world without death?

With sensitivity and acute perceptiveness Brown explores such questions to their fullest, mediating them through a group of regulars who meet every Tuesday night at a pub called The Fleece. The group's roster keeps shifting but one member remains constant throughout, Khalid Azzam, a doctor whose calm, reasonable voice guides the reader from one chapter to the next and whose own moment in the spotlight, "The Wisdom of the Dead", is a neat little whodunit that owes a debt, albeit not a crippling one, to the Sherlock Holmes story "The Problem of Thor Bridge".

Kéthani takes place against the backdrop of the Yorkshire moors in winter. The physical landscape is constant across all the stories: snowy, cold, barren, bleak. Inside The Fleece, however, a fire is always blazing and the conversation is as warm as the beer. Brown's characters reflect this contrast. They're outwardly reserved, chilly even, but with a strong brew of emotions fermenting inside.

This is unfashionable SF, steering clear of the often cumbersome space-operatic conventions of size and spectacle, written in an unfashionable style, the sentences meticulously well balanced and the language articulate. On those grounds alone, *Kéthani* deserves to be read.

The Graveyard Book by Neil Gaiman (2008)

Characters in Neil Gaiman's fiction inhabit a world of shadows and gloom, but mostly (and the notable exception to this is *Sandman*'s Morpheus) they do not mope around wallowing in morbid melancholy. They engage with the dark, or at the very least adopt a pragmatic attitude towards it.

So it is with Bod, whose story forms the backbone of *The Graveyard Book*. As an infant, Bod wanders into a graveyard on the night that the rest of his family are murdered in their beds. He's swiftly adopted by the resident ghosts and christened Nobody. He is also taken under the wing – literally, one might say – of Silas, whom we are given to infer belongs to the night-flying, blood-sucking fraternity, although the v-word is never mentioned.

Episodic in structure, the novel follows Bod from infancy through to young manhood, introducing him along the way to ghouls, night-gaunts, a werewolf, some kind of guardian-creature out of Celtic folklore, a witch, and more besides. He also meets members of the mortal realm, most of whom prove to be bigger monsters than any of the beings he shares his necropolis home with. One who isn't is Scarlett, a girl Bod befriends and later in life must protect from the bad guys who killed his family and who still want him dead.

Said bad guys, the Order of the Jacks of All Trades, are a worldwide cabal of magic-assisted hoodlums passing themselves off as wealthy philanthropists. Admittedly their motivation for wanting to kill Bod is somewhat sketched-in and vague, seeming almost an afterthought to their role in the novel as a plot-driving force of pure malignance. They remain creepily compelling villains nonetheless, cold men with no souls in contrast to the humane warmth of the incorporeal spirits in the graveyard.

Two versions of *The Graveyard Book* are being published, a children's edition illustrated by Chris Riddell, of *Edge Chronicles* fame, and an adult edition illustrated by long-time Gaiman collaborator Dave McKean. Neither set of illustrations appears in review copies, so no specific comment can be made on them here, but it would be surprising if artists of such sterling pedigree turned in anything less than a spectacular job.

Even without pictorial accompaniment, though, this is a captivating work, light as fresh grave dirt, haunting as the inscription on a tombstone. The title and narrative structure may emulate Kipling and *The Jungle Book*, but the tone evokes Ray Bradbury in his whimsical-macabre pomp, and really there can be no higher praise than that.

Drood by Dan Simmons (2009)

The Mystery Of Edwin Drood is an anomaly in the Dickens canon. Famously it was left uncompleted at the time of the author's death in 1870. It was also his first and only attempt at writing a murder-mystery, heavily influenced by Wilkie Collins' *The Moonstone*, which was published a couple of years earlier and which most critics regard as the *ur* detective story.

Dan Simmons' *Drood* is set during the evolution and creation of both novels, and explores the close and often combative relationship between the two great writers.

The novel purports to be a manuscript left by Collins to be published a century and a quarter after his death. He narrates. Dickens takes centre stage.

The plot opens in 1865, at the scene of one of the most remarkable events in the latter's life, the terrible train crash at Staplehurst in Kent which he only narrowly survived. In the aftermath Dickens reports meeting a pallid, spectral figure moving among the dead and dying, who introduces himself as Edwin Drood.

Thereafter Dickens is drawn into a feverish pursuit of this sinister creature through London's rookeries and opium dens, dragging the reluctant Collins with him. His obsession leads both of them into mania, exacerbated in Collins' case by inordinate amounts of laudanum, and also into acts of literary pioneering and murderous abandon.

The scale and scope of this novel can't be faulted, except in so far as Simmons' utter immersion in his subject matter results in a few too many digressive forays into historical detail which slow the pace (a similar problem bedevilled his previous opus, the otherwise superb *The Terror*).

Drood is not only a kind of dual biography, it's a compendious exploration of several of the mid-Victorian era's signature fascinations (opium, mesmerism, the theatre, Oriental mystics), a forensic dissection of the creative process, a horror story, a study of the genesis of the detective novel as we know it, a superior specimen of metafictional pastiche, and a cunning gloss on Dickens' final work, whose catchword – 'Unintelligible' – recurs throughout, a dark, ironic refrain.

It is undeniably brilliant, absorbing in its immensity, shot with flourishes of Gothic genius.

We'll Always Have Paris by **Ray Bradbury (2009)**

Ray Bradbury, nigh on 90, continues to put out collections, although their contents are not in the strictest sense new. He is on record as saying that for every short story he has had published there's another that, for reasons of his own, he put away in a drawer. Recent books – such as *One More For The Road, The Cat's Pajamas* and *Summer Morning, Summer Night* – have seen him raiding that drawer pretty extensively.

And so it is with *We'll Always Have Paris*. In the introduction Bradbury tells us that these stories "came to me throughout my life – from my young age through my middle and later years". Might we then not feel short-changed? If these never-before-published tales were any good, wouldn't they already have seen the light of day? Are we being fobbed off with inferior material?

Not with an author of this calibre and this fecundity. While nothing in *We'll Always Have Paris* is Bradbury at his absolute pyrotechnic peak, nothing in it shames him in any way. Glints and firefly-flashes of the old master are in clear evidence. Every few paragraphs comes a simple yet arresting image. A couple sit down on a porch swing "which hung like a special scale weighing them, and them afraid of the total" – the precarious uncertainty of their relationship captured in a subtle snapshot. A woman who has just enjoyed adulterous sex has "a look of philosophic tiredness on her face". A haughty young man is imagined as wearing an invisible cape and mask, a Zorro in his own mind. A street scene is so silent, "the only sound was the sun burning in the sky".

Familiar Bradbury themes abound. There's a Mars story, "Fly Away Home", in which pioneer astronauts are saved from being driven mad by homesickness when a small-town main street is built on the sands of the Red Planet. It could have slotted neatly anywhere into the pages of *The Martian Chronicles*.

In the horror-tinged "Ma Perkins Comes To Stay", a neglected wife immerses herself all too literally in the world of radio drama. Guy Montag's wife in *Fahrenheit 451* does much the same with her TV soaps, and likewise the children with their virtual reality nursery in the sinister classic "The Veldt".

A number of the stories deal with romances and marriages that have grown stale or hit the rocks. Twice, in "Doubles" and "Un-pillow Talk", a game of tennis features as the salvation of, or at least a salve for, failing love. In "The Twilight Greens" we meet 'golf widowers', ageing husbands who prefer eighteen holes in the near dark to the dull comforts of hearth and supper. In "Miss Appletree And I", a wife generously pretends to be the fantasy mistress her husband, in the throes of midlife crisis, yearns for.

As if to counterbalance these rather dour, dark meditations on domesticity gone wrong, metaphors of birth and rebirth feature elsewhere, in the guise of ghost stories. "When The Bough Breaks" has newlyweds haunted by the sound of a baby crying. Realising it is their own not-yet-conceived child begging for life, they perform what may be described as a sexual exorcism.

"The Reincarnate" inverts this idea. A man rises from the dead for a reunion with his true love. After, he returns willingly to the grave and surrenders up his soul, which transmigrates to become the new life that the woman is carrying inside her.

As always, there are reminiscences of mid-Western idyll, the unashamedly nostalgic evocation of a time and place that are long gone and probably never were, the fictive vision of America-as-Arcadia for which, surely, there can now be just one accurate epithet, Bradburyesque. This we find in "Remembrance, Ohio" and, most heart-wrenchingly, in the father-and-son vignette "Pietà Summer".

One story is a distinct anomaly, not just in the book but in the whole Bradbury canon. The title tale tells of an abortive homosexual encounter in the French capital, and reads like lived experience, a true anecdote, a confession even. As curios go, it is very odd indeed.

That rueful miscue aside, *We'll Always Have Paris* demonstrates that Ray Bradbury's drawer still contains a wealth of gems and trinkets worth unearthing. Overall the collection is whispers and echoes of other, better work, but where Bradbury is concerned even whispers and echoes have more substance and value than most other authors' loudest shouts.

Journey Into Space by Toby Litt (2009)

It's always a slightly unnerving proposition when a mainstream literary author takes an unexpected sidestep into science fiction, having not shown any tendencies in that direction previously.

First of all there's the fear that he or she will deny the work is in any way science fictional, as though SF is somehow tainted and, by association, tainting. In the past this has given us the unedifying spectacle of Margaret Atwood and Jeanette Winterson, to name but two, putting themselves through contortions in their efforts to disavow the SF aspects of novels – respectively *The Handmaid's Tale* and *The Stone Gods* – that are plainly, full-bloodedly SF. Why choose to employ the tools and tropes of the genre if you're only going to flap your hands afterwards and claim you didn't?

There's also the danger that the author doesn't fully understand SF – where it comes from, how it works, what it's for. Then he or she will make a half-hearted stab at it, as if idly scratching an itch (Philip Roth's counterfactual *The Plot Against America*), or botch it altogether (Paul Theroux's turgid satire on consumerism, *O-Zone*), or, perhaps worst of all, hit upon some concept that to him or her seems new and revolutionary but to even the most casual SF reader is old hat – a case, one might say, of reinventing the warp drive. For instance, critics in the literary pages lionised Martin Amis for the time-in-reverse conceit of *Time's Arrow* while SF greybeards sighed and pointed out that, as is so often the case, Philip K. Dick did it first (in *Counter-Clock World*) and did it better.

Toby Litt's *Journey Into Space* is, happy to report, wholeheartedly and unashamedly an SF novel. The title is at once a tribute to the pulp magazines that were the genre's cradle – imagine it in a dramatic, up-sweeping font, perhaps suffixed with an exclamation mark – and an accurate if somewhat prosaic summation of the plot. This *is* a book about a journey into (and ultimately back from) space. It's that straightforward. But within the edifice of a scenario that has been done, let's face it, a million times before, Litt finds new and interesting rooms to explore.

UNSS Armenia has been travelling outward from earth for decades. The destination of this kilometre-long starship – capable of nearlightspeed but built, ironically, in the shape of a slug – is a habitable world which, when they reach it decades hence, the crew will colonise. Since cryogenic suspension has not been perfected, generations are born aboard the *Armenia* who will not live to see planetfall.

The story opens by focusing on teenaged cousins Celeste and August, who pine for an earth they have never known and who are finding it hard to come to terms with the fact that they will spend their entire lifespans as passengers in space. As an antidote to claustrophobia and ennui they conjure up descriptions of natural landscapes familiar to them only through literature and art, gradually distilling these into an imaginary paradise, which happens to be an idealised version of the Lake District.

Their collusion in this shared fantasy is a seditious act in the ship's rigidly controlled environment, where everything is monitored and broadcast by means of the all-pervasive onboard computer system known only as *it* (a clever play on the acronym for Information Technology). And when collusion becomes physical consummation, and a child is conceived, the way is paved for a collapse of moral purpose and a breakdown of order.

The fruit of Celeste and August's union, Orphan, is a drooling congenital idiot whose simple, hedonistic outlook is rapidly elevated to an ideology, and himself to Captain of the ship, and then King. Sexual restraint is superseded by orgiastic free-for-all. A sense of mission is discarded in favour of the missionary position (and, indeed, emissions). During this same period, earth itself convulses in a spasm of inter-religious war and civilisation is annihilated. This leaves the crew of the *Armenia* a deracinated race, isolated, pathologically depressed.

Eventually, naturally, a new order of discipline and asceticism emerges. The next generation of the crew form a nihilistic cargo cult that views the ravaged, polluted homeworld as an object of shame and scorn. The outcome is as inevitable as it is apocalyptic.

Journey Into Space's basic premise, of lunacy and decay occurring during an interminable spaceflight, has a direct antecedent in Brian Aldiss' 1958 novel *Non-Stop*. Litt, though, is to be commended for playing the whole thing absolutely straight and for using SF for what it does best: the examination of politics and society through futuristic and/or otherworldly metaphor. Not only that but he handles well the sense of sheer scale – spatial, temporal – in which SF exults and excels.

Sometimes his questing, inventive use of language strives for heights that it does not achieve, going from artful to arch. What is, one wonders, "an almost-sobbing form of sleep"? What advantage is there in describing something as 'different-differing'? Which is it, different or differing?

Nevertheless *Journey Into Space* is a rich, bold foray into the unknown for this author, from which he comes back triumphant, his literary reputation intact and his SF credentials, if he wants them, securely established.

Lavinia by Ursula Le Guin (2009)

Lavinia is something of a curiosity in ancient literature. She is Aeneas' second wife, and of royal blood, and it is her decision to marry him, an outsider recently arrived on the shores of Italy, rather than a local noble, that sparks a brutal conflict between the Trojans and her countrymen. From the ashes of this battle on the banks of the Tiber rises the city that will one day be called Rome.

Virgil intended his *Aeneid* to hew closely to both of its Homeric templates, the *Iliad* and the *Odyssey*. The initial wanderings of Aeneas and his fellow Trojan refugees echo those of Odysseus and his men. The war with the Italians is roughly analogous to the siege of Troy.

Lavinia, then, ought to be a figure of considerable importance and stature in the *Aeneid*, given that her role in the story corresponds to that of Homer's Helen. Yet she is scarcely mentioned. She is a walk-on part in Virgil's epic. A handful of lines describe her blonde hair and her grief at her mother's suicide. She is a shadow in the myth the poet was celebrating, glimpsed, thinly imagined.

Ursula Le Guin has taken it upon herself to put flesh on the barely-there bones of this character, to transform a thumbnail sketch into a fully-painted portrait. *Lavinia* gives us Lavinia's life in its entirety, from girlhood to old age, and illuminates her role as royal daughter, her joy as the betrothed of a hero, and her struggles as the widowed mother of a future king. The novel is a poised, distaff take on the usual male-dominated classical blood-and-thunder. It gives a voice to all the quiet women, the steadfast wives, the stalwart matriarchs, whose lot is to sit on the sidelines while the men make war and history.

In its early passages, *Lavinia* dwells on the day-to-day details of its heroine's young existence – the household duties, the sacrifices to the gods, her adoration of her father, King Latinus, and her strained relationship with her mother, who has never recovered from the deaths of her two infant sons from fever. A world rich in ritual and piety is evoked, a world teeming with divine omens and auguries much as a river is with currents. It's beautifully done. It's also, perhaps, a tad repetitive and dull.

Things liven up once Aeneas appears. Till then Lavinia has been busy fending off suitors, chief among them her self-regarding cousin

Turnus. With Aeneas' arrival, her destiny – and that of the region – is set, and the narrative takes flight with impressively described fight scenes and a true sense of how it might have been to live at such times, in the dawn-grey overlap between barbarism and civilisation.

The *Aeneid* ends (unfinished, some say) with Aeneas' slaying of Turnus. Le Guin continues and concludes the tale, ramping up Lavinia's part in the founding of Rome as she strives to keep her and Aeneas' son Silvius away from the malign influence of his older stepbrother Ascanius.

Being an SF and fantasy author, one rightly lauded for such novels as *The Left Hand Of Darkness*, *The Lathe Of Heaven* and in particular the *Earthsea* series, Le Guin has a further trick up her sleeve. She makes Lavinia aware of herself as a fictitious, illusory construct. Several times, Virgil visits Lavinia in her dreams and tells her of her future, as he is writing it. Lavinia therefore knows that she does not truly live, and at the same time that she will live for ever, certainly as long as the *Aeneid* is read. She knows, too, that she is only a footnote in the poem, lacking the vibrancy of, say, Dido. "[Virgil] did not sing me enough life to die," she says, conscious of this immense irony. "He only gave me immortality."

It's an unusual, poignant touch in this intriguing and often luxuriantly well-realised novel.

Transition by Iain Banks (2009)

The term 'multiverse' will be familiar to readers of Philip Pullman's *His Dark Materials* and Michael Moorcock's fantasy sagas. It's the theory that reality consists of an infinite number of divergent, coexistent parallel universes.

This unequivocally SF conceit is central to *Transition*, yet, curiously, the book is billed as an Iain Banks novel, not an Iain M. Banks novel. The absence of the middle initial implies one of the author's mainstream works, and yes, *Transition* is firmly engaged with contemporary culture and has acerbic comments to make about our age of global terror, financial collapse and state-sanctioned torture. But it is at heart SF, exploring outlandish Big Ideas as only SF can.

Temudjin Oh is a 'Transitionary' who can, with the aid of a drug called septus, project his soul between worlds, taking over the bodies of unsuspecting individuals much as though commandeering stolen cars. He works for the Concern, a vast, nebulous organisation described at one point as "a multiversal niceness-enforcement force". The Concern is there to police the alternate Earths and help them develop along the right track.

Or so it seems, but very little in *Transition* is to be taken at face value. From the outset Banks disorientates and wrongfoots with a rolling rota of disjointed, nonlinear and apparently unconnected narratives. How do the experiences of Patient 8262, an anonymous amnesiac stuck in a care home, dovetail with the reminiscences of wideboy coke-dealer-turned-hedge-fund-manager Adrian? How does the tale of the torturer known as The Philosopher relate to the storyline focusing on paranoiac sophisticate Madame d'Ortolan, a power player in the Concern, and her nemesis, the renegade Mrs Mulverhill?

Banks has terrific fun shuffling the cards of the plot and dealing them in a pattern that at first makes little sense but eventually takes meaningful shape. His customary punning wit and scatology are to the fore (a London gentlemen's club, for instance, is called The Perineum). There is also the playful suggestion that everything in the novel could be one character's fevered imagining, a dream.

For all that it might be just one long elaborate shaggy-dog story, *Transition* is nonetheless Banks at his exuberant, flamboyant, head-spinning best.

Under The Dome by Stephen King (2009)

Under The Dome reworks two novels Stephen King attempted to write earlier in his career. The first, also called *Under The Dome*, was a late-1970s draft he didn't get far with. He completed nearly 500 pages of the second book, *The Cannibals*, in the early 1980s before abandoning that project too.

The Cannibals was, as King says on his official website, "a kind of social comedy" about a group of people trapped in an apartment complex. The title provides a pretty big hint as to what they end up doing to one another. As for the original *Under The Dome*, the manuscript is long lost but King's memory of the first chapter remained so clear that, his afterword informs us, he was able to "re-create it almost exactly" when he sat down in 2007 to embark on the book one more time.

Under The Dome, in its present form, doesn't betray any evidence of being a fix-up of old material. It does, though, understandably hark back to vintage King, evoking the eschatological tone of *The Stand* and the small-town-in-peril framework of *'Salem's Lot*. Unlike more recent offerings such as *Lisey's Story* and *Duma Key*, there isn't the impression here of an author late in a long and well-rewarded career keeping a weather eye on posterity and his literary legacy. What we have is a pacey, balls-out tale of lives in a pressure cooker and the evil done by bad men convinced they have the best of intentions.

King rolls up his sleeves and gets straight to work in the opening pages. A light aircraft crashes for no obvious reason; a truck collides with an unseen barrier on what appears to be an open road. Some kind of invisible forcefield has descended over the Maine town of Chester's Mill, like a glass lid over a cakestand, cutting the residents off from the rest of the world.

The forcefield is as impenetrable as it is inexplicable. The military try burning through from the outside, burrowing underneath, a cruise missile strike, all to no avail. Trapped, the townsfolk begin by pulling together and making the best of their predicament, but caged-rat panic sets in soon enough. That's when a figure emerges to exploit the situation, Big Jim Rennie, used-car salesman and town Selectman (a kind of councillor in New England).

Rennie is a splendid villain, fat, ruthless, with cardiac arrhythmia and a cast-iron Christian piety which manifests in plenty of Bible quoting and the use of Bowdlerised profanity such as 'cotton-picker' and 'clustermug'. He was running a lucrative sideline in crystal meth manufacture before the Dome came down. Now he wants power, and with the aid of a psychotic son and a makeshift police force, he grabs it.

Every good dictator needs a scapegoat, and Rennie picks on diner cook and Gulf War veteran Dale Barbara. One can easily imagine Barbie – his gender-disorientating nickname – as a long-haired drifter in the original novel, a peacenik trying to forget Vietnam, like Rambo. Here he's haunted by dreams of prisoner abuse in Fallujah and, being an outsider, he's the ideal fall guy for what's going wrong in the town.

Through its long gestation, then, *Under The Dome* has matured into a critique of post-9/11 America. There are clear satiric parallels to be divined in a plot that centres on a self-deluded, religiously inspired leader pointing the finger at a spurious 'enemy within' in order to control a frightened populace. Global warming is a theme too. The atmosphere under the Dome rapidly becomes polluted and overheated, and at the climax a fiery manmade apocalypse destroys nearly everything.

Flaws are few. Prophetic visions experienced by a number of characters, principally children, serve as somewhat clumsy foreshadowing, and the rationale for the Dome itself is the kind of ironic payoff a *Twilight Zone* episode might conclude with. Set against that, though, is the aplomb with which King marshals a huge cast; his expert ratcheting of tension as he puts the people of Chester's Mill through the, ahem, mill; and his ability to sustain the liveliness of his narrative across almost 900 pages.

Towards the end of the book one character contemplates a possible future as a novelist, before baulking at the idea. "What if," she wonders, "you spent all that time, wrote a thousand-pager, and it sucked?"

Under The Dome doesn't suck.

Hergé: The Man Who Created Tintin by Pierre Assouline, translated by Charles Ruas (2009)

Tintin, with his plus fours, trademark quiff and faithful terrier sidekick Snowy, is one of the few truly iconic comicbook characters.

The man who invented him was born in Brussels in 1907. Georges Remi began his career as a graphic designer but soon was providing comic strips for the juvenile supplement of *Le Vingtième Siècle*, a newspaper administered by the conservative wing of the Belgian Catholic Party. Here, Hergé was born, the pseudonym generated by reversing Remi's initials and pronouncing them phonetically.

Tintin himself debuted in 1929 in an ongoing two-page strip. Billed as a 'boy reporter', he never seemed to do much actual reporting. Rather, he embodied his creator's belief in the ideals of the Scout movement, of which Hergé had been an enthusiastic member in his youth. His values also reflected those of the newspaper's editor, Norbert Wallez, a priest who became a father-figure and mentor to Hergé. Visiting "The Land Of The Soviets", Tintin was appalled by the atheist Bolsheviks. On his next adventure, in the Congo, he preached the virtues of colonial rule to the natives.

Later strips moved away from conformism and didacticism, and the best Tintin stories, published between the 1930 and 1950s, were straightforward, rip-snorting adventure yarns. By this time Hergé was leavening the action with humour, thanks to a supporting cast of memorable characters such as the irascible dipsomaniac Captain Haddock with his streams of eloquent invective, the befuddled, half-deaf scientific genius Professor Calculus, and the politely ineffectual bowler-hatted detective duo Thomson and Thompson.

However, a readiness to sacrifice anything for the sake of his art led Hergé to make moral compromises that would complicate his life and damage his happiness. The most compelling passages in Pierre Assouline's adroit biography cover the war years and their aftermath. In German-occupied Belgium, artists and writers were confronted with a stark choice: go along with the dictates of the regime or find other employment. Hergé decided, for the sake of Tintin's many fans, to continue providing weekly strips for tacitly collaborationist newspaper *Le Soir*. In the wake of liberation, while revelling in material success, he would struggle long and hard to rehabilitate his professional reputation. Later still, from the 1970s onward, he would find it difficult to answer critics who decried the blatant anti-Semitism which had occasionally reared its head in his earlier work. His somewhat diffident response was to say that Tintin and his adventures simply reflected the world as it had been during the middle of the century.

Le Monde journalist Assouline, who has also written a biography of that other famous Belgian Georges Simenon, is interested less in providing a 'life of' than in addressing the discrepancies and consonances between the artist and his art. Happily, the author never loses sight of the fact that, for all Hergé's personal shortcomings and sometimes blinding naïveté, he left us with a series of graphic novels that are visually beautiful, painstakingly well crafted, warm-hearted, thrilling, and capable of being enjoyed by readers of any age even today – no small achievement.

Smoothly and unobtrusively translated from the French by Charles Ruas, *Hergé: The Man Who Created Tintin* is to be commended for its even-handedness, lack of sensationalism, and also brevity. Given the vogue for biographies so compendious they seem to take as long to read as their subjects' lives were to live, Assouline has sketched a portrait of Hergé that is as clean, clear and concise as one of the man's own drawings.

Embassytown by China Miéville (2011)

Embassytown is China Miéville's seventh novel and his most pure science fictional work to date. Up until now, the author has traded predominantly in urban fantasy. For his trilogy of novels beginning with *Perdido Street Station* he created New Crobuzon, a Dickensian metropolis teeming with different races and species, some of them supernatural. In *King Rat*, his debut, and *Kraken*, he presented a vision of contemporary London layered with occult substrata.

These and other books have not only won Miéville countless prizes, including the prestigious Arthur C. Clarke Award for best SF novel of the year no fewer than three times, but also brought him a wide audience among mainstream readers as well as genre fans. Miéville, whose exotic name belies an upbringing in Norwich and Willesden, brings a rigorous intellectual high-mindedness to his work, which he combines with a sense of playfulness. He openly adores the tropes of SF and fantasy but also regards them as vectors for serious ideas and radical politics. He is one of a small but thriving band of British SF authors who see no reason why tales of space flight and alien worlds shouldn't tackle the same down-to-earth human questions that mainstream literary fiction has been dealing with for centuries.

In his new novel, set in the distant future, we are taken to another planet; the Embassytown of the title is a kind of citadel, a far-flung outpost of humanity perched amid a larger city that's inhabited principally by an indigenous race called the Ariekei, also known as the Hosts. The city's quirks and interstices are explored in typically loving detail, its various different quarters painstakingly mapped out. The Ariekei themselves are more of a mystery, but they and the human population, along with a few other alien races, have learned to rub along together.

Resembling a hybrid of winged insect and horse, the Ariekei have two mouths and converse using both at once. (Rather wonderfully, Miéville renders their dialogue as parallel phrases arranged one above the other like the numerator and denominator in a fraction.) Theirs is a double language, but the delicious irony is everything they say has only one meaning. Their syntax is such that it can only permit statements of truth, with no scope for duplicity or nuance.

Certain humans, known as Ambassadors, have been specially engineered by our own kind so as to be able to communicate with the Ariekei. Each Ambassador is a duo of test tube twins fitted with technology that links their minds and allows them to vocalise in unison. Thus interspecies trade is possible and humans have access to, among other things, the Ariekei's biotechnological machinery.

However, through centuries of exposure to human nature, the Ariekei have begun developing the ability to dissemble. As part of this process, they have taken the step of choosing certain ordinary humans to serve as what are known as similes. The Ariekei make someone perform a seemingly banal act – a man goes for a swim with fishes once a week, for example – then incorporate descriptions of these actions into their language. In some indefinable way the similes enrich their vocabulary and permit them to say what they don't mean as well as what they do.

Avice Benner Cho is selected to become one such simile while a child. We don't find out what exactly is done to her. All we are told is that she is somehow caused pain and made to eat something she doesn't want to. It's an uncomfortable and degrading experience which nonetheless earns her the admiration of the Ariekei. We then follow Avice as she grows up and leaves Embassytown to become a pilot in the 'immer', a kind of subspace ocean that permits relatively easy faster-than-light travel between worlds.

Returning home with a husband in tow, Avice learns that a new Ambassador is due to arrive in the city. It soon becomes apparent that this conjoined pair are not like the others. The Ariekei listen to them with rapt attention, becoming addicted to their dual voice as though to a drug. What with their crippling junkie-like dependency on the speech of this pair of human clones and a new-found capacity for falsehood, the Ariekei are no longer the docile, compliant indigenes they once were. Conflict inevitably breaks out between human and alien, a war both sides abhor but are powerless to prevent. At this point the novel threatens to become a somewhat didactic parable about how contact with civilisation degrades and corrupts 'primitive' cultures.

Miéville, though, is smarter than that. In fact, throughout the book he delights in wrongfooting us. Whichever way we anticipate he's going to turn, he turns the other. For example, Avice's husband, Scile, who seems to be a well-meaning revolutionary firebrand, turns out instead to be the Lucifer of the piece, its 'devil *ex machina*'.

This is a novel about language – in particular Miéville's love of language, evident in the neologisms, portmanteau words and allusive derivations he uses throughout. His prose scintillates with verbal invention; in places it becomes a sort of dense, gleeful, polyglot poetry:

The immer's reaches don't correspond at all to the dimensions of the manchmal, this space where we live. The best we can do is say that the immer *underlies* or *overlies, infuses,* is a *foundation,* a *langue* of which our actuality is a *parole,* and so on.

But there is also the underlying theme of language as a means of social control. Words can bridge gulfs of understanding but sometimes, deliberately or otherwise, lead to tragic misunderstanding.

At times, particularly in its early passages, *Embassytown* comes across as a linguistic thought-experiment more than anything, a book-length crossword clue, something to be mulled over and decoded, its pleasures solely cerebral. There is enough narrative action in the later stages, however, to offset this, and the characterisation is sharp and engaging from start to finish. What emerges from the wordplay and the exotic drama is an argument for tolerance. Anything alien is not to be shunned but rather interpreted, empathised with and, when possible, embraced.

In Other Worlds: SF And The Human Imagination
by Margaret Atwood (2011)

Margaret Atwood has published three novels, out of twenty so far, that can be classified as science fiction. All three – *The Handmaid's Tale*, *Oryx And Crake* and *The Year Of The Flood* – are admirable, and one, *The Handmaid's Tale*, is considered a modern SF classic.

Yet Atwood has long seemed to have an ambivalent relationship with the genre, claiming that this portion of her oeuvre cannot be science fiction, which is, in her words, "fiction in which things happen that are not possible today". She prefers the description 'speculative fiction', whereby an author takes some aspect of present-day life, exaggerates it, often for satirical effect, and extrapolates it into a future setting.

Such niceties of distinction aren't of great interest to the layperson. It's like specifying the difference between milk and dark chocolate. We can tell which is which usually just by looking, and we know already whether we like either or neither or both.

Happily, there isn't much of this sort of academic nitpicking in Atwood's new nonfiction collection, *In Other Worlds*. Instead, she has produced a wonderfully readable and accessible clarification of her relationship with SF and the SF tradition.

The book is split into four parts. The last two are bitty and ephemeral: a selection of brief excerpts from Atwood's own fiction to illustrate points she makes elsewhere in the book; and an open letter to a library followed by a short commentary on the 'brass brassieres' worn by women depicted on the covers of 1930s pulp magazines. It's the first and longest two parts which contain the real meat.

The book opens with the texts of three lectures the author delivered at Emory University in Atlanta, Georgia, in 2010. The first portrays her as a child, growing up in a remote region of Canada where she read voraciously and omnivorously and drew superhero comics featuring flying rabbits. Next comes a disquisition on mythology, incorporating her experiences of university where she was equally in thrall to literary theory and bad SF B-movies.

The third and final lecture, "Dire Cartographies", maps out her ideas about utopian and dystopian fiction and how she came to write the above-mentioned three novels, each of which fits into one of those two categories. She forges the somewhat ungainly term 'ustopia' to demonstrate that the distinction between utopia and dystopia – the perfect imagined world and the imperfect – is far from clear cut. In her view, "each contains a latent version of the other", just as each half of the yin-yang symbol bears an element of its opposite.

The lectures are insightful and cogently argued and boast a neat comic turn of phrase. For example, when discussing a purely mechanistic view of the universe which denies the existence of gods and reduces human life to a meaningless set of biological imperatives, Atwood wryly acknowledges that this isn't in any way whatsoever comforting: "... we don't like it much. It isn't cuddly. There aren't many tunes you can hum in the shower."

The second part of the book consists of reviews and critical analyses, focusing on works of – let's use her own coinage – ustopian fiction. Notable among these are a fascinating reading of Wells 'The Island Of Doctor Moreau; a detailed analysis of the Laputa section of Gulliver's Travels and its formative influence on the 'mad scientist' figure found in countless novels and films since; and penetrating examinations of Nineteen Eighty-Four and Brave New World.

The latter two novels deal with totalitarianism, but of contrasting kinds. Orwell described control of society being imposed from above, through oppression and force, whereas Huxley saw totalitarianism arising from the state assuming management of physical desires, principally materialism and sex in the mid-20th century when they were published it seemed plausible that every nation in the world could end up under the jackboot of one or other of these forms of dictatorship, and Atwood chillingly makes the case that it seems no less plausible today.

In Other Worlds sees Atwood finally demonstrating a willingness to adopt the mantle of SF author, as though accepting that there is no shame in joining the ranks of luminaries such as Orwell, Huxley, Wells and Swift. Her writing here shows someone revelling in the genre's many facets, be they highbrow or cheesy, with an enthusiasm and a level of intellectual engagement that is second to none.

Railsea by China Miéville (2012)

Railsea is billed as an 'all ages' novel, and is the second book by China Miéville, after 2007's *Un Lun Dun*, designed to appeal to younger readers as well as adults. At heart it is an adventure yarn in the mould of *Kidnapped, Treasure Island, Robinson Crusoe* and all those other classics of fiction that children today will most likely have heard of, if not actually read. There are reversals of fortune, breakneck escapes, narrow scrapes, pirates, even an abnormally intelligent animal sidekick – all the ingredients for a tasty stew of action and plot.

The problem is, there's a great deal of literary tricksiness as well. It is as if the author doesn't trust himself, or is too high-minded, to deliver a straightforward rollicking yarn. He has to deck out the narrative with references to famous novels and with interludes which directly address his readers and break the spell by reminding them that, yes, they are merely witnesses to a tale he has invented.

Miéville has imagination to burn and his genius at conjuring up striking fantasy landscapes and bizarre baroque technology is second to none. Frustratingly, beneath *Railsea*'s clever-clever, punsome writing, there's a terrific story struggling to breathe.

The world of *Railsea* is one where endless, countless crisscrossing rail tracks cover the land and are used by trains of different kinds – diesel, steam, even sail-powered. Some trains belong to salvagers, others to groups of nomads, while certain specialised ones are ridden by crews hunting gigantic monstrous moles that burrow beneath the ground. The moles are the whales of this earthy ocean, prized for the meat, oil and hide their carcasses provide.

One mole in particular, an albino specimen known as Mocker-Jack, is pursued obsessively by a moletrain captain who blames him for the loss of her arm in case you miss the point, consider this character's name, Abacat Nipha – an anagram of Captain Ahab.

Miéville embraces his near-namesake Melville wholeheartedly. *Railsea* is *Moby-Dick* recast as steampunk fantasy. There are brief informational passages that mimic the factual sections of Melville's epic. Similarly, the name of *Railsea*'s cabin-boy protagonist, Sham, echoes that of *Moby-Dick*'s narrator Ishmael (add 'lie' to 'sham' and you have another anagram).

Sham's name, however, is also indicative of the self-consciousness of *Railsea*, a repeated nudge in the ribs telling us that it's all fake. Adding to the general impression of artifice are the thickets of portmanteau words and neologisms the reader must negotiate – 'flatograph', 'scholarocracy', 'rumourbook', 'wartrain', 'ferronaval', 'gallimaufrayan', to list just a few – and Miéville's use of the ampersand throughout instead of just plain 'and' (a justification is provided for this but fails to convince).

In the end, you wish Miéville would have more faith in his own formidable storytelling skills and not place so many unnecessary barriers between reader and text. *Railsea* is brilliant. The pity is, the author wants you to know just how brilliant.

The House Of Rumour by Jake Arnott (2012)

What links Rudolf Hess to L. Ron Hubbard? Aleister Crowley to Ian Fleming? Kurt Waldheim to the Reverend Jim Jones? More than you'd think, at least according to Jake Arnott's sixth novel, which delves into the secret history of the latter half of the twentieth century and unearths all manner of connections, both factual and fantastical, between players in some of the pivotal events of the age.

If *The House Of Rumour*'s fragmented, multi-stranded narrative can be said to have a central protagonist, it is Larry Zagorski, an American science fiction writer of Arnott's invention who comes to prominence during the genre's Golden Age. This was the early 1940s, when SF shook off its trashy pulp-magazine associations to become a vector for big, serious ideas, exploring not just far-flung planets and the future but the human condition.

Larry's life and career meander through SF's many phases, taking in the 1960s New Wave, when optimism failed and cynicism took over, and the cyberpunk movement of the 1980s, which restored some of SF's techno-fetish gloss. Of all the known SF greats he most closely resembles Philip K. Dick, losing his way amid a welter of pharmaceuticals and paranoia while forever chasing after gnostic revelation.

Alongside Larry and his circle of acquaintances, Arnott juxtaposes a host of real-life figures who inhabit underworlds that are no less murky and arcane than that of science fiction and its adherents – demimondes where lies, stories, ideological argument and harebrained speculation are likewise the main currency. We meet Fleming, pre-Bond, in his role as wartime spymaster, recruiting the Great Beast himself, Crowley, for a covert operation to derail the Nazis' march to conquest using occult means. We also look in on the Cuban revolution, the Jonestown Massacre, the rise of the alien abduction phenomenon, and, most importantly, the abortive attempt by Rudolf Hess to broker a peace treaty between Germany and the West, which resulted in him spending the rest of his life in captivity at Spandau Prison as a bizarre kind of living talisman shared among the victor nations.

At the heart of the story are two further stories. One is a novel by an English SF writer, *Swastika Night*, which appears to predict Hess' mission. The other is a manuscript penned by a senior member of British counterintelligence which purports to tell the truth about Hess but may be fake, a piece of disinformation. There is little that we can take on trust in *The House Of Rumour* and much that we must look at askance as the viewpoints of extraordinarily unreliable narrators. The novel revels in this ambiguity, suggesting that what we accept as history is just a consensual fabrication, a version of events agreed upon retrospectively but by no means accurate. Nothing is what it seems. Everything is open to more than one interpretation. The made-up might be the reality, and vice versa.

The books takes the form of twenty-two interlocking short stories, some of them little more than character studies. Each is based on one of the Major Arcana of the tarot deck, drawing its theme from the symbolism of the card. On occasion the conceit does not quite work, Arnott straining to make it fit his purpose. The chapter named after the Tower card, for instance, hinges on Larry's first published story rather conveniently being called "The Tower", while the chapter named after the Moon card begins by asserting "Hitler had always despised the moon" and goes on to aggrandise our lunar satellite's role in helping Hess navigate his Messerschmitt through the night skies to Scotland.

Nonetheless the tarot motif is a neat sleight of hand, adding an extra layer of intrigue and esotericism to the book, a frisson of literary legerdemain. All said, *The House Of Rumour* is an astonishingly clever and thought-provoking piece of work. Arnott made his name with crime novels such as *The Long Firm* and *He Kills Coppers*, but they were as much about deception and double lives as they were about crooks and thieves. His interest is those ideas here reaches apotheosis. The novel is brilliantly written, meticulously researched, wise but not jaundiced, full of skilful literary ventriloquism and the occasional loving pastiche (the Fleming section deftly parodies that author's own pragmatic prose style). Above all else, it is forgiving – of humankind, of our high aspirations and our failure to meet them, of our low behaviour and our unwillingness to take responsibility for it.

Alif The Unseen by G. Willow Wilson (2012)

With the headlines still full of the events of the sputtering, tumultuous Arab Spring, G. Willow Wilson's first novel seems remarkably timely, even prescient. *Alif The Unseen* is set in an unnamed Middle Eastern country where revolution is fomented using the tools of the digital age – social media, phone-camera footage, instant messaging. This being a fantasy tale, however, there are genies and demons as well, making for a heady mix of the traditional and the contemporary.

Our hero is a hacker known as Alif. It's his online handle, and also the first letter of the Arabic alphabet and the first character of the first *sura* of the Quran. His real name is not revealed until near the end of the story. He is, by choice, a cipher, a person who exists primarily in the immaterial realm of cyberspace.

Alif's talent lies in creating software that protects anonymity and thus allows radicals and dissenters to operate freely online, safe from government crackdowns and censorship. He is as gauche in real life as he is confident at the keyboard – so callow that he fails to realise that the girl next door, Dina, whom he treats like a sister, is the right girl for him. He pines instead for haughty, rich Intisar, with whom he has had an affair but who is now promised to another man.

After their breakup Intisar sends Alif a beautiful leather-bound book of stories, the *Alf Yeom*. Its title translates as *The Thousand And One Days*, and it is purported to have been dictated to a human by a *jinn*. The book serves as plot MacGuffin, fought over, sought after, pursued, lost, found again. Most importantly, its language and use of metaphors inspire Alif to create a system-sabotaging program so powerful as to pose a direct threat to the oppressive aristocratic regime that rules his homeland.

The passages in which Alif writes his magically dangerous software are among the most vivid in *Alif The Unseen*. Wilson lets rip with her imagination, presenting the mundane nuts-and-bolts act of typing code as a trance-like, out-of-body experience: "The numbers themselves, like stories, were merely representative; stand-ins for meaning that lay deeper, embedded in pulses of electricity within the computer, the firing of neurons in Alif's mind..." This is cyberpunk taken to the next level, hacking as sublime, transcendental uplift.

Inevitably, the might of the authorities comes down on Alif's head, in the form of the state cyber-security specialist known as the Hand and his jackbooted minions. Alif seeks sanctuary in a mosque, and although he has a formidable champion in a *jinn* he has befriended, a fearsome creature nicknamed Vikram the Vampire, even that cannot save him. He is caught, imprisoned, and nearly broken by psychological torture. Wilson spares us no detail of the indignities and deprivations Alif suffers in captivity. Her novel may be fantastical but it is grounded in brutal realities.

Alif manages to escape and goes on to discover what it takes to be a hero, learning the lesson that 'most problems had very simple solutions, if one was willing to make sufficient sacrifice'. After taking a sidestep into a brilliantly realised otherworld where spirits and mythical beasts dwell, *Alif The Unseen* romps home to a satisfyingly dramatic and triumphal conclusion.

American-born Wilson lived in Egypt for several years and is a Muslim convert, so brings to her novel a broad and enlightening knowledge of Islamic tradition and culture. Her most notable previous work is the graphic novel *Cairo*, a similar blend of ancient mysticism and modern life. *Alif The Unseen* is a more fully-formed story, richer in characterisation and detail. Themes of the clash between truth and fiction, secrecy and revelation, are elegantly, maturely explored.

What lingers in the mind after reading this marvellous tale, however, is not Wilson's prose, for all that it is poised and lyrical, nor her storytelling, for all that it is skilful. What lingers is her message of hope for a region which to many seems trapped in an inescapable social and political quagmire. She shows us both the exotic Arabia of old and the energetic, striving Middle East of today, and puts forward the possibility of a stable, egalitarian future arising from a fusion of the two.

Ash by James Herbert (2012)

Ash is James Herbert's first new offering in over half a decade, a considerable silence for this hugely popular British horror author who since 1974 has averaged a book every other year. The novel's long gestation seems to be reflected in its elephantine proportions. Plenty happens within its nearly 700 pages, but *Ash* nonetheless feels cumbersome and unwieldy.

David Ash is a paranormal investigator already known to Herbert fans from earlier novels *Haunted* and *The Ghosts Of Sleath*. He is a paradoxical character, a determined sceptic who is also a psychic sensitive, capable of seeing ghosts.

Ash is hired to look into a series of spooky, violent events at Comraich Castle in a remote location on the Scottish coast. It's a highly secretive place that appears to be a retreat for burned-out celebrities, disgraced politicians and multimillionaires wishing to flee scandal – like rehab but with electrified fences and armed guards.

The castle has a bloody history and a curse laid on it. Hordes of animals, from Highland wildcats to oversized spiders, succumb to the malign influence permeating the building and grounds and pose a hazard to life and limb.

The true evil lurking at the heart of the story, however, is human. Some of the inmates of Comraich Castle are real-life hate figures, among them Colonel Gaddafi, Lord Lucan and Robert Maxwell. Others are the fictional offspring of royalty or fascist dictators. All are detained there for the sinister purposes of the Inner Court, a secret cabal described as "the powers behind the powers that be".

Herbert has great fun drawing together conspiracy theories that have circulated about the British establishment for decades and weaving them into his story. *Ash* works well as a black-hearted satire on the shameless misdeeds of the so-called great and good. The author depicts their acts of incest, rape, sodomy and corruption with a prurient, Hogarthian relish.

Unfortunately, the seething scorn and the supernatural scares aren't sufficient to sustain interest through a book of such length. Put simply, *Ash* is in dire need of a good pruning. There is too much description – particularly of people's clothes and physical appearance – and too many chunks of undigested Wikipedia research. For instance, do we really need to know the details of how a glow stick works? Is there any call for countless references to clinical pharmaceuticals and their uses and side effects? *Ash*, cut by half, would have been twice as good.

The Ocean At The End Of The Lane by Neil Gaiman (2013)

It begins with a funeral and ends with a death. *The Ocean At The End Of The Lane*, however, isn't a morbid novel. Neil Gaiman, one of the premier fabulists of our age, knows that not only is telling stories a good way of keeping the dark at bay, but also that the stories which do the job best are those with plenty of the dark already in them.

Our narrator, unnamed, returns to his native Sussex to bury a relative, unidentified. Driving to visit the house he lived in between the ages of five and twelve, he finds all the changes you might expect after forty-odd years have passed: fields are now housing estates, muddy country lanes now tarmacked roads. Unchanged, though, is the red-brick farmhouse once inhabited by his childhood friend Lettie Hempstock.

Viewing the duckpond at the bottom of the farmhouse's garden, the narrator is drawn into a reminiscence about his past, specifically about the year he turned seven. The pond serves the same function as Proust's madeleine, propelling him back in time.

Shortly after his seventh birthday his family takes in a lodger, an opal miner from South Africa who then, overcome with guilt at gambling away the savings entrusted to him by friends, commits suicide. The car in which the man kills himself is parked by the Hempstocks', and that is how the narrator meets Lettie, a strange, self-confident country girl, slightly older than him, with "a soft Sussex accent and sharp grey-blue eyes". She introduces him to the duckpond, which she calls an ocean. In it floats a fish which has choked to death on a sixpence. The association of death with money is a core theme of the novel.

It soon becomes clear that the three Hempstocks – Lettie, her mother and her grandmother – are otherworldly beings, gifted with clairvoyance and the kind of skills and wisdom that in olden days would have been called witchcraft. They are a homespun, rustic version of the classic female trinity of folklore and myth, Robert Graves' pagan triple goddess: the Maiden, the Mother and the Crone. This trio of archetypes have appeared in Gaiman's work before, notably as the housemates Thessaly, Hazel, and Foxglove in the *A Game Of You* storyline in his epic comicbook saga *Sandman*.

When the narrator wakes up one morning with a shilling

mysteriously stuck in his throat, he runs to the Hempstocks for help, fearing the ghost of the opal miner is haunting him. In fact he has been singled out for attention by an altogether more sinister creature. Lettie, guided by a hazel wand, leads him into another realm where the sky is "the dull orange of a warning light" and plants look "as if they have been beaten from gun-metal". Here they encounter a gargantuan, ragged monster which claims it wants to make humans happy by giving them what they want – principally money. They think they have convinced it to leave the narrator alone, but the monster has other ideas and manages to worm its way into his foot and thus gains, almost literally, a toehold in our world.

The monster manifests in the form of Ursula Monkton, a young, attractive housekeeper who is hired by the narrator's family and is soon working her wiles on his father and alienating the narrator from his nearest and dearest. A scene where the father, in a fit of maddened rage, almost drowns the boy on purpose in the bath is chillingly rendered. Later, as our narrator spies on his father and Ursula in an adulterous tryst, Gaiman artfully evokes the pragmatic, moralistic mindset of a seven-year-old. The youngster is neither enthralled nor repelled by what he sees. Nonetheless he senses instinctively that there has been a violation of the proper order of things.

Defeating Ursula entails sacrifice and loss, and so does growing up, and that is what *The Ocean At The End Of The Lane* is really about. It's about how our certainties fall away as we age and how our innate belief in magic and love of imagination wane but, tragically, nothing replaces them. Adults are merely "children wrapped in adult bodies, like children's books hidden in the middle of dull, long books. The kind with no pictures or conversation".

The novel is itself a children's book, in the sense that it's a book about childhood. A child could read and enjoy it, but only an adult will appreciate its bittersweet nuances and subtle sadnesses. In prose as delicate and diaphanous as a cobweb, and with a painstakingly precise use of symbolism, Gaiman traces one boy's journey from innocence, through fear and regret, to experience. In doing so, he traces all of ours too, and beautifully.

Doctor Sleep by Stephen King (2013)

The Shining, published in 1977, is one of Stephen King's best-known and most celebrated novels. Many years and many millions of published words have passed between then and now, not to mention many millions of sales, and as King says in the afterword to this sequel, "the man who wrote *Doctor Sleep* is very different from the well-meaning alcoholic who wrote *The Shining*". Yet *Doctor Sleep*, while not as feverishly suspenseful as *The Shining*, is a more than worthy successor, a sombre study of amok talent and inherited sins. It is, in fact, one of the best things the author has produced in some while.

The phrase 'well-meaning alcoholic' is key. Alcoholism lies at the core of *Doctor Sleep*, much as it did with its forebear. In *The Shining*, disgraced English teacher and aspiring playwright Jack Torrance is an abusive husband and father with a drink problem. His inner demons are as much a threat to him and his family as the ghosts which haunt the Overlook Hotel where Jack takes a caretaking job and where, snowbound in winter, he gradually goes insane. His son Danny and wife Wendy bear the brunt of his mania. Both are lucky to survive, saved when the hotel's faulty boiler explodes and the building burns down with Jack in it.

This, of course, is a different ending to that of the stately and much-lauded Stanley Kubrick film, which climaxes in a more downbeat way with Jack – a role that seemed tailor-made for the batty charisma of Jack Nicholson – dying of hypothermia in the hotel's hedgerow maze. There are other small differences between adaptation and source material, and those who know of *The Shining* only through the movie should note that the sequel cleaves solely to the action of the novel, which King maintains is "the True History of the Torrance Family".

Doctor Sleep picks up Danny's story not long after *The Shining*'s denouement, and for its first hundred-odd pages it somewhat ploddingly traces his life as he grows up and develops a crippling drink habit of his own, while King carefully tidies up the any leftovers from the previous novel and clears the stage to make way for the next act.

Danny – now Dan – has an addiction-prone personality that is in part innate, a genetic legacy. But he drinks, too, in order to quieten and dampen his psychic powers, dubbed his 'shining' by the Overlook's chef Dick Hallorann, who possesses those same abilities himself (and who survived in the original novel but was brutally axe-murdered in the movie). Dan is cursed with precognition and acute telepathic sensitivity. He is also still harassed by some of the horrifying spectres he encountered at the Overlook, who pursue him everywhere he goes until with Hallorann's help he devises a method for neutralising them. Alcohol, though, remains his preferred coping strategy: "The mind was a blackboard. Booze was the eraser."

Dan reaches rock bottom when he steals a girlfriend's last few dollars while she is sleeping off a cocaine binge. Riddled with guilt, he stumbles into a New Hampshire town called Frazier and falls under the benign influence of Casey Kingsley, a recovering alcoholic who offers him a job and, more importantly, persuades him to join Alcoholics Anonymous and becomes his sponsor.

As Dan struggles to beat his addiction, he finds work at a hospice, Helen Rivington House, and here he discovers a use for his shining, a purpose in life. Whenever a resident of the hospice is close to death, Dan is able to comfort them and ease their passing. With his powers he shows them that there is nothing to fear; there is more to come. Soon the nursing staff have dubbed him, with kindly euphemism, Doctor Sleep.

Meanwhile another, more sinister group of addicts is roaming the highways and byways of America in an innocent-looking convoy of recreational vehicles and camper vans. They are the True Knot, and they are vampires of a sort. They feed off the shining of children, which for them takes the form of a silvery mist they call 'steam'. Inhaling this rejuvenates them and effectively grants them immortality. The children, alas, have to die, and in great pain, in order for it to be released.

The True Knot have piratical, gangsterish names – Crow Daddy, Barry the Chink, Snakebite Andi, Jimmy Numbers. They are a makeshift but close-knit family, and King is at pains to show them not as purely evil, rather as desperate and needy, monsters with human failings, "more than people, *worse* than people". Deprived of regular doses of steam they age, degenerate, and eventually flicker into nonexistence like a torch with a drained battery.

Their leader, beautiful but terrifying matriarch Rose the Hat, becomes aware of a young girl with an immensely powering shining, Abra Stone. Rose knows that Abra's steam would feed her and her people for a long time once she matures.

Abra and Dan forge a telepathic connection, tentative at first but increasingly strong. By the time she reaches her teens Abra's supernatural abilities are so great they pose a danger to herself and those around her, much like Charlie McGee, the pyrokinetic girl in King's *Firestarter*.

When Rose deems Abra finally ripe for plucking, Dan senses the danger, and the two of them, with a handful of allies, move to confront the True Knot and end their menace once and for all. This entails a showdown at the site of the former Overlook, now a campground called the Overlook Lodge. It's more than just ironic coincidence. "Life was a wheel, its only job was to turn, and it always came back to where it had started." The climax brings, for Dan, a touching grace note, a moment of final reconciliation.

The ideology and mantras of AA flow through *Doctor Sleep* like a river current. This is a novel about making amends, admitting and accepting one's past wrongs, and surrendering to one's 'Higher Power' – literally so, in Dan's and Abra's case. King is himself a recovering alcoholic and substance abuser. His successful battle with booze and drugs is well documented, and he has addressed it frankly and compellingly in his memoir *On Writing*. His novels are often exercises in self-exorcism; writer's block, a persistent fear, has featured in many of them, not least *The Shining*. Here we have him ousting one more demon from residence in his mind, bringing it screaming into the daylight to burn to ashes.

Doctor Sleep clocks in at just under 500 pages, which for Stephen King is concise. The bloat and self-indulgence which have afflicted some of his recent output, such as *Under The Dome* and *11. 22. 63*, is largely absent, and after a slightly awkward opening that's like starting a car after it has been lying idle in the garage for too long, the story gets into gear and pulls you along on a remorseless ride. This is a gripping and powerful novel, all the more so for being patently heartfelt and *meant*.

Dark Entries by Robert Aickman (2014)

Robert Aickman's literary reputation, like that of M. R. James, rests on the few dozen horror stories he published during his lifetime. Like James, Aickman was a cultured aesthete, delivering scares in a precise, somewhat lofty style as though addressing the reader from behind a veil of erudition. Because he belonged to a later, more liberated generation, however, Aickman was able to introduce deep, swirling undercurrents of sexuality into his haunting tales.

Indeed, sex is what leads people astray in almost all the stories in *Dark Entries*, a collection originally published in 1964 and now appearing in a new edition as part of a reissue by Faber of all of Aickman's books on the centenary of his birth (he died in 1981). As protagonist after protagonist is undone by temptation and lust, one can't help but divine a sinister double entendre in the book's title – something nocturnal and obscene. In "Choice Of Weapons" a man abandons his heiress girlfriend, and the secure future she represents, in order to chase after a girl he glimpses across a restaurant. His obsession leads him to cross swords with a dangerous otherworldly rival for her love. The hero of "The View", meanwhile, meets a beautiful, enigmatic woman on the ferry from Liverpool to the Isle of Man and is soon sharing her stately home and her bed. Such is his infatuation that he is not deterred by the way the landscape around the house is constantly transforming or by the weird, shambling figure – like some sort of nameless pagan god – who roams the grounds.

In perhaps the best-known and most anthologised tale in the collection, "Ringing The Changes", Gerald Banstead and his new, much younger wife Phrynne are honeymooning in a remote East Anglian seaside town where the church bells peal insistently one night a year. The purpose behind this is gradually revealed: they are summoning the dead from their graves. Common sense urges Gerald to flee before it is too late, but Phrynne's amorous demands – "Lie still instead, and love me" – persuade him against his better judgement to stay. A grotesque *danse macabre* of reanimated corpses and living townspeople winds its way into their hotel room, sweeping them both up in it. Phrynne emerges with "a nightdress so torn that she stood almost naked" and an erotic flush to her face. The experience, it is implied, will forever colour the rest of the marriage.

Cold, wintry settings contrast with the heat of passion. Neuroses become embodied as ghosts, caged demonic entities, doppelgangers, shape-shifters. Aickman's peculiar talent as an author is never making explicit the nature of the evil that ensnares his characters; what he does show is that they are at least half complicit in their own doom, drawn towards the hideous and the unknown as though in a dream, like sleepwalkers.

These 'strange stories' (Aickman's preferred description) are supernatural detective mysteries without a clear solution, each ending on a plangent, cracked note of ambiguity which sounds in the mind for a long time after. Often it is hard to decide whether the hauntings are genuine or merely manifestations of psychosis – nervous breakdowns projecting themselves outward onto the world. In that respect they speak to a modern reader more vibrantly than, say, James' donnish, Christmas-sherry entertainments. They are emanations manifesting from the dark heart of a fearful, uncertain century.

Moriarty by Anthony Horowitz (2014)

One of the smaller but more intriguing subsets of the Sherlock Holmes pastiche industry is stories featuring the great detective's nemesis, Professor James Moriarty. Michael Kurland has, to date, produced five very entertaining novels in which Moriarty is called on to solve crimes, poacher turning gamekeeper, while Kim Newman's *The Hound Of The D'Urbervilles* is a riotous romp focusing both on the Napoleon of crime and his pet thug Sebastian Moran.

Anthony Horowitz's *Moriarty* is, as the title suggests, another Moriarty-centric book. To all intents and purposes, however, Moriarty is barely present in it. Neither does Holmes appear, except for in a linked but discrete short story at the end. Both characters are like shadows cast over the novel, ghosts loitering at the edges.

The story takes place in the aftermath of the final, fateful showdown between the two men which led to Moriarty plunging to his doom at the Reichenbach Falls and Holmes disappearing for three years, leaving the world to presume he was dead. Barely has Moriarty's corpse been pulled from the water than a Pinkerton's agent from New York, Frederick Chase, arrives in Switzerland to examine it, as does Athelney Jones of Scotland Yard.

Even the casual Sherlock fan should recognise that name. Inspector Jones is the hapless copper in *The Sign Of The Four* whose ham-fisted attempts at deduction are archly derided by Holmes, although the sleuth does concede that Jones is "not a bad fellow". Here, Jones has taken Holmes' criticisms to heart and devoted himself to emulating his analytical methods. In fact, Sherlock Holmes has become something of an obsession with him. His study at home is a shrine to his newfound idol, littered with forensic equipment and copies of the *Strand Magazine* and Holmes' own monographs. Physically, Jones is not a well man, suffering the consequences of a serious bout of rickets, but it is suggested that he might also be mentally unbalanced, desperate at all costs to prove his worth after being portrayed on the page by Watson as a pompous, plodding buffoon.

Chase, meanwhile, has come to Europe from America in pursuit of a mysterious Chicagoan criminal mastermind called Clarence Devereux who, in the manner of a Bond villain, has a freakish distinguishing characteristic: crippling agoraphobia. It appears that Devereux and Moriarty were in league, and with the latter now dead, the former looks set to take advantage of the power vacuum in the London underworld and establish himself as the capital's new crime boss. Jones and Chase (who narrates) swiftly form a partnership whose dynamic in many ways resembles that of Holmes and Watson, the sharp-witted detective always one step ahead of his slower-on-the-uptake sidekick. At one point Jones even chastises Chase using one of Holmes' familiar formulations: "You see but you do not observe."

Their investigations draw them into the orbit of some particularly nasty American criminals who, like Mafiosi, masquerade as legitimate businessmen and whose penchant for torture and execution is decried as distinctly un-British. Though Horowitz dishes up the gore and violence with relish, he also offers all the tropes one might expect from a Holmes yarn, including baffling coded messages, impossible murders and clever red herrings. There are nods to the canonical works, too, not least a robbery which explicitly references that in "The Red-Headed League", while in one beautifully orchestrated scene the author assembles together just about every Yard detective who ever graced the pages of Conan Doyle's original tales, including Gregson from several adventures, most notably *A Study In Scarlet*; MacDonald from *The Valley Of Fear*; Bradstreet from "The Man With The Twisted Lip" among others; Gregory from "Silver Blaze"; and last but not least good old Lestrade. It's a moment of trainspotter heaven for Sherlockians.

Horowitz, best known for his Alex Rider spy series for teens, produced a previous Holmes pastiche three years ago, *The House Of Silk*, a sombre but bracing novel which took the character into unusually dark territory. *Moriarty* is a different beast, its plotting just as brilliantly gnarly but its tone more self-aware and laced with wry in-jokes. Frederick Chase is a classic unreliable narrator, and towards the end the author pulls off a wonderful prestidigitatory coup which few, one suspects, will see coming but which plays entirely fair with the reader and makes perfect sense.

The Peripheral by William Gibson (2014)

When William Gibson debuted as a novelist with *Neuromancer* in 1984, he rapidly became SF's new great prognosticator, the Wells or Clarke of our times, writing of near-futures where capitalism has run rampant like a weed and humans are intimately interfaced with technology. His early novels established the template for the cyberpunk genre with their exhilarating fusion of film noir tropes, vibrant urban subcultures and post-abundance decay.

By the turn of the century, events seemed to have caught up with Gibson's imagination – we were now living in a cyberpunk world – and he turned his attention to the present day. 2003's *Pattern Recognition* and its two sequels are contemporary, more or less mainstream thrillers where corporations and brands, rather than nations and governments, are the power blocs.

The Peripheral sees the author making an emphatic return to pure SF. Here are not one but two futures, the narrative interleaving a pair of storylines, one set in America a couple of decades hence, the other in London some seventy years after that. Dividing the two eras is a global watershed known euphemistically as 'the jackpot', a slow apocalypse arising from a perfect storm of environmental and economic collapse which results in an 80% reduction in world population levels and immense prosperity for the remainder.

In the nearer-future storyline, professional gamer Flynne Fisher witnesses what she at first assumes to be a fictional death, the gory disintegration of an in-game avatar on a balcony of a giant London skyscraper. To her horror, she learns that she has seen an actual murder taking place and only she can identify the culprit.

This information is conveyed to her by a resident of the further future, Wilf Netherton, a human resources expert variously described as a 'chronic malcontent' and a 'bullshit artist', who is in the employ of a wealthy kleptocratic family of Russian origin. The bridge between the two periods is a process, only vaguely explained by Gibson, known as 'quantum tunnelling' which among other things allows people in the future to affect events in the past through communications and the manipulation of money markets. Such interference creates a 'stub', the bud of a new, divergent timeline.

The run-down semirural Middle America which Flynne inhabits is a vivid and all too plausible vision of a nation going down the pan. Drug dealers generate their own product on 3-D printers, injured war veterans rely on robotic prosthetics, homespun militias act as law enforcement, a single corporation has a monopolistic lock on the retail industry, and Homeland Security is an all-seeing, all-powerful agency. Gibson's great strength is his ability to sketch in these details so that they are organic, integrated into the characters' dialogue and experiences. We see their world familiarly, as they live in it, the prose embedded with slang terms and little eye-catching references that indicate how things have moved on: "the cork-patterned paper on the squashed filter of a legally sold cigarette, older than she was"; the smell of pancakes which "meant they were printing with that plastic you could compost".

The further-future London is more exotic and Gibson seems correspondingly less comfortable conjuring it. It's a city dotted with sleek towers known as 'shards' which vault above empty, vegetation-choked streets and contrast with a Victorian theme-park Cheapside populated by costumed androids and tourists. Here, his deftness at creating credible texture rather withers and he resorts to elaborate, overlong descriptions of furniture and clothing as a substitute. There are cherishable inventive touches nonetheless, such as Lego bricks that move and morph of their own accord, mobile tattoos of extinct animals adorning a character's skin, and artificial bodies, the peripherals of the title, which serve as ambulatory telepresence units.

The back-and-forth interplay between the twin narrative strands is complex and tangled, the plot hinging on getting Flynne to a party via peripheral so that she can formally ID the murder suspect, which in turn may prevent the jackpot from becoming the flat-out disaster it was in Netherton's history. There's still not really enough story to sustain a book of nearly 500 pages, however, and one finds oneself missing the terse precision and nippy pacing of Gibson's earlier work. While it's good to see the author going back to the future, if only his crystal ball were that little bit more sharply focused.

Forewords

Foreword to Jupiter Magnified by **Adam Roberts (2002)**

"Poetry has never been about the world ending. I wonder why not?"

So says Stina Ekman, poet, protagonist of Adam Roberts' *Jupiter Magnified*. Strictly speaking, she's wrong. Eliot's "The Hollow Men", Yeats' over-quoted "The Second Coming", Edwin Muir's sinister yet hopeful "The Horses", Peter Porter's deadpan, cynical "Your Attention Please" – these are all poems of peculiarly twentieth-century doom, verses from an era when the world balanced time and time again on a perilously sharp knife-edge (the same knife-edge persists today, albeit somewhat blunted).

Less strictly speaking, she's right. A poem of the apocalypse, any artwork which depicts the subject of The End, is not so much about the destruction of the mundane than about the destruction of the self. The poet, the artist, is really addressing his or her own mortality, the termination not of *the* world but of *a* world, the eventual, inevitable demise of mind and spirit and the whole nurtured artefact of a life. The twentieth century, when God died too, heightened our anxiety about death. Magnified it, you might say. Externalising the internal, creative types responded by extrapolating their own fears to encompass the entire planet. With extinction for oneself a certainty, and extinction for all a real possibility, why not conflate the two? The one might quite readily be mistaken for the other.

Jupiter Magnified is about The End, or a perceived End. It opens with a sudden, startling portent in the sky, the kind of omen that throughout the centuries we have been warned to look for. All at once, with this irruption of the impossible into the fabric of the everyday, the life of Stina Ekman is thrown into disarray. The whole world, accordingly, falters and quivers. Her response, everybody's response, Roberts carefully and convincingly delineates. He has a sharp and candid eye for the truths of human nature. Stina snaps at her boyfriend, and then:

He looked a little crestfallen, so I was moved to try and comfort him. I hate that impulse; I feel weak and stupid, but it gets me every time.

Even as things fall apart, people remain people.

But the crisis, Stina's crisis, has been brewing since even before the beginning of The End. Stina is suffering from writer's block – a death, of sorts; a perpetual inner stillbirth; the collapse of purpose. She is struggling against an oppressive sense of meaninglessness, while, with savage irony, Meaning writ large hovers overhead in the form of the titular planet – redolent with symbolism, immune to a single interpretation, a cosmic poem. Her efforts to re-ignite her creativity are the spine of *Jupiter Magnified*. The novella's unusual shape, as you will see, reflects her fight and embodies in its very format the triumph of art over annihilation.

Adam Roberts is an academic, a Reader in Nineteenth Century Literature no less, but carries his learnedness lightly. His fiction is not robed in donnish fustian. It combines steely, disciplined prose with liveliness of imagination. Roberts, unlike many science fiction authors, is steeped in more than just science fiction. You can tell. He is not part of that Campbellian school that has been recycling gung-ho intergalactic clichés since the 1950s. He brings a literate sensibility, a breadth of interest, to his work, and does not allow himself to be hamstrung by convention or by rigorous adherence to the dictates of science. In his novel *Salt*, he posited a planet covered entirely in salt. Not geologically very likely, but as a metaphor for conflict, sublimation, the fusion of opposites? Brilliant. In *On*, he created a world where gravity runs sideways. Physically impossible, and yet, in fictional terms, skewed and compelling. And the same is true of *Jupiter Magnified*, whose central phenomenon is explained in various plausible ways but remains, at heart, numinous and unknowable. Roberts understands the need for getting the minutiae right but isn't constrained by it. The idea matters more. The idea rises above.

In this respect he becomes a literary author who just happens to write science fiction. If he had chosen to, he could easily have gone down the mainstream route, and with results just as successful. You would doubtless then be reading about his work in the books pages of the Sunday supplements. But the McEwans of this world, the Amises, the Ishiguros, the ones who do get the fawning attention of newspapers' literary editors, brilliant though they are, write within a narrow field. They, as it were, have restricted themselves to the rainbow, whereas authors like Roberts have correctly intuited that there is a whole further range of colours out there beyond either end of the visible spectrum, a palette imperceptible to the unaided eye but rich and strange when discovered and disclosed. Roberts is part of an upcoming generation of novelists who have seen that there is something to be gained by shedding a literary light on the occult traditions of SF, and that if SF has a future – a real future, not one of its many imagined ones – it lies in taking itself seriously and looking outside itself for inspiration.

Jupiter Magnified demonstrates clearly this shedding of light. It is, indeed, a story about light. It is about shades of light, and of darkness as well. In theme and execution it reflects, almost literally, *Pale Fire* by Nabokov (another academic). That book extrudes a novel from the footnotes to a poem. This book effectively inverts the process, and its power resides in its openness to interpretation, its refusal to give tidy answers, in the manner of the best poetry. In tone it is more saturnine than jovial, shot through with an immutable melancholy. One could almost believe it is genuinely a translation from the Swedish, gloomily Scandinavian. At the same time, it carries a weirdly uplifting conclusion, a touching reminder that not every end is The End. Stina's fate is not written in the stars. No one's is. *Jupiter Magnified* gives you the haunting, thrilling sensation that there is no situation, however dire, that cannot be transcended.

Foreword to *The Halloween Tree* by Ray Bradbury (2009)

A small confession. I didn't like *The Halloween Tree* when I first read it.

I was in my early twenties. I'd been a massive Ray Bradbury fan since I was 11 or 12. Fan? That word hardly begins to cover it. Bradbury was the author who'd sustained me through my teens, encouraged me to believe that the science fiction and comics I loved were worth loving, and kindled the flames of my nascent ambition to become a writer. Bradbury was everything to me. His books were my sword and my shield. I'd read them all, several times...

Except *The Halloween Tree*. Mainly this was because no mass-market edition had been published recently enough in the UK. it just wasn't available then. Also, I knew it was a kids' book, and as a teen I didn't want to read a *kids'* book. (I didn't really want to read kids' books as a pre-teen, either. Once I'd had a taste of stronger meat – Conan Doyle, Ian Fleming, Robert E. Howard, Michael Moorcock – I had no wish to eat baby food any more.)

Finally, around 1990, I bought a Bantam edition of the novel, imported from the US, at Forbidden Planet in London. *I'll give it a go*, I thought. *It's Bradbury. I'm sure there'll be something I like about it.*

But there wasn't. The book seemed too... schematic, I think's the word. The way the plot was laid out, the box-ticking jaunt through history, the linear leaps from era to era. Too didactic. Too contrived.

I admit all this simply to demonstrate how wrong a twenty-something young man can be.

The Halloween Tree was unmistakably Bradbury, that much I could see. It had all his trademark tropes – the dynamic language, the imaginative flights, the towering use of sustained and incidental metaphor, the thrilling, unabashed enthusiasm, the prose that launched itself off the page on springboards of italics, exclamation marks and new coinages to hit you again and again smack dab in the inner eye.

But I felt there was something missing. Because it was a story for children, it seemed like a cocktail with all the alcohol taken out, a Shirley Temple of a book. The dark, throbbing undertone found in *Fahrenheit 451* and *The Illustrated Man* wasn't there. Sweet, but no back-of-the-throat hit. All dandelion, no wine.

Now, almost twenty years on, my view has changed. Radically. Now, I'm a grownup, or a boy masquerading as one at any rate, and I have two children of my own, and I understand better the purpose of children's fiction, as someone who's penned his fair share of it.

I know what the point of *The Halloween Tree* is. It isn't just a history lesson couched in pyrotechnic prose-poetry. It isn't just an explanation of the whys and wherefores and what-the-hells of Halloween. It isn't just another of Bradbury's hymns to the habits and haunts of his youth in Waukegan, Illinois. It's all those things, but it's more, much more.

The novel began life in 1967 as a screenplay for a cartoon to be animated by the great Chuck Jones. That project did not come to pass, and so we have never got to taste the fruits of what would surely have been a glorious collaboration between the grandmaster author and the creative genius behind Bugs Bunny and Daffy Duck. Eventually, in 1993, a feature-length cartoon was made, directed by somebody called Mario Piluso. But for all that it boasted Bradbury himself providing the narration and Leonard Nimoy voicing the role of Moundshroud, the result was disappointing – a scratchy shadow of what might have been – although the script nonetheless garnered Bradbury an Emmy.

Bradbury turned screenplay into book in 1972, and the influence of Chuck Jones can be clearly felt in several places: Moundshroud-as-mummy's sudden pratfall, for instance, and the scene in which the boys conjure a staircase out of nothing to get to the top of Notre Dame. One can imagine each of the book's setpieces segueing into the next in a feverish swirl of hand-drawn lunacy, *Merrie-Melodies*-style. Imagine, and drool.

But as a prose piece, *The Halloween Tree* has so much more to offer than its visual coups. There's Moundshroud himself – let's honour him with his full name, Carapace Clavicle Moundshroud – who is a vector of seductive wish-fulfilment like Mr Dark from *Something Wicked This Way Comes*, but more besides. He's the firefly-eyed embodiment of our deeper fears, particularly the deepest fear of all, that of death; yet charming with it. He wants to educate our eight young heroes, most of all Tom, the book's autobiographical Bradbury-as-boy persona. He also, at the end, wants to exact a steep price from his pupils in return for imparting this knowledge. He's genial but amoral, as any instructor in the school of sinister studies should be.

Then there's the book's restatement of a classic Bradbury theme, which is summed up in a single line of dialogue uttered early on by Joe Pipkin, the official plot MacGuffin:

"This *summer*! Before you know, bang! – it's gone! Quick!"

Pipkin is youth and summer incarnate. He's a fleeting moment of sunshine and delight. He's the infinite possibility of boyhood. And he's self-aware enough to know that life must be grasped, *now*, while you're young, and must be relished, and cherished, because it's never going to be this good again. His near-fatal illness, which impels his eight friends to rescue him with Moundshroud's aid, is the brush with mortality that brings a chill to the sunlight. It's what Halloween is about – the recognition that summer is, must be, finally over, autumn is here, and the cold, dark months are coming. Youth is all the sweeter if you understand and accept this hard truth. The heedless, headlong days cannot last, so make the most of them. Adulthood isn't nearly as much fun, and death's wintry breath blows constantly through it.

Finally, there's the Halloween Tree itself, its branches hung with flickering jack-o'-lanterns. It's the symbol that roots the entire book. Death and life in one. A growing thing laden with the shells of things that once grew, things carved in a mimicry of life, in each of which a semblance of life burns, all in celebration of a day of death. It's both ornament and warning. Alluring and alarming. Haunting. Haunting in its beauty. Haunting like a ghost. Bradbury has often declared himself an author, not of any particular genre of fiction, but of fiction that deals in pure metaphor. The tree is pure metaphor.

All of which leads me to revise the addle-pated opinion of my early manhood. *The Halloween Tree* has a place at the heart of Bradbury's oeuvre, not in spite of but because of its being a children's book. It exists to tell children to treasure what they have, and it exists to remind adults to treasure the memory of what they used to have. It is a novel about boys, for boys, and for the men that boys become. (The cartoon made the mistake of including a girl in the cast of characters. Bad move. Girls have their own enchanted circle to dance in, and it's not the same enchanted circle as the boys'. Responsibility comes much earlier to them, and they welcome it. Bradbury knows that boys are freer longer, and at liberty to go crazy, in a way that girls can't and don't wish to.)

The Halloween Tree speaks to the boy who still raves from time to time inside me, and tells him that he's had his moment in the sun and, pray to God, he made the best of it. It also speaks to the father that I am and reminds me to let my two sons be as mad and impulsive and wilful and blithe and dreamy and fantasy-led and reckless with their own wellbeing as they can be (within limits). They will never get another chance like this. Over its short length the novel rips my cynical old self out of the driving seat and plants someone wide-eyed and wild-haired there instead, someone whose feet only just reach the pedals, and invites him to hit the accelerator hard and steer like a nutter. Which he does, if only in tribute to the time, that manic golden age, long gone, when safe driving wasn't a concern.

Foreword to Witches' Tales vol. #4 (2012)

This piece, which I entitled "Tomb Of The Unknown Writer", provides the introduction to a collection of reprints of issues from the classic Harvey horror anthology comic.

It's crazy to wish you were older, but whenever I read 1950s horror comics, I do.

I wish I had been born twenty years earlier and had stumbled across copies of *Chamber Of Chills*, *Tomb Of Terror*, *Adventures Into The Unknown* and the like at the age of nine, ten, eleven. The sweet-spot age. The impressionable age. The golden age.

I would have lapped them up. I would have devoured them. I would happily have allowed my pliant, still developing brain to be warped by the feverish dementia of the strips they contained. I would have applauded and appreciated them in the way that only a kid can – unthinkingly, unquestioningly, uninhibitedly. I wouldn't even have minded the sleepless nights they doubtless would have caused. Braving unseen fears in the bedroom dark is one of the true heroic feats of childhood, and the victory is incalculably gratifying.

Not that I'm complaining, I hasten to add. My 1970s upbringing had its share of decent horror comics. Weaned on the Marvel reprints of the old, milkily sanitised Atlas-era horror anthologies, I soon graduated to stronger, spicier stuff. "Monster superhero" series such as *Tomb Of Dracula*, *Werewolf By Night* and *The Living Mummy* were my gateway to the black-and-white Marvel/Curtis magazines – *Vampire Tales*, *Monsters Unleashed*, *Tales Of The Zombie*, *Dracula Lives!*. These boasted great artwork from Marvel's stable of Filipino talent – Tony DeZuniga, Sonny Trinidad, Alfredo Alcala, Rudy Nebres – and sometimes great stories to match.

Then came the discovery of the Warren titles which the Marvel mags were trying so desperately to ape: *Creepy* and *Eerie*. This was the motherlode, the throbbing jugular, the atom-bomb epiphany. They showed explicitly the gore which the Marvel magazines, for all that they were liberated from the constraints of the Comics Code by their size and format, still only hinted at. They had truly twisted twist endings. They were vile and violent and giddyingly, exhilaratingly *wrong* – and therefore just right.

One tale continues to linger with me. It was from an issue of *Creepy*. Unaided, I do not recall which number, but internet research tells me it was #85. The story was called "Orem Ain't Got No Head Cheese", and it was about a family of cannibal hillbillies – you know, *those* guys – who get more than they bargain for when their latest victim turns out to have terminal brain cancer. The tumour somehow takes over all the bits of offcut and offal that the hillbillies have tossed into a slops pit. It assembles a crude, squamous body which slithers out to exact awful vengeance.

Icky, nasty, perverted, sick. Brilliant. I was maybe twelve when I read it. The copy of *Creepy*, with its spectacular Abominable Snowman cover by Ken Kelly, had been doing the rounds at school, but I honestly felt I was the only person on the premises who genuinely relished it, understood it, needed it. Thirty-four years on, "Orem Ain't Got No Head Cheese" remains an indelible part of the makeup of my own head cheese. It was a classic horror-comic squib as good as any in these PS Artbook collections – as transgressive, as weirdly moralistic, as unforgettably skin-crawling.

Something else about it that I cannot recall unaided is who wrote and drew it. Again, the internet comes galloping to the rescue: the script was by Bill DuBay, the art by José Ortiz.

Warren titles at least credited their creators. That courtesy was denied the people who purveyed the majority of the content of Harvey and ACG horror comics.

Which brings me to my sort-of point.

As a diehard, old-school Marvelite, I grew up taking the splash-page credits box for granted. I had no reason not to assume that everyone involved in the making of a comic, even the letterer, automatically received acknowledgement in print for his or her contribution. Nowadays we're used to seeing the entire editorial staff, the publisher, even the publisher's dog name-checked on the frontispiece or at the back of every issue and reprint collection. It was not ever thus. In the good old bad old days, comics creators were low-waged, deadline-doomed hacks who were treated like slaves and, like slaves, were deemed unworthy of the dignity of a name. They toiled in obscurity, paid by the page, receiving a dismal flat-rate fee for the sweat of their brow. We know now who they were largely thanks to the diligent efforts of comics historians who have trained themselves to recognise this particular person's style, that particular person's quirks.

The artists – pencillers *and* inkers – are almost invariably identifiable. But the writers? Not so the writers. Seldom are they remembered and named. Look at the credits in these volumes. How often is the writer of a strip listed as "Unknown"? Peruse the Grand Comics Database. See how many times the poor, lowly scribe of a Harvey or ACG strip is recorded only as a mere plaintive question mark.

It's generally accepted that most of the stories were penned by the anthologies' editors, men such as Sid Jacobson and Richard E. Hughes, along with the occasional slumming-it prose author such as Frank Belknap Long. The assumption must be that the remainder were banged out by jobbing nonentities who perhaps had once had an ambition to write the Great American Novel, only to see their dream founder on the rocks of ineptitude – or possibly the rocks of a whisky-on-ice.

Yet what if – *what if* – all these wonderful, mad, depraved, irony-laden supernatural sting-in-the-tale jobs were the brainchildren of one single man? What if there was only ever one Unknown?

Picture him at work at his desk. I say 'desk' but it could just as easily be 'packing crate' or 'park bench' or 'bar'. Behold how he hammers relentlessly at his portable typewriter, filling up page after page with reanimated corpses, revenging revenants, frightened superstitious wives, ancient curse-carrying tomes, crumbling castles, deadly dream homes, bewitching zombies and zombifying witches. All these tales of mystery and imagination – all these visions – spring fully-formed like Athena from his head. One lone man originates them all.

His eyes are so bloodshot, their sclera show hardly any white, only overlapping webs of red. His hair is wayward and torn from the number of times he runs an agitated hand through it. He sweats. Oh, how he sweats. Great globular beads of perspiration cling to his skin, pearling his face. His collar is askew and his tie, half-undone, dangles round his neck like a hangman's noose.

Something drives him, some satanic goading impulse that will never let him rest. The tales keep coming. They have to. The next batch of commissions appears, as does the next batch of bills and mortgage interest payments. He meets demand. Meagre dollars slip into and through his fingers. He cannot stop.

He is haunted by language, hounded by fiction. Exaggerated punctuation marches past his eyes in a staggering parade.

The exclamation marks! Oh God, the exclamation marks!!!

Not to mention -- the double dashes.

And the ellipses...

This book, like its companion volumes, stands as tribute to the tireless efforts of poor, penurious Unknown. It is the slab of headstone marking his final resting place. With its solid binding and its smooth glossy pages it celebrates and commemorates all that he achieved during his long, laborious, broken life.

But what's this?

The grave is unquiet. The soil stirs. A wormy hand bursts forth from the dirt, clutching a sheaf of rotting, tattered script pages...!

For, in truth, Unknown can never die. As long as you or I read his captions and speech bubbles, thrill at his sometimes surreal turns of phrase, and let the nightmare logic of his plotting beguile us, he is damned to live.

Anonymous, yet eternal, immortal.

Foreword to Carrie **by Stephen King (2014)**

Bullies never win.

That's the lie that we're sold by well-meaning teachers and parents, and by cheap fiction and mainstream cinema.

Bullies get their comeuppance. They always come a cropper. Really they're just cowards at heart, lashing out at the world because (a) they're lacking in the smarts department, (b) they've been abused by their parents, (c) they're jealous of those cleverer and more articulate and socially adroit than they are, or (d) all of the above.

Bullies are to be pitied, that's the subtext here. Getting them to back off and leave you alone is simple: you just have to stand up to them. Confront them, meet their violence with a little implied violence of your own, and all of a sudden they'll be whimpering like whipped dogs and wanting to be your friend.

Bullies are kids with bodies too big for their brains. They're clumsy, oafish, masking their inadequacies with snark and aggression. That wedgie – it's a cry for help. That Chinese burn – they may be hurting you but they themselves are hurting worse, on the inside. When they duck you under in the swimming pool – they're the ones drowning in their own misery. When they exclude you from their group – they're loners too, they just can't admit it.

We should feel sorry for bullies. We should report them to the authorities and hope they receive the care and counselling they need, they deserve. We should understand them. Empathise. Give them a hug.

Bullshit.

Good fiction, interesting fiction, *true* fiction shows us that, contrary to received wisdom, bullies do win. In fact, by and large they prosper. Look around you. The evidence is there. The kid who ruined everyone else's lives at your school – he's a major success these days. He simply grew up into a bigger bully and now he's editing a national newspaper or chairing the board of a FTSE 100 company or wielding a movie director's megaphone or – Jesus, why not? – running some tinpot dictatorship. He made it. He's in a position of power where he swaggers around and yells at people and makes them do his bidding, and his word is spittle-flecked law and anyone who disagrees with him, who fails to kowtow, loses their job or even their head.

The world loves bullies. It welcomes them with open arms. It gives them everything it has to give: money, status, sex.

Literature's best known bully is Flashman in *Tom Brown's Schooldays* (1857). He tortures Tom at Rugby School, even to the extent of burning him in a fireplace. Soon the tables are turned, but a century later the character would become the antihero of a series of rollicking romps by George MacDonald Fraser which depict him as a rogue, a bounder and a scoundrel but invite us to admire and even envy him.

In the Roald Dahl short story "Galloping Foxley", a commuter meets his boarding-school nemesis on the train to work. He recalls how he was appointed personal servant to this Foxley and how the senior boy mentally and physically abused him. But when he plucks up the nerve to confront the man sitting across the carriage from him, all he gets is denial. Either it isn't Foxley after all, or Foxley is blithely pretending to be someone else. In other words, even now Foxley still has the upper hand, whether deliberately or in absentia.

In the early Spider-Man comics, high-school jock Eugene 'Flash' Thompson makes 'puny' Peter Parker's life hell. Yet, with wonderful irony, he is the number one fan of Parker's superheroic alter ego, not realising that his web-slinging idol is the science nerd he regularly belittles and ostracises. Later on, Flash becomes a wounded war hero and, more recently, following a brush with a certain alien symbiote, takes on the role of super-powered government agent Venom. He loses his legs but, as it were, falls on his feet.

Bullies don't get punished. That's the lesson, the moral of the tale, the incontrovertible fact. They coast through life, getting rewarded for their unthinking self-confidence and vicious streak.

Stephen King knows this. In his novella *The Body*, a gang of delinquents threatens narrator Gordie and his three friends, and subjects them all to appalling beatings. They get away with it, too, leaving the younger kids battered, bruised, bandaged, and "looking like the remains of a Korean assault force". Gordie and chums don't snitch on them. In fact, Gordie's friends are the ones who end up badly off. Fate has a trick in store for them. None of the three makes it to adulthood. They all die young, leaving Gordie as the only one to go on to lead a successful, productive life.

And then there's Carietta White and the ghastly treatment she undergoes at the hands of her peers, principally spoilt rich-kid Chris Hargensen and Chris' compliant thug-boyfriend Billy Nolan.

Carrie is targeted because she's dumpy, gauche, immature and a little bit creepy. She's a sixteen-year-old girl who doesn't know what menstruation is, whose personal and social development has been stunted – deformed – by her mother's sexual repression and raving religious fundamentalism. Carrie is a runt, a victim, a butt: "the elusive stamp of hurt was already marked clearly in her eyes". She gets everything wrong, and is taunted for it, and the harder she tries to get everything right, the more wrong she gets it and the more she is taunted. It's a self-perpetuating vicious circle.

Someone takes pity on Carrie – Sue Snell, a girl with a conscience. She decides to help the ugly duckling. Her motives are not pure. Sue feels remorse because she, too, has teased Carrie, and she is keen to redeem herself. For all that, she behaves nobly, sacrificing her place at the school prom, persuading her guy, Tommy, to take Carrie instead of her.

That's when the shit hits the fan, or rather the bucket of pig blood hits the king and queen of the Ewen High School spring ball.

I'm not going to insert a spoiler alert here. I'm not going to pretend that you don't know anything about *Carrie* and that I'm giving away the novel's big dramatic pivotal moment.

Of course you know about *Carrie*.

Either you've already read the book, or you've seen Brian de Palma's zesty and faithful 1976 movie adaptation (or either of the markedly inferior remakes, the 2002 TV film or last year's big-screen 'reimagining'). Maybe you're even one of the few foolhardy souls who caught the short-lived late-eighties stage musical version. Believe me, if you aren't, you didn't miss anything. Take it from one of those few foolhardy souls.

Failing that, you must at least have picked up by osmosis the basic gist of the story of *Carrie*. You know what happens to the novel's protagonist and how she reacts, because someone will have told you or you'll have stumbled on a reference to it on a TV show or online or in a newspaper article.

Carrie is a modern classic, and Carrie White has entered the cultural lexicon as an archetype of the downtrodden sad-sack who exacts gruesome, overwhelmingly disproportionate revenge on her tormentors. The telekinetic worm who turns. The fucked-up laughingstock who teaches her haters a deadly lesson.

The deep irony of the novel – King's publishing debut, the first step on his road to mega-bestsellerdom and worldwide renown, forty years young this year – is that Carrie White ultimately becomes the biggest bully of all. She doesn't kill just the conspirators who played a vile prank on her; she murders most of her school year, innocent and guilty alike. She all but destroys her hometown. She is as indiscriminate in her retribution as God Himself. She is a one-woman Plague of Egypt, a natural disaster in human form, the atomic bomb embodied in a bovine teenager with bad hair, Godzilla in a homemade ballgown.

The bullies have pissed off the wrong person, and they pay for it with their lives. But so does everyone else – the teachers who let them get away with their bullying for so long and the classmates who may not have participated in the persecution but failed to help by turning a blind eye.

After her slaughter spree Carrie limps back to the family home, to be greeted with a kind of divine justice. By this point, can we truly say she is any better than the girls who threw tampons at her in the locker room or the pig blood pourers?

It's not an easy call to make. Carrie has been provoked. She has been pushed beyond endurance. She snaps. Something inside her, a power, breaks out and goes on the rampage. She could control it. She chooses not to. And once it's unleashed, she knows she can't go back:

She was unaware that [...] she was weeping even as she laughed, or that one hidden part of her mind was keening over her final and utter ruin.

Because she was going to take them with her, and there was going to be a great burning, until the land was full of its stink.

Carrie is a tragic figure up until the moment she moves from being an individual sufferer to an inflictor of wholesale suffering. She crosses that line consciously, willingly, and after that, even if we can't blame her, neither can we forgive or condone her.

Therein lies the brilliance of *Carrie*. The novel tells us that the only genuinely effective way to stand up to bullies is to make yourself a far worse bully. Beat them at their own game. Bring a gun to their knife fight. Drop napalm on their jungle. Respond to their suicide bombing with shock and awe. For every one of yours they take, take ten of theirs.

It's how our world works. It's how the human race has functioned since time immemorial. It's our history, which is, remember, written by the victors – the bullies.

Don't like it?

Fuck you, squirt. Whiny little bitch. Shut your mouth, or I'll shove your punk-ass head down the toilet.

Essays

Tackling The End Of The World (2003)

The astute and acerbic SF-cinema critic Nick Lowe drew attention, in a recent issue of the magazine *Interzone*, to the difference between American and British attitudes to apocalypse, as exemplified in the movie *Reign of Fire*. The British characters in that film are a ragtag band of survivors who have taken refuge at a remote gravel works and converted it into a fortress where they hold out against the dragons that have destroyed most of humankind and turned the planet into a blasted, ashen wilderness. Under a pacifist leader, played by Christian Bale, they have re-created a miniature feudal society. Not for nothing does the converted gravel works resemble, from certain angles, a castle.

Then along come the Americans, with tanks and helicopters, an armed force presided over by bald, big-bicepped, basically bonkers Matthew McConaughey. The Yanks have made the transatlantic trip for one reason alone: to kick some serious dragon butt. Bale and McConaughey clash in a most manly fashion, but eventually settle their differences. Having suffered a devastating assault by the sole male dragon, the Brits realise the Yanks' approach is best, and so everyone troops off to London, the dragons' lair, in order to resolve the situation once and for all or die in the attempt.

The merits of *Reign of Fire* as a piece of entertainment are mixed. It has its exciting moments and the sets and special effects are fine, but it is let down by budgetary constraints and by inconsistencies and poor pacing in its plotting. Lowe, however, hits the nail on the head when he comments that in modern apocalypse tales, British people faced with the end of the world tend to hunker down and grow tomatoes (as they do in *Reign of Fire*), while the American instinct is much more "Why is the world ending? What is responsible? And how can we stop it?"

Consider *Independence Day*, that thoroughly infantile and meretricious piece of nonsense. In the London cinema where I saw it, the audience delivered its loudest and most derisive laugh during a brief scene where a stiff-upper-lip British army type gets off the radio and says, with relief, something like "Thank God the Yanks have come up with a plan." How typical! How deserving of mockery! But of course, the Yanks *have* come up with a plan, and it sees off the alien invaders before Earth is reduced to a complete smouldering ruin, and no one in that auditorium would have laughed so heartily, I suspect, if there hadn't been an uncomfortable ring of truth to the scene, in so far as waiting for the Americans to weigh in is, these days, an integral part of any British defence game-plan.

And then there's *Armageddon*. Another big, loud, ludicrous planet-in-peril movie. But at least Bruce Willis and co. are up there in their space shuttles, drilling nukes into the asteroid of doom, doing something while the rest of the world sits at home and bites its nails.

To take a more recent and more highbrow example, Jeff Long's novel *Year Zero* posits the unleashing of a terrible, quasi-Biblical plague which spreads rapidly across the globe while a group of scientists holed up at Los Alamos work desperately to develop a vaccine. The scientists' choice of location is pungent with irony. The site of the creation of the greatest manmade scourge of the modern era becomes the site of hope's last redoubt, where every effort is being made to defeat rather than manufacture mass destruction. The novel is hampered by its over-ambitiousness, just as Long's previous offering *The Descent* was, but its winding plot is pleasingly unpredictable and its exploration of the messianic impulse fascinating. Best of all, it is entirely serious in intent, unlike the last two films just mentioned.

Naturally, American-produced works of fiction will want to show Americans as heroes, combating and conquering the forces arrayed against them, however insuperable those forces might seem. Furthermore, the positivism on display in *Armageddon* and the like is never wholly naïve, never seen to be without price. Sacrifice is invariably required if the end of the world is to be averted. It is, in effect, a tax on redemption from extinction. Both McConaughey and Willis in their respective films give up their lives to the cause, as does the addled ex-alien-abductee pilot played by Randy Quaid in *Independence Day*, along with countless other nameless flyboys. They die so that the rest of us might live. And the same fate befalls the main protagonist of *Year Zero*, although his demise, in the event, is more symbolic than transformative.

So then compare and contrast, if you will, this rage-against-the-dying-of-the-light national trait with the grin-and-bear-it national trait demonstrated in British apocalypse fiction. For the ur-archetype of this we must go back to H. G. Wells. In *The War of the Worlds*, the Martians are not defeated by the military but by an agency outside human control, a bacterial *deus ex machina*. Until that happens, it seems almost a foregone conclusion that nothing will stop the annihilation of the human race.

Then there's John Wyndham, who in the nineteen-fifties and sixties cornered the market in end-time scenarios with novels such as *Day of the Triffids* and *The Kraken Wakes*. When worldwide disaster strikes, be it the blinding of almost all humankind by a strange meteor shower or the rising of the tides engineered by a mysterious sub-sea foe, the Brits retreat to the countryside. Cities lie abandoned. In small rural communities, society is perpetuated in microcosm, and ordinary people keep their heads down and live at subsistence level until the danger, for whatever reason, passes. This is what interests Wyndham – the effect of cataclysmic events on ordinary people, the character arcs of the victims rather than the heroes. The battle against the apocalypse, if it happens at all, takes place elsewhere, largely off-page.

Likewise in the apocalypse novels of Wyndham contemporary John Christopher – *The Death of Grass*, *The World in Winter*, *A Wrinkle in the Skin* – we see characters for the most part accepting rather than resisting the inevitable. Surviving is deemed to be more important than overcoming. Civilisation must go on at all costs, in however enfeebled, however etiolated a form. Entropy will be beaten by fortitude, not by opposition.

It isn't hard to divine the long shadow of World War II, and particularly the Blitz, looming over the Wyndham/Christopher mindset. Civilians in Britain during wartime were encouraged to turn their back gardens into vegetable patches, to Dig for Victory and become self-sufficient in order to compensate for the heavy rationing of food and other basic necessities. Urban children were packed off to rural areas so that they might be spared from the nightly bombing raids by the Luftwaffe. People on the Home Front, hard pressed in their struggle against possible obliteration by the Nazis, went back to the land, even as, overseas, British troops did their brave, beleaguered best against the superior might of the Wehrmacht.

We might also see the US side of the paradigm expressed in the eventual entry of America into the war. Across the Atlantic came the GIs, not unlike McConaughey and his cohorts in *Reign of Fire*. Enough was enough. Plucky resistance was all well and good, but in the end nothing was going to be solved without the application of vast (i.e. US) military firepower. And so the tide of the war was turned.

Nowadays, one wonders whether British prime minister Tony Blair's unhindered support for George Dubya in his determination to prosecute a war against Iraq isn't a deliberate attempt to move away from the UK's post-war self-image as a proponent of the passive-aggressive response to (alleged) global menace. Mind you, the British contribution to any proposed attack against Saddam will be minimal, so perhaps it's easy for Mr Blair to be so gung-ho.

What is clear is that the US will always fight back against anything which it perceives as a threat to its, and the world's, continued existence. In most American works of apocalypse fiction, this is unequivocally portrayed as a good thing. In reality, the waters are murkier. International terrorism and the 'Axis of Evil' may indeed present civilisation, specifically western civilisation, with the most pressing danger it has ever faced, and thus must be vanquished. Equally, it may be that the provoked bellicosity of the government of the most powerful nation on Earth is what proves, at the last, to be the undoing of us all.

Either way, if you want me, I'll be out back, planting lettuces by the kitchen door and harvesting plums from the tree that shades the summerhouse.

The Omega Man (2004)

This was written for Cinema Macabre, *an anthology edited by Mark Morris which gathers together fifty genre authors and asks each to champion his or her favourite horror movie.*

It's almost a Hollywood subgenre: late-60s/early-70s apocalyptic SF movies starring Charlton Heston. The actor featured in three of note, *Planet of the Apes* (1968), *The Omega Man* (1971) and *Soylent Green* (1973), and while the middle of these is by any objective reckoning the weakest, it's far from being the piece of cheapo, gun-happy schlock that most critics would have us believe.

The Omega Man is also the first film that genuinely gave me nightmares, and for that it has my undying gratitude.

I was eight when I first saw it, and although in the past I had been unnerved by scenes in certain films – the creepy way the trees move downhill during the landslide in *The Railway Children*, for instance, or the chained slaves getting thrown into the lava pit in *She* – I had never been so thoroughly, engrossingly frightened as I was by *The Omega Man*. Not just some of the movie but all of it, from beginning to end, had me peering through my fingers, scared to know, and at the same time eager to know, what was coming next.

It was my first term at boarding school and some bright spark in the staffroom had decided that, for our fortnightly Sunday evening cinematic presentation in the library, a violent shocker about a world that has been ravaged by bacteriological warfare and overrun by scarred albino mutants was suitable entertainment for a hundred-odd eight-to-thirteen-year-olds. Schools like mine hired actual films in those days, three reels of 16mm celluloid, which were run through a rattling and often temperamental projector. Just a single projector, moreover, so that there was a five-minute break between reels as the finished one was rewound and the next spooled in.

We kids didn't mind. The wait gave us a chance to chatter about what we'd just viewed and speculate on what would happen next.

During reel changes on *The Omega Man*, however, there was stark silence. A roomful of children, dumbfounded. Any parent will know how remarkable a phenomenon that is.

And when the film was over, I recall everyone trooping off to the dormitories in a state not un-akin to shock. There may have been a wet bed or two that night. If that was the case with me, I would never admit it. I will admit, though, that for the next week my dreams were peopled by white-faced, dark-robed figures straight out of the movie. They were coming to get me, and not even Charlton Heston could save me. I felt, in my sleep, like the last child alive.

I've watched *The Omega Man* several times since, as a grown-up, and increasingly I've perceived its weaknesses, as we tend to with the things that made an impression on us as children.

The film is set in an all but deserted Los Angeles, and the plot – a wafer of a plot – follows Robert Neville (Heston), apparently the last normal human on Earth in the wake of a germ war, as he combats the maddening effects of solitude and also the aforementioned vampire-like creatures. These bacteriologically mutated people shun the daylight, favour sunglasses and natty black robes, call themselves the Family and are led by one Matthias (Anthony Zerbe), a former newscaster, now a prophet-figure. Matthias has an understandable hatred of technology, on which he blames all the world's present ills and to which he refers, demonisingly, as "The Wheel".

The Family constantly ambush and besiege Neville. He in turn, when he isn't cruising LA in his convertible searching for their nests and exterminating them, takes refuge in the splendid isolation of a well-fortified brownstone penthouse apartment, from where, in between taking sips of fine wine and making moves in a chess game against a bust of Caesar, he picks off his nocturnal foes using a nightscope.

Alas, the Family finally get the better of Neville and take him captive. They humiliate him and are all set to burn him at the stake, and then rescue comes. Neville, it transpires, is not alone after all. There are other human survivors, who soon come to look on him as a saviour.

Now, to my adult eyes the film's flaws are many. For starters, there's Heston's early seventies wardrobe, all neckerchiefs and shirts unbuttoned to the navel. For such a macho actor in so manly a role, he looks deeply, disturbingly camp. Then there's the fact that the movie espouses an antiwar sentiment – witness Neville showing *Woodstock* at a cinema and hollowly echoing the utterances of the hippies onscreen – and yet pacifism barely gets a look-in the moment Heston lays hands on an automatic rifle. (And of course the germ war was between Russia and China. You'd never get America being so belligerent, would you?)

But the worst offender of all, as far as flaws go, is the crude and cloyingly rendered religious subtext. Neville is immune to the effects of the bacteriological plague because, as we learn in flashback, he has injected himself with an experimental vaccine. By means of transfusion, the antibodies in his bloodstream can counteract the disease's mutagenic effects in others. In other words, Christ-like, Neville can literally redeem the world with his blood.

All very well and fine, but director Boris Sagal and screenwriters John William Corrington and Joyce Hooper Corrington ladle on the message with a trowel. At one point a child lispingly asks Neville if he's God – well, no, but Heston *was* Moses, will that do? – and the film's closing image is of Neville spreadeagled in a fountain, dying, the water around him stained crimson with his blood. Sagal solarises the shot, just in case we may have missed the point. In starkly contrasted hues, Neville's pose is shown to be, yes, unmistakably one of crucifixion.

It's too shallow a movie for such weighty preoccupations. In the novel on which it is based, Richard Matheson's *I Am Legend*, Neville's final martyrdom is a much more subtle affair, the iconography implicit, unstated. Indeed, over-all *I Am Legend* is a wonderfully clever and concise construct. Matheson uses actual vampires instead of the movie's mutated vamp-alikes and explores his basic theme – if everyone else in the world is a monster and one person is not, who then is the monster? – with intelligence and wit.

Intelligence and wit are not to the fore in *The Omega Man*. What the film does display, in copious amounts, is brio, energy, a grittiness, a low-budget, down-and-dirty readiness to get to wherever it is going. The scenes depicting the ruined, unpeopled city are well executed and hauntingly memorable (rather than go to the expense of building sets, Sagal simply used downtown LA locations early on weekend mornings when there was nobody about). The relationship between Neville and the human survivors' leader, Lisa, played by Rosalind Cash, is daring for its era, in that it pairs whitebread Heston with a black woman who is almost his equal in the fighting-moves department. (Refreshingly, the miscegenation is hardly commented on. Nor, unsurprisingly, is the age gap between 47-year-old Heston and twentysomething Cash.) Meanwhile Zerbe steals the movie, acting at a level far higher than the material deserves. He imbues Matthias with a pathos, a wounded honour, that makes it perfectly possible to empathise with him and his Family. Indeed, thanks to Zerbe the nominal bad guys start to look like the good guys, victims as much as villains.

The downbeat ending – hero dead, hope just about living on – is affecting if you overlook the clumsy Christian parallels, and is interesting in that downbeat endings are a feature of all three Heston-at-the-end-of-the-world flicks. Maybe there's a streak of *après moi le deluge* in ol' Chuck. *The Omega Man* also wears its disgust for the military-industrial complex like a badge of pride, even if it does fudge the issue at times.

These are all noble attributes.

For me, though, above anything else, *The Omega Man* is where I learned the exhilaration of fear, the excitement of being scared vicariously, the strange delight that comes from mixing dread with eagerness, the power of horror films to enthrall even as they terrify.

Eight, I would say with hindsight, is just the right age at which to make that discovery.

Spot The Title (2006)

This cunning little squib appeared in the BBC's excellent but short-lived MindGames, *a glossy monthly for the serious lover of puzzles, conundrums and brain-teasers, edited by Jonathan Wright. I also contributed a regular column to the magazine about how to solve cryptic crosswords.*

Writers spend their whole lives wrestling with words, placing them painstakingly one after another to produce prose and poetry. So it's not surprising that some scribes should seek to toy and tinker with the tools of their trade.

Old English verse favoured alliteration over rhyme. Every line of *Beowulf*, for instance, consists of two half-lines, each of which is tied together by an alliterated consonant or vowel, much as in the sentences in the paragraph above. So wordplay in literature can claim a long and noble lineage, all the way back to Anglo-Saxon times.

Really, though, it was the Victorians who elevated the practice into an artform, and the arch exponent in this field was Lewis Carroll. Carroll's "Jabberwocky" is a babbling brook of neologisms and portmanteau inventions (e.g. 'slithy', which evocatively fuses lithe and slimy), while the short dedicatory poems attached to "The Hunting of the Snark" and *Through The Looking-Glass* form acrostics of the names of the young girls who inspired the works.

During the twentieth century the baton was taken up by the likes of Nabokov, who loved the intricacy and malleability of the English language as only a fluent non-native speaker could. In his short story "The Vane Sisters" the narrator delves for hidden meanings in Shakespeare's sonnets, "checking the first letters of the lines to see what sacramental words they might form". Interpretation of the entire tale hinges on an acrostic embedded in its closing paragraph.

Pale Fire, meanwhile, Nabokov's novel of 1962, features a character who likes reversing words to create palindromes, along with a narrator who enjoys word golf, the pastime of changing one word into its conceptual opposite a letter at a time, as in HATE, HAVE, HOVE, LOVE.

Less fond of word games, by his own admission, was Ogden Nash. Nevertheless his comic verse abounds with puns and groan-worthy

Spoonerisms ("...when I throw rocks at sea birds I leave no tern unstoned").

And then there's the Oulipo movement, a loose collective of predominantly French authors and mathematicians who came together in the early 1960s with the aim of producing works using constrained writing techniques. Oulipo is an acronym of *Ou*roir de *li*ttérature *po*tentielle, which translates roughly as "workshop of potential literature". Its best-known members are Italo Calvino and Georges Perec.

You only have to look at some of the tasks Perec set himself to wonder whether he was crazy. His novel *La disparition* is a lipogram – a composition which eschews the use of a single letter of the alphabet, in this case the commonest of all, *e*. (It has been translated into English, by clearly-just-as-crazy Gilbert Adair, as *A Void*.) Perec then began *Les lettres d'Eve*, in which the only vowel permitted is *e*, in order, as he put it, "to use up all the ones I had left over". He did not get very far with this ambitious enterprise.

While not as explicitly and rigorously experimental, another Perec novel, *Life: A User's Manual*, is set in an apartment block and hops about the building from location to location in a manner known as the Knight's Tour, a technique employed in certain word search puzzles requiring the solver to move like a knight on a chessboard, one square in one direction then two at 90°, or two then one. A dense and dizzying book, it also features acrostics and maths problems and appears to be about ... well, absolutely everything.

Recent wordplay novels include Lorrie Moore's witty and inventive *Anagrams*, whose central character, Benna, attempts to make sense of reality by various methods, not least by jumbling up letters ("One gust of wind and Santa becomes Satan").

In a similar vein, there's Mark Dunn's *Ella Minnow Pea* – think about that title – which describes itself as a 'progressive lipogrammatic epistolary fable'. This lively satiric tour de force depicts the efforts of the inhabitants of an island off the coast of South Carolina to communicate with one another by mail while being forbidden to use an increasing number of letters of the alphabet.

Gyles Brandreth, no less, has managed to rewrite several of Shakespeare's plays lipogrammatically: *Macbeth* without *a* or *e*, *Othello* without *o*. More originally, avant-garde Canadian poet Christian Bök (pronounced 'book') has produced a clever collection of univocalic poetry – that is, poems employing only one particular vowel. Its title is *Eunoia*, the shortest word in English that contains all five regular vowels.

Hopelessly unignorable in this context is *The Da Vinci Code*, which, if you're one of the three Kazakhstani goatherds who haven't read it yet, is littered with anagrams and riddles. Dan Brown's achievement, colossal sales aside, is to have successfully welded a thriller plot to the cerebral gymnastics of wordplay and code-breaking. The combination of overarching conspiracy mystery and smaller, swiftly-solved puzzles has proved well nigh irresistible.

The greatest wordplay trickster of all, however, is Shakespeare himself. Or rather, if Ignatius Donnelly is to be believed, Francis Bacon. Donnelly's thousand-page opus *The Great Cryptogram* (1888) subjects the Folio edition of the Bard's complete works to arithmetical scrutiny and comes up with a *Bible-Code*-style 'proof' that Bacon authored the plays, with Shakespeare in the role of front man and patsy. Needless to say, it's one of those theories that crumble under any kind of serious analysis, and a CIA cryptographer easily demolished it in the 1950s. Wherever there are men of genius like Da Vinci and Shakespeare, though, there will inevitably be those who'll hunt for and find a subliminal significance in their work that simply doesn't exist.

Speaking of subliminal…If you haven't spotted it yet, the proper title of this article may be found by initial examination of the paragraphs.

The Terrestrial Alien – *Air* by Geoff Ryman, *The Execution Channel* by Ken MacLeod, *Black Man* by Richard Morgan, *Brasyl* by Ian McDonald (2007)

Science fiction has traditionally looked to space to find metaphors for otherness. Aliens of every conceivable shape, hue and limb-count populate the history of a genre "fascinated by the encounter with difference", in the words of critic and SF author Adam Roberts.

Consider the Martians. For a century, contemporary hopes and fears have been projected on to them. They've been a weathervane of the mood of successive eras.

To H. G. Wells, the Martians are a conquering foreign power. In *The War of the Worlds* (1898) they are analogous to Russia or Germany, but equipped with terrifyingly superior technology. They're imperial Britannia's worst nightmare, a foe whose weapons make her mighty navy and artillery look like toy boats and popguns.

Ray Bradbury's Martians in *The Martian Chronicles*, by contrast, are gentle, spiritual and wise. When astronauts arrive from Earth to colonise their planet and remake it in the image of the American Midwest, these ethereal aboriginals give way almost graciously, sensing their time is up. These 1940s stories were written as Native American culture was in decline and seemed in danger of vanishing – Bradbury's spacesuited settlers simply trailblaze a new Frontier.

Kim Stanley Robinson's massive *Mars* trilogy of the 1990s represents a shift in perspective. Here the Red Planet is a dead planet. Over the course of 200 years, men and women from Earth struggle to tame it and make it habitable. Their environment shapes them in turn, until they end up at home on their new world. These former Earthlings have themselves become the Martians.

Robinson's epic acknowledges the uncomfortable truth laid bare by the ever-stretching gaze of astronomers: that there are no inhabited planets in the vastness of space, at least not within easy reach. There is no life on Mars. There's nothing out there. Unless it's us.

Contrary to received opinion, SF's preoccupation has always been the here and now. Its far-flung planets and future timelines are merely a way to analyse the contemporary. In this respect, SF is the most politically engaged of all literary genres. Motifs that may appear trashy to the uninitiated – space exploration, extraterrestrials, futuristic technology – can in fact be surprisingly sophisticated tools for dissecting and examining the world as it is.

It's interesting, then, that a distinct trend has emerged in modern science fiction. While the urge to address state-of-the-world concerns remains, the approach is altering. The emptiness of space, coupled with the fragility of our increasingly fevered home planet, has led these writers to lower their telescopes and aim them directly at life on Earth.

SF is still intrigued by notions of otherness, defining ourselves against what we are not. This manifests now, though, not through tales of bug-eyed monsters from beyond, but by measured scrutiny of 'aliens' closer to home. Science fiction is written predominantly by white Western males. For them, the alien may be found beyond borders, across continents. The Other is someone with a different language, skin colour, set of cultural signifiers, even gender.

Geoff Ryman's *Air*, which hoovered up virtually every SF award going in 2006, perfectly embodies this trend. It is set in a remote village, Kizuldah, in a fictional kingdom next to China, and depicts the impact of 'Air', a new communications technology, on the villagers. Air is essentially an über-internet, beamed directly into the brain. Like some sort of inescapable Bluetooth, it affords constant access to information without the need for computers or mobiles phones.

A disastrous trial run leaves the residents of Kizuldah panicked and disorientated. Ryman conveys the sudden, shocking sensory overload his heroine experiences: "Mae smelled wine, perfume, sweat, onions, rain on cobbles, scorched rice, old shoe leather. Colours danced in her eyes; green-yellow red-blue, as if colour had become a kind of toffee to be stretched and mixed. And there was music – all kinds of music – as if hundreds of radios were being played at once, and a rearing-up of screeching, tinkling sounds like thousands of birds."

It becomes apparent that Air threatens both the villagers' sanity and their entire way of life. Air is the portal to a slick-shining realm of materialism – the ultimate instrument of globalisation. It proffers everything that the West holds dear: designer outfits, consumer goods, pop music, ephemera. The price is tradition and individuality – and it's a price Mae is loath to pay.

Mae retaliates by selling the local culture back to the West in the form of fashion accessories. But the creeping tide of homogeneity cannot be halted. And that's where the power of Ryman's narrative lies: in his eloquently expressed contention that the Other in our globalised economy is an endangered species. We want to make it like us. Perhaps it even wants to be like us. But what is the cost to diversity?

Throughout the book Ryman seeds references to famous fictional utopias. One character is called Mr Oz, while a near-extinct tribe is known as Eloi, the elfin, sheeplike race in Wells' *The Time Machine*. He also namechecks two great avatars of modern capitalism: Gates and Saatchi. In the book, the former is a Windows-style operating system, the latter a fatcat bank manager. These satirical touches help point out the gulf between consumerism's intangible dreams and the realities of life as it is lived in Kizuldah, with all its mundane muddle and mire.

Air portends the end of the world for Kizuldah; it's as much of an elemental catastrophe for the village as crop failure or flood. The novel belongs, then, to the well-established SF school of apocalyptic-warning narrative. Ken MacLeod's *The Execution Channel* sits in the same school, but the apocalypse MacLeod warns of is more conventional: all-out global conflict.

The Execution Channel opens with the well-realised detailing of a nuclear attack on an RAF base. MacLeod doesn't gives us a huge bang and a mushroom cloud, but rather the effects of the event on people just too far away from ground zero to be eyewitnesses. It's a concatenation of seemingly unrelated events: a flash in the sky, phones going dead, power cuts, all leading to the slow-dawning realisation of the horrible truth.

In the aftermath, chaos ensues. No one is sure who launched the attack or why. The hunt to discover the truth – before it's too late – enmeshes IT expert and sometime spy James Travis, along with his peace campaigner daughter Roisin and his son Alec, a soldier. Sundry intelligence operatives are on the trail of the Travis family. But when the attack itself turns out to be not the straightforward act of provocation it first appeared, the consequences for the Travises are grave. Alec, in particular, learns the chilling disregard his own government has towards the human rights of its citizens.

MacLeod makes clear the parallels with current confusion over the detention of terrorist suspects and the use of 'legitimate' torture methods such as stress positions and water-boarding. He also wittily and cynically points up the mistrust between nations that profess to be allies. In this novel, France is the last bastion of geopolitical integrity – a beautiful irony – while deceit and self-interest drive the US, UK, Russia and China.

In the end, Russia and China are revealed to be striving for a nobler goal than the endemically corrupt West – the lurch towards war is an unfortunate by-product of their true aim. MacLeod is no apologist for the sins of communism, but in all his novels radical left-wing ideology is the key to betterment. Hence *The Execution Channel*'s late-stage sucker punch, a twist that lifts the book suddenly and brilliantly from day-after-tomorrow thriller to hard-SF novel of ideas. Most of the book has the pace and streamlining that one would expect of a Tom Clancy or Michael Crichton blockbuster, if subtler. Then, at once, we see that MacLeod has been playing a cleverer game, layering his narrative with a political message the average airport novel wouldn't touch.

At its climax *The Execution Channel* demonstrates a belief that, just as the failure to see things from another's viewpoint may be our downfall, mutual co-operation can elevate us. In the crucible of potential Armageddon, a capitalism-shunning paradise may be forged.

Black Man by Richard Morgan also presents a form of paradise on Earth – an early-22nd-century feminised, pluralist future where equality is the order of the day. You shouldn't mistake this for a perfect world, though. Corporations still hold sway, and political correctness is more pointed then ever (when a male character assumes a vicious killer must be a man, a female colleague insists the murderer could as easily be a woman).

The novel's hero is the antithesis of the global culture he inhabits. Carl Marsalis is a 'variant thirteen', one of a small minority of people who have been genetically modified for aggressive, sociopathic tendencies. He's a science-created throwback to pre-civilised hunter-gatherer times, designed to be a soldiers or lawman, and vital to the establishment of a stable, peaceful world. Now that that goal has been achieved, variant thirteens are redundant, ghettoised, universally despised. The nickname for them is 'unluck'.

Carl is not just a variant thirteen, he is also black. In the context of the novel, this is commented on but not remarkable in itself – most characters are non-white, including the female protagonist, Sevgi Ertekin, an American policewoman of Turkish ethnicity.

However, Carl's blackness plays a crucial role in our understanding of the almost visceral hostility that other characters feel towards him. It's a visual emblem of being an outsider, an Other. Carl has no choice about his 'unluck' status. He can't change it any more than he can change his skin colour. But he must curb his resentment and his sense of dispossession – especially when the UN hires him to track down and kill another rogue variant thirteen.

Morgan's fast-paced, ultraviolent cyberpunk thrillers have always had an added layer of intellectual rigour, with serious discussion in the lulls between the bloodletting. Morgan is confident his readers will appreciate that, in this book, he is not equating black malehood with racist notions of violence and savagery. He is, instead, using racist prejudices of our own time to inform us about the genetic prejudices of his imagined future. It's a risky tactic (too risky, it would seem, for his US publishers, who are releasing the book under the less provocative title *Thirteen*).

In Ian McDonald's *Brasyl* we find racial outsiderdom inverted. One of the central characters, Marcelina Hoffman, is a loira, a white woman of Germanic descent, which makes her an oddity in her native Brazil. She is also a producer of reality TV shows – a subset of Homo sapiens that the rest of us can safely feel contempt for.

Marcelina's story is one of three strands in *Brasyl*. Hers takes place in the present day while the other two strands, also set in Brazil, occur in a seething, tech-riddled 2032 and in colonial-era 1732. McDonald's future Brazil is so hyperlinked, so videoclipped together, that there is scarcely any room left for God. Who needs an all-seeing deity when everyone constantly watches everyone else anyway? His historic Brazil, meanwhile, is experiencing an influx of Christianity. Indigenous faiths are being harrowed into extinction, while the Enlightenment is stirring even in the depths of the rainforest.

The three strands run concurrently, forming a larger picture. The author likens this literary structure to the famous adage about the three blind men feeling an elephant: "Each imagines an elephant is like a tree trunk, like a snake, like a whale." The elephant in *Brasyl* is an immense, marvellous beast whose shape comes slowly, majestically into focus, constructed out of a welter of thematic elements such as quantum computing, multiverse theory, and the clash between science and religion.

McDonald inhabits Brazil so thoroughly and uses its language so liberally that the prose at times reads closer to Portuguese than English (there is a handy glossary at the back). Above all he hammers home the protean strangeness of his chosen setting: "Brazil is not like other places", "Brazil is not like anywhere else", "Brazil is not as other places".

The search for aliens, then, has turned inward. The Other is no longer up there in the stars. He's our neighbour with the faith-based dress code. She's the person with the tinted skin and unfamiliar accent. Modern science fiction is putting out the unexceptionable message that we should gladly embrace him or her, if we are to have any kind of future.

Someone else's Other, after all, is us.

Séance Friction – *Conan Doyle: The Man Who Created Sherlock Holmes* by Andrew Lycett, *Servants Of The Supernatural* by Antonio Melechi, *Ghost Hunters* by Deborah Blum, *Conversations With Eternity* by Victor Hugo, translated and with a commentary by John Chambers (2008)

The Victorian era may be characterised as a time when the warring factions of science and religion did their best to set aside their differences and sue for peace. The tools of empiricism were brought to bear on mysticism, and vice versa, in an effort to achieve a synthesis of fact and faith. This is the period when Darwin vacillated over publishing his *On the Origin of Species* for fear that the theory of evolution might oust God from the world once and for all, and when he did publish it he made sure to note that evolution could only have come about through the ministrations of a benign Maker. Likewise, as spiritualism took off and séances and table-turning became respectable parlour pastimes, there was a concerted effort by broader-minded scientists and academics to investigate such supernatural phenomena and determine one way or another whether there was any validity in them.

If there's one eminent Victorian who seems to embody the contradictions of the age and the desire to reconcile them, it's Arthur Conan Doyle. Here was a man full of sharp paradoxes and only too aware of it. Brought up in a strict Catholic household and educated by Jesuits, he nonetheless embraced materialism and was eager for worldly success. He was a would-be Bohemian who was happy to use his fame to promote worthy and not-so-worthy causes. He was a shrewd bargainer, always haggling with publishers for more money, and yet a terrible investor, frittering his income on one harebrained business scheme after another. He was a firm believer in the sanctity of marriage, but that didn't stop him keeping a mistress while his wife declined into poor health. Above all he was the creator of the most rational character in all of literature but was himself notoriously susceptible to paranormal fraud, credulous to the point of gullibility.

These contrasts are wonderfully brought to life in Andrew Lycett's biography, *Conan Doyle: The Man Who Created Sherlock Holmes*. Lycett takes pains to demonstrate how Conan Doyle was committed, right from the start, to the pursuit of reason while "maintaining an essential belief in a higher being". His mother's taste in fiction had steeped him in the tradition of Walter Scott and other Celtic romantics, and many of his early stories exhibit a strong Gothic influence. As a medical student, though, he was trained in the art of precise factual observation, notably by Dr Joseph Bell whose deductive methods Conan Doyle would openly acknowledge as a formative influence in the creation of Sherlock Holmes.

In short, Conan Doyle was almost ineluctably fated to become an ardent advocate of spiritualism and to try and treat it as a science. His upbringing and training would appear to have shaped him for nothing else.

Lycett demonstrates, too, with woeful irony, how growing up with a deranged, alcoholic father would later lead Conan Doyle into his greatest folly. Charles Doyle's career as an illustrator was sabotaged by his uncontrollable drinking habit, and in his latter years, confined to an asylum, he would sketch phantasmagorical visions of fairies, monsters and similar otherworldly beings. Not surprising, then, that his son should fall hook, line and sinker for the Cottingley fairy photographs, a palpable hoax carried out by two young sisters. As Lycett puts it:

Arthur had a strong motive to corroborate this story. If he could prove its truth, he would go a long way to rehabilitating the memory of his father and showing that, far from being mad, Charles Doyle had the evolved sensibility to communicate with higher spiritual beings.

But in writing *The Coming of the Fairies*, all Conan Doyle did instead was make himself a national laughing-stock.

The picture that emerges from Lycett's compendious, meticulously detailed tome is of a genial, bluff personality who was prepared to plough his considerable energies and resources into campaigning for what he felt to be true, even if that meant squandering a great deal of the fund of goodwill he had built up with the public. Antonio Melechi's *Servants of the Supernatural* opens with a thumbnail sketch of Conan Doyle, giving much the same impression. Conan Doyle lived during what Melechi aptly calls "the golden age of the Victorian séance".

Servants of the Supernatural, though, is concerned with tracing the origins of the phenomenon right back to its eighteenth-century roots in mesmerism.

This, of course, was a pseudoscience invented by Franz Anton Mesmer, basically a variant of the old 'laying on of hands' cure, dressed up with the use of magnets and talk of an invisible force, "a medium of reciprocal influence between celestial bodies, the earth and living things", which might be harnessed to restore balance to disordered minds and physiologies. Nonsensical as this was, what Mesmer did (inadvertently) discover was the power of the subconscious to effect changes in the self and health of an entranced subject.

Mesmerism was championed in Britain in the early nineteenth century by Dr John Elliotson, who was able to use it for, among other things, carrying out surgery on patients anaesthetised by 'mesmeric sleep'. Still it failed to gain traction among the medical and scientific establishment. Mesmerism could not shake off the whiff of charlatanism. Nor could it remain untainted by the claims that it unleashed clairvoyant powers in certain individuals, enabling them to communicate with the dead.

Elliotson fought hard and in vain to extricate mesmerism from its association with "those poor creatures who believe in spirit-rappings and spirit-table-movings". But the spiritualist movement, as Melechi shows, was too strong and had too many celebrity proponents like Wilkie Collins and Elizabeth Barrett Browning, and later Conan Doyle. With hindsight we can see that mesmerism was the forebear of modern psychotherapeutic practices like hypnotism, but for the Victorians it was an idea whose time had yet to come, or rather an idea that ended up swamped by the craze it inspired. Séances, with their cryptic messages from beyond the grave and their bizarre physical manifestations – glowing hands, ectoplasmic extrusions, and so on – were simply more *entertaining* than a hard-to-quantify quasi-medical procedure.

Servants of the Supernatural pursues its argument well and with an understated wit. If there's a flaw, it's that Melechi's tone is too austere, at times sober verging on teetotal. Some of the more eccentric and colourful figures who haunt his book's pages, for example the mediums Daniel Dunglas Home and Leonora Piper, don't fully come to life. They're more phantoms than flesh and blood.

This isn't a criticism that can be levelled at Deborah Blum's *Ghost Hunters*, which covers much the same ground but brings a transatlantic perspective to the proceedings. Blum chiefly focuses on William James, older brother of Henry the novelist. The senior James sibling was an early member of the Society for Psychical Research, and later its president, and as a psychologist spent much of his life applying scientific methodology to spiritualism. If inclined towards scepticism at first, James became a convert after the death of his infant son Herman.

It's a pattern that recurs repeatedly throughout *Ghost Hunters*, and may be found in Melechi's and Lycett's books as well. The man or woman wary about but still interested in spiritualism suffers a sudden, terrible bereavement and is understandably impelled to seek evidence of the continuation of life after death, more often than not finding it. It happened to Conan Doyle after his son Kingsley died during the Spanish 'flu epidemic of 1918. It happened to Frederick Myers, a founder of the SPR, when the love of his life Annie Marshall committed suicide in 1876. Grief propels us into strange places and makes us clutch at straws of hope, however flimsy. In James' case, that hope came in the somewhat portly form of Mrs Piper, whom he reckoned to be the one verifiably genuine medium in a field littered with impostors. "If you wish to upset the law that all crows are black," he wrote, "you mustn't seek to show that no crows are; it is enough if you prove a single crow to be white."

Mrs Piper was his white crow. Years of repeated and intensive testing by the SPR and its American offshoot failed to find fault with her talents. Even when being subjected to all manner of undignified probings and jabbings while in her mediumistic trance, this middle-class Bostonian shopkeeper's wife was calmly able to furnish information she could not have come by through normal means, facts known only to her investigators or the impartial witnesses they brought with them. It was theorised that her abilities might be the result of telepathy rather than dialogue with the inhabitants of the hereafter. Either way, she remains an extraordinary presence, the heroine of Blum's book, the heart of the story, where William James is its head.

It's reasonable to speak of *Ghost Hunters* in novelistic terms because Blum is a terrific storyteller and has a masterful, writerly turn of phrase, as in this descriptive passage:

The surrounded wooded hills were set with the gemstone colours of autumn – amber

151

and carnelian, garnet and citrine – heart-stoppingly brilliant against a clear blue sky.

Taking a fictive approach to her material, far from diminishing it, makes it all the more compellingly readable. Her book remains even-handed throughout, presenting the facts straight and leaving the reader to draw his or her own conclusions.

Would that such neutrality could be found in *Conversations With Eternity*. This is a distillation of transcripts of table-turning sessions carried out by Victor Hugo and family while in exile on Jersey. The Hugos fled the tyrannical regime of Napoleon III in 1851, and having fetched up on the Channel Island, they set about holding séances. It's possible Hugo was precipitated into this activity by the death, nine years earlier, of his daughter Léopoldine, although equally boredom may have played a part. For two years, at any rate, the family were in regular contact with the ethereal realm, and *Conversations With Eternity* details the tidings that came in from the other side.

Anyone wishing to see the problems that researchers like James were up against need look no further than this book. Various spirits, including the shades of such luminaries as Hannibal and Shakespeare, visited the Hugos to convey statements of either mind-numbing banality or bewildering obscurity, sometimes both at once. The one, just-about-coherent theme that emerges is the notion of the world as a prison for human souls, which become reincarnated as lesser organisms if their owners were insufficiently well behaved during their lives. This leads to a lot of high-flown, repetitious gobbledygook and the odd, unintentionally hilarious assertion such as "The plant is the grimmest of the soul's prisons. The lily is sheer hell."

One can see that exiled expats might well be preoccupied with matters of confinement and imprisonment, and one may well infer that the spirit message could have had their origins, if only unconsciously, in the minds of the people taking part in the séance, those whose fingers were holding the small tripod table one leg of which was tapping its way painstakingly letter by letter through the alphabet to form words and sentences. One may even conclude that Hugo himself was at least in part responsible. He was not a man lacking in a sense of self-importance, and several times the spirits come across as being no less convinced of his genius than he.

It falls to the book's translator and commentator John Chambers to make sense of the spirits' garbled effusions, and this he signally fails to do, several times contorting logic out of shape in order to interpret what is frankly meaningless. But then a man who describes temperate Jersey as being surrounded by ice-floes in winter may not be the most reliable of guides.

What *Conversations With Eternity* does well, with its Channel Island channellings, is reinforce the maddening truth about séances and mediumship. Nothing that comes through from beyond the veil makes much sense, at least not to the unbeliever. Even the utterances conveyed by a plausible source like Mrs Piper often lapse into downright gibberish. There is never clear, conclusive, concrete proof that there really are spirits and they really are talking, and this is the issue which vexed Victorians to distraction.

Then again, to a man such as Conan Doyle, the words of his own fictional arch-rationalist might well offer some comfort in this context: "How often have I said to you that when you have eliminated the impossible, whatever remains, *however improbable*, must be the truth?"

Bibliodiversity (2008)

A guest editorial for the Winter 2008 issue of genre-fiction anthology PostScripts.
*It was written well before (and failed to foresee) the current self-publishing boom, but
I stand by its arguments nonetheless.*

Forgive me if I'm about to ramble here. I'm sure that by the end I will
have made a point. Possibly even a good one.

But have you walked into a high street bookstore lately, and walked
out again half an hour later empty-handed and disappointed? You
know, you've got a few spare quid on you, you need something to read,
you've no idea what you're looking for but you'll recognise it when you
see it...

Only, you don't see it. That book you're after, with its indefinable,
ineffable something, the one it seems you've been waiting your whole
life to discover? Not there.

What *is* there is a horde of serial killer novels, stacked high like
corpses in a basement. And a dozen pallid Dan Brown clones with titles
along the lines of *The Nebuchadnezzar Conundrum*. And a hundred pastel-
toned chick lit offerings about the agony of high heels and, to a lesser
extent, heartbreak. And any number of post-Potter teen wizardly wand-
waving escapades. And a myriad misery memoirs, a.k.a. cryographies,
whose authors vie to outdo one another in the level of childhood
suffering they endured, not so much a pissing contest as a pissed-on
contest (my rapist daddy's bigger than yours). And huge steaming piles
of celeb stuff. God, the celeb stuff! So essential to the publicity
portfolio of the modern actor/singer/model/human car crash. You
can't call yourself famous these days if you don't have a book out. Or,
in the case of Katie 'Jordan' Price, several books – and I'm sure she's
looking forward to reading them sometime, arf arf. Still, at least she's
keeping a few ghost writers in gainful employment, along with all those
plastic surgeons.

(Brief sidebar. I once knew a crime writer in Chicago in the mid-90s.
He told me he'd been offered the opportunity to ghost a novel on
behalf of Michael "Lt. Worf out of *Star Trek*" Dorn. The deal was, the
actor would get $90,000, the author would get $10,000, with the
royalties split likewise. In other words, simply for signing a contract and

lending his name to the project, Dorn would earn nine times as much as the man who would sweat and toil for weeks to generate the artefact on which that name would appear. Naturally, and admirably, my acquaintance turned the job down. But the moral of the story is: as a ghost writer you're treated like an imaginary, ethereal entity, and should expect to be paid as such.)

What I'm getting at, pre-sidebar, is that the stock in your average modern high street bookstore exhibits a dismaying lack of choice. What's being pushed at the customer is basically more of the same old same old.

Oh, now and then there's a work of maverick genius there, a left-field bestseller that no one saw coming, a quirky word-of-mouth hit that's had its publisher scrabbling to keep up with reprint demand after the initial run vanished abruptly from the warehouse. But this is the exception rather than the rule – the rule being: if people like something, booksellers will insist on foisting upon them 1,001 variations on that theme till they're heartily sick of it.

It's market forces, of course. 'Market forces'. An oblique way of saying fate, or the herd instinct, or the will of God. A buzz phrase that's the business equivalent of throwing up your pudgy hands and giving a broad shrug and a wry wink. *Give 'em what they want. And keep flogging it to them long after they've stopped wanting it.*

Except it isn't market forces. It's a collective loss of nerve.

The root of the problem lies, I would submit, in the collapse of the Net Book Agreement fifteen-odd years ago. For non-UK readers, the Net Book Agreement was a gentlemanly collusion between publishers and booksellers whereby the former set book prices and if the latter chose to offer a discount on a title they would no longer be supplied by the publisher in question. It was, on the whole, a mutually beneficial arrangement, bringing profit to both parties. It contributed to the growth of the midlist, those titles which are well regarded, critically acclaimed, but without an instant, easy appeal. It also meant that a publisher had the resources to spend time developing authors, nurturing their work, building them a readership, and fostering their careers. It was a cartel, yes, but a benign one.

With the Agreement gone, the balance of power shifted and the benign cartel was replaced by another, not so benign one. All at once, publishers were no longer in charge of determining what the public

155

might or might not like to read and how much they should pay for it. Booksellers were. And the booksellers decided that what they wanted to do was maximise the volume of stock throughput. They wanted to expand their market share and minimise overheads. They wanted books to become a commodity rather than an art form – washing powder with pages, baked beans with a jacket and spine. The big chains wanted to get bigger and buy out or bury the smaller chains and the independent retailers. It was a deregulated free-for-all. Booksellers now set prices, and chose what titles they would promote on the basis of commerciality alone. They also considered knowledgeable, literature-loving staff to be a liability rather than an asset (doubtless because discussing books with a customer uses up time, valuable time, time that could otherwise be spent running the laser scanner over the barcode of yet another item of merchandise). They wanted McWorkers, minimum-wage slaves for whom slinging paperbacks across the counter at Borders wasn't much different from slinging paper cups across the counter at Starbucks.

So what we're left with is books being sold as loss leaders at supermarkets, books being discounted so heavily that neither the publisher nor the author makes much in the way of a percentage cut, books being displayed prominently in all branches of a chain only on condition that the publisher stumps up some ridiculous sum, as much as £45,000 for a week's promotion, which chews a significant chunk out of the marketing budget for a lead title.

This has meant, in turn, that the major publishing houses have had to become painfully risk averse and are obliged to focus their attention on product which they feel confident will sell in quantity. The midlist has been squeezed almost into nonexistence, and many authors now feel constrained to turn out formulaic, less innovative work than they otherwise might in order to meet demand and remain in employment.

We all know about biodiversity. We all know that scientists consider a broad range and variety of life forms as vital to the health and survival of an ecosystem. If large numbers of species become extinct, if biodiversity is lost, then the ecosystem is in trouble and could well collapse. This is happening right now in our world, thanks to human activity, our intervention in the balance of nature. It's one of the reasons why the planet is so fucked.

The book trade is facing a similar crisis. The increasing lack of what I shall term *bibliodiversity*, the gradual disappearance of the less immediately saleable forms of literature, is undermining the wellbeing of the business and threatening its destruction.

I'm writing here not as an author concerned about his own career – I'm doing okay, thank you very much – but as a reader. As someone who's finding it harder and harder to walk down into town and stumble across, almost serendipitously, some unforeseen literary treat. Someone who's thirsting for fiction and nonfiction that is out of the mainstream, sometimes so far removed from the mainstream it's not even in a tributary, it's in a remote alpine spring way above the treeline. Someone who hankers after material that challenges, provokes, refuses to play safe, messes with form and genre, crosses boundaries, experiments, sometimes disappoints, sometimes infuriates, but always does what is least expected and even the polar opposite of what is expected, while still being highly entertaining, of course. And it's in short supply.

But it is out there. It can be found.

To paraphrase Winston Smith, "If there is hope, it must lie in the small presses and indie imprints."

You already know this, because you are holding a copy of *PostScripts* in your hand (and no doubt are chafing to get to the end of this editorial so that you can move on to the meat of the magazine, the great stories that follow – not much further to go now, I promise). Most likely you are a subscriber to this esteemed periodical and are therefore aware of the existence of PS and its ilk, not so much publishing houses as publishing cottages, one-man-and-his-QuarkXPress outfits whose aim is not pumping out pap by the bucketload but crafting beautifully presented editions of truly new fiction, novels with novelty, in addition to reissuing established or unjustly neglected classics. Their philosophy isn't big bucks; it's breaking new ground and breaking even, no less, no more.

Such imprints are the obscure creatures who are continuing to keep the literary gene pool deep and ensure bibliodiversity and the future of this industry. They're the hardy little mammals who are in a good position to escape the looming mass extinction and may well evolve into the next dominant species.

They're not easy to track down. Their product can't necessarily be found in malls and pedestrian precincts. Their natural habitat is specialist bookstores on side-streets and weird little one-ended alleyways, and dealer sites on the misty uplands of the internet.

But they exist. And they will breed and multiply. They will thrive, and we will all be better off as a result.

American Gothic – *American Fantastic Tales: Terror And The Uncanny From Poe To The Pulps,* *American Fantastic Tales: Terror And The Uncanny From The 1940s To Now,* both edited by Peter Straub, *The Black Heart* by Patrick O'Leary, *Just After Sunset* by Stephen King (2008-2009)

A body is discovered in woods in rural Indiana, skinned from the neck up, leaving the head looking like "the cupped husk of a peeled orange". The detective investigating soon unearths evidence that this grisly murder is linked to a war between two ancient secret cults, one celebrating laughter, the other despondency. The victim, a circus clown, was an adherent of one cult. His killer, from the opposing cult, removed his face – clown makeup and all – in order to appease a joyless deity and help usher in a dismal apocalypse.

This deft short story, "The God of Dark Laughter" by American author Michael Chabon, is an archly witty and chilling tale which plays neatly on coulrophobia – a fear of clowns. It was first published in 2001 and is included as one of the later entries in *American Fantastic Tales*, a two-volume anthology compiled and edited by the Wisconsin-born horror novelist Peter Straub.

The volumes contain 86 short stories between them, and offer an intriguing overview of how the supernatural short story has grown and developed in the US over the past 200 years. The common thread throughout is that of authors revelling in the bizarre, the outré and the grotesque. As Straub says in his introduction to volume one, "one expects a bit of wildness, of exaggeration and dramatic effect" from the American supernatural story. What we find in his anthology are not genteel hearthside yarns; they are stories that belong round campfires in dark woods.

Aside from a couple which touch on science fiction, these are broadly speaking horror tales. They're there to disorientate, to alter a reader's perceptions and deliver delicious, sharp jolts of unease. Their aim is to suggest how thin the veneer of civilisation is, how close to the surface savagery and madness lurk. For a nation whose founding fathers tamed a whole continent and shaped an identity for themselves from scratch, such loss of control must have been a pre-eminent fear.

In Britain, when we think of the supernatural short story we think of the 'cosy' ghostly tales of Dickens and MR James – quaintly eerie relics of a smoggy, candle-lit era. In the US, though, the genre has waxed and waned in popularity but never lost its appeal. During the 1800s spooky tales by Edgar Allan Poe, Nathaniel Hawthorne and Herman Melville would feature in esteemed literary periodicals such as *Harper's Monthly* and *New England Magazine*. In the early 20th century, the pulp magazines, most notably the periodical *Weird Tales*, provided a home for writing by the masters of the uncanny such as HP Lovecraft, August Derleth and Robert E. Howard. Today, examples of American fantastical storytelling, such as the tale by Chabon, appear in magazines as prestigious as *The New Yorker*.

A recurrent theme in the first volume of *American Fantastic Tales* is that of people losing their way – straying off the safe path, surrendering to the temptations of the flesh, or falling under the thrall of some sinister, often pagan influence: witchcraft, in the case of Hawthorne's cautionary tale "Young Goodman Brown" (1835); material greed, in Harriet Prescott Spofford's "The Moonstone Mass" (1868); and the hell of industrial mechanisation, in Melville's "The Tartarus Of Maids" (1855).

As we proceed through the late Victorian era into the early 20th century the tone of the stories moves away from morality and didacticism. The tales cease to focus on a dangerous transgression from the proper, Christian order of things. More and more, they are informed by the fear of psychological imbalance. Malign forces no longer manifest in the guise of vampires, ghosts, voodoo curses and the like. The presiding theme becomes the dread of mental instability – a sense of the character losing grip of his sense of self.

Or indeed *her* sense of self: the protagonists are as likely to be women as men, usually depressed or high-strung women. Charlotte Perkins Gilman's celebrated "The Yellow Wall Paper" (1892) is a fine example of a progressive feminist take on the supernatural – a fascinating, sympathetic study of a 'hysterical' wife, who breaks down under the pressures of domesticity, fancying there is a woman crawling around behind the wallpaper in her bedroom, having found refuge there. Joan in John Cheever's "Torch Song" (1947) is seemingly a kind of blighted 'black widow' who brings death to every lover she has, although she could equally just be a lonely good-time girl who's having extraordinary bad luck with men. Her beguiling influence draws the story's (male) narrator to her as surely as a Siren draws sailors onto the rocks. And what about the jilted woman in Shirley Jackson's "The Daemon Lover" (1949)? Is she genuinely pursuing a faithless fiancé or simply obsessed with some phantom man of her own imagination?

The fragility of the psyche is a typical vein in American fantastical fiction and achieves its most eloquent expression in Nabokov's "The Vane Sisters" (1951), which tells of an academic's fascination with a pair of sisters, one of whom commits suicide, the other of whom becomes obsessed with spiritualism. In the final paragraph, we are given a cryptic clue which casts all that has gone before in a new and spectral light. Unless, that is, you prefer to see it as the punch-line for a self-lacerating literary joke from its playful narrator. In other words, this is a ghost story which hinges on the reader's complicity in believing it to be one. Straub, in his introduction to his second volume, calls the Nabokov a 'meta-ghost story' as if to make it clear it deserves its place in his grand anthology.

Today, American horror authors are clearly at home with the possibility of the supernatural tale being as much about the exploration of neurosis as encounters with paranormal phenomena. With psychoanalysis a commonplace feature of American life, people are ever more aware of the possibility of being derailed, and indeed betrayed, by the subconscious.

Thomas Ligotti, Tim Powers, Jonathan Carroll and Kelly Link excel in their ability to convey mental disorientation through subtle shifts between the real and the unreal, so smooth that at first you aren't aware of the transition. The strangeness of these stories, so enmeshed in the fabric of everyday life, only seems logical if you accept that either the world is mad, or you are yourself. In the best way possible, they fail to make sense. As such they increasingly reflect the western experience of modern life – atomised, fast-paced, overloaded by information and innovation and seemingly configured to drive us crazy.

It does seem that, in the second volume, Straub has been pushed to find material which truly merits the appellation supernatural. In the later stories, actual ghosts and ghouls remarkable by their absence. Hence, one supposes, the use of the word 'fantastic' in the title, which can be applied equally to altered states of mind as to otherworldly beings. In a predominantly rational and secular West, our demons are inside us, or else they are the people around us.

That, certainly, seems to be the approach of American SF/fantasy author Patrick O'Leary, who employs a consistently dreamlike and psychological approach to the modern supernatural tale in his collection of short stories *The Black Heart*. In "What Mattered Was Sleep", a father surrenders his son to the government because the boy has tested positive for some kind of disease. What disease? What becomes of the boy? O'Leary never reveals the answers, but the doom-laden, fatalistic tone of the story suggests we are better off not knowing. Similarly "The Me After the Rock" consists of a dialogue between two quarantined astronauts who've returned from a mission to Mars where something went badly wrong. We're given only teasing glimpses as to the nature of the mishap. However, that we are reading a *transcript* of the conversation is a clue to what lies in store for the astronauts.

The flinty brilliance of *The Black Heart* lies in its understatement and its willingness to leave its stories open-ended and ambiguous. O'Leary, a Detroit resident and former creative director of an advertising agency, hints that life in his homeland nowadays is so bewildering that it cannot readily be decoded in fiction. There are horrors aplenty, but they're no longer concerned with the external or supernatural. They come from within – apparitions summoned by fractured minds unable to cope with life.

Stephen King, by contrast, has kept the flame of the good, old-fashioned spine-tingling tale burning throughout his long, vastly prolific and immensely successful career. He has become the supremo of the horror-fiction world largely because he fuses respect for classic supernatural storytelling with a modern sensibility.

In the second volume of *American Fantastic Tales*, King is represented with a late-1990s tale entitled "That Feeling, You Can Only Say What it is In French". It could have fit seamlessly into his latest collection of short fiction, his eighth, *Just After Sunset*. Here, he employs several revered horror tropes: ghosts, voices from beyond the grave, people with paranormal powers, a cat as an instrument of supernatural vengeance (shades of Poe's "The Black Cat"), and dreams that foretell the future.

King uses these spooky elements to address contemporary issues in subtle fashion. "Stationary Bike", for example, satirises American attitudes towards fitness and physical perfection: an overweight man pedals an exercise bike so obsessively he ends up in another world. In "N. ", a man with OCD believes that counting objects is the only way to prevent a malevolent, Lovecraftian entity breaking through from its plane of existence to ours. As his account of events is mediated to us via notes taken by his psychiatrist, we cannot tell if it is truth or delusion. It could, disturbingly, be either.

In "The Things They Left Behind", written a month after 9/11, King tackles the fall of the Twin Towers. The narrator, an employee of a company with offices in the World Trade Center, decides to play truant on that fateful day. Afterwards, personal possessions belonging to dead work colleagues turn up mysteriously in his apartment. He can't get rid of them. It's an inventive, if sad, metaphor for survivor guilt.

Nearly all the stories in *Just After Sunset* pick at scabs from wounds inflicted by the modern American age – albeit with wit, panache and glee by a writer who loves to raise a goosebump or two. Where his contemporaries dig deep into the human mind to find their horrors, King prefers to gaze out into the darkness beyond the reach of the campfire glow, as so many others have done in the past.

There's definitely something sinister, something unmentionable, creeping around out there.

Biting Commentary – *Pride And Prejudice And Zombies* by Jane Austen and Seth Grahame-Smith, *Patient Zero* by Jonathan Maberry, *World War Z* by Max Brooks, *The Living Dead* edited by John Joseph Adams (2009)

The ball at Netherfield is going well. Mr Bingley is charming company, though haughty Mr Darcy, in Elizabeth Bennet's opinion, is a highly disagreeable fellow. Then, suddenly there's an interruption: "A chorus of screams filled the assembly hall, immediately joined by the shattering of window panes." In come a horde of shambling, flesh-hungry zombies – and the evening is quite ruined...

If that doesn't sound quite like Jane Austen's famous novel, it's not. Instead, it's a passage from a new pastiche, *Pride And Prejudice And Zombies* by Seth Grahame-Smith.

Though it takes place in a world of empire-line dresses and exquisite etiquette, the scene is not so much classic novel as classic zombie-siege attack. And the book goes on in this manner: the freshly self-exhumed undead lurch in from the outside to gorge themselves on the living. For this is not the 19th century but a new world – and *Pride And Prejudice And Zombies* is just one of a recent glut of books that brings that very modern supernatural monster, the zombie, clawing and groaning its way into our 21st century lives.

Zombie fiction may be relatively new but zombies themselves are not. The idea originated in Africa and during the slave trade in the 15th and 16th centuries was brought over to Haiti, where it became an established part of voodoo culture. In this tradition, a reanimated corpse is mystically given a shuffling semblance of life – the *zuvembie*.

The present-day pop culture version of the zombie dates back only to the late 1960s and has a single point of origin: the film *Night Of The Living Dead*. Directed by George Romero, this seminal horror movie – and the sequels and countless imitations that followed – quickly established the 'ground rules' for the modern zombie archetype. The dead rise from their graves, for reasons no one can fathom, and crave human flesh – preferably brains. One bite from a zombie, and you become one too. How can you stop them? Only with a bullet to the head or outright decapitation.

Night Of The Living Dead came out in 1968, a year of worldwide social upheaval. Many critics divined satirical parallels between the film and the Vietnam War, the death of the hippy dream, and the student protests in the US and Paris.

Why, then, have the last few years seen a rise in the number of zombie-related movies, computer games, comic books and novels?

In their mutilated, decomposing frames, zombies seem to embody the great anxiety of the age we live in. As in 1968, they are symbols of all that we dread: conformity, mindlessness, disease, apocalyptic calamity.

Eras get the horror myths they deserve, which reflect them like distorting mirrors. The Romantic period had the scientific nightmare of Frankenstein and his creation. The Victorians, obsessed with sex and death, had the vampire. We, in our jittery, post-9/11 age, have zombies.

The zombie is an archetype still in flux, however. It has not yet matured to become fixed and rigid. This is an interesting moment precisely because, depending on the novelist's perspective, its meaning is still malleable. The zombie is as nebulous and unformed as many of our own fears and horrors of the early 21st century.

In *Pride And Prejudice And Zombies*, the zombie enhances and exaggerates the social critique already present in Austen's novel. But it's also outrageously transgressive and subversive – which is why Grahame-Smith's mash-up of kickass horror-action tropes and literary comedy of manners is such a winning idea, in theory if less so in execution.

Here, the Bennet sisters aren't hapless damsels waiting to make a good marriage. They're skilled in martial arts and able to wield sword and musket as well as any man. They wouldn't need to inherit their father's money, even if that were an option: "All five of them were capable of fending for themselves... they could make tolerable fortunes as bodyguards, assassins or mercenaries if need be."

Injecting zombie references – and some smutty double entendres – into Austen's text is amusing, albeit scandalous to some Janeites. The trouble is the joke doesn't sustain itself over the length of a novel.

The unadulterated Austen constitutes about 80 per cent of the book. When Grahame-Smith makes radical changes or invents whole scenes, they're bold and funny: Darcy cripples Wickham as punishment for mistreating Lydia; Elizabeth and Lady Catherine fight a duel to prove the former's worthiness to marry Darcy.

It might have been better, if the author had written an all-new zombie novel featuring Austen's characters. As it is, the contrast between gory undead ultraviolence and mannered gentility loses its potency.

Pride And Prejudice And Zombies has been an unexpected bestseller, and publishers have been quick to emulate it. Zombified versions of *A Christmas Carol* and *The War Of The Worlds* are soon to appear.

Zombies aren't useful to authors simply as a means to inject comic bathos into the classics, however. Jonathan Maberry is a horror writer whose books include *Vampire Universe* (2006) and *Bad Moon Rising* (2008). In *Patient Zero*, Maberry takes the zombie more seriously than Grahame-Smith. Fully cognisant of, and reverential towards, the existing lore, he also puts his own spin on the monster.

Patient Zero is a fast-paced techno-thriller which posits a genetically engineered disease communicable via bodily fluids – and therefore by bite. The plague engenders all the standard Romero-zombie attributes in its victims: apparent death, raging appetite for flesh, inhuman strength and near-invulnerability to harm.

Further reinforcing the association between zombies and modern fears, Maberry's novel sees al-Qaeda terrorists use the disease as a bio-weapon to strike against the Great Satan, America. That the terrorists are the dupes of a greedy Western pharmaceuticals magnate adds a further layer to the metaphor.

This is a wonderfully overblown novel. Its indomitable hero, Joe Ledger, is prone to the odd moment of self-doubt but, by and large, he gets the job done, swiftly, lethally, with minimum fuss. His best friend is a psychiatrist, and therapy is repeatedly invoked to deal with the ghastliness of combating the walking undead.

That peculiarly American quirk notwithstanding, the novel delivers zombie mayhem aplenty. The duration and intensity of the living-versus-unliving set pieces escalate all the way to a crazy climax at a July 4 celebration where the president's wife, no less, is under threat from a crowd of sightseers-turned-biteseekers.

Implicit in *Patient Zero* is the notion that zombies could be – indeed are – us, the clumsy, milling rabble we may degenerate into if we're not careful. And that's one reason why the zombie archetype is so effective:

zombies represent the worst in humans – the only difference is that zombies, of course, are dead.

Echoing our contemporary fears – not least with the current swine flu outbreak – zombies and disease are good partners. Max Brooks' *World War Z* (2006) also employs disease as the root cause of the zombie affliction.

Here the contagion is not manmade but a natural pathogen that mutates beyond control. But when it spreads, encompassing the world in a matter of weeks, this transmission is indeed down to human failings. Again, we see the horrors of our time projected onto fiction: a solitary, localised outbreak becomes an unstoppable planetary pandemic because of people-trafficking, trade in illegal organs, government corruption and inefficient bureaucracy.

The novel is told as an oral history. Through excerpts of interviews, people recall their involvement in pivotal moments over several years of the crisis in which the walking undead almost overwhelm the living, and the human race shrinks. Amid the turmoil and slaughter, some are prepared to do anything to survive. A Canadian woman recounts how her father traded a radio with neighbours for "a big bucket of this steaming hot stew" – that's human hot pot, we assume.

The humour, of which there is a surprising amount, is pitch-black and laden with irony. Israel, for instance, gathers as many Jews inside its borders as it can, then builds a huge wall around itself, in effect making a Gaza Strip of itself; a black South African describes a plan to save his nation, an updated version of a real-life scenario once drafted to protect Afrikaners in the event of a black uprising.

World War Z is the epitome and pinnacle of zombie fiction. Brooks, son of movie director Mel, treats the subgenre with respect and intelligence and does everything right. Where most zombie fiction narrow-focuses on a small band of humans battling to survive, *World War Z* is a widescreen vision, and all the better for it. Brooks' zombies are credible and horrible, and there are just so many of them – million upon million.

Sheer numbers is another reason why zombies are so scary and so pertinent to their 21st century audience. Earth, after all, is perilously overcrowded. And the arrival of great numbers of the undead means even less space to go round and more mouths to feed – and we, the animate, are on the menu.

To our contemporary palate, then, the fear is not of single villains so much as multiple horrors. This idea is played out in an anthology of zombie stories, *The Living Dead*.

The authors in this anthology are mostly fantasy or horror writers of some kind – some specialise in science fiction, others in horror or gothic novels. And though these genres are typically dominated by male authors – and have a primarily male readership – nearly a third of the contributors in this instance are women.

The best pieces here are those in which zombies appear en masse; they work because the stories stick to Romero's template and follow his satirical lead. And again, these narratives bring the zombie to life – in more ways than one – through the world's problems.

In Dan Simmons' truly outstanding "This Year's Class Picture" the zombies are school children into whom a possibly deranged teacher is trying to instil some learning. In Michael Swanwick's "The Dead" zombies are the social underclass.

The zombies of Poppy Z. Brite's "Calcutta, Lord Of Nerves" are India's untouchables. In Norman Partridge's "In Beauty, Like The Night" they are porn-mag centrefolds. The best known writer in this collection, Stephen King, tells a lovely tale of islanders off the coast of Maine who contend with a Romeroesque zombie uprising.

In 1988 Kim Newman, film critic and sometime horror author, published *Nightmare Movies*, a compendious survey of modern horror cinema. He wrote then that zombies can "at once epitomise and chastise any number of vices: conservative complacency, consumerist frenzy, mindlessly instinctive political positions, random violence, pointless greed".

Zombies, in that sense, are nullity, the proverbial blank canvas. And as the 21st century advances, more and more zombies keeps shambling our way. Onto the empty deadness of their faces we may project everything that we hope we are not – and everything we fear we may be.

Apocalypse Soon (2009)

Michael Crichton's *State Of Fear*, an anti-environmentalist diatribe fashioned roughly in the shape of a thriller, concludes with an 'Author's Message'. In part, this asserts:

> I suspect the people of 2100 will be much richer than we are, consume more energy, have a smaller global population, and enjoy more wilderness than we have today. I don't think we have to worry about them.

The late – and admirable – Crichton was a far smarter man than I will ever be. His intellectual superiority, especially in matters scientific, means his opinions on climate change and global warming carry considerably greater weight and authority than mine ever will. I'd like to believe his prophecies to be accurate.

I just can't.

Something in my gut tells me his optimistic outlook is wrong. More than that, *any* optimistic outlook is wrong. If you ask me, humankind is doomed to a future of rising sea levels, extreme weather events, mass starvation, resource wars, unsustainable mass-migrations from poorer to wealthier nations, animal extinctions, power shortages, rampant pandemics, and markedly reduced life quality and life expectancy. A hundred years from now I see a global population reduced by a few billion, sheltering from rampant flood waters in quasi-feudal enclaves, surrounded by husks of redundant technology and fighting off invaders with a mix of modern and medieval weaponry. A little bit *Mad Max*, in other words, and a little bit *A Canticle For Leibowitz*.

The stars? Intergalactic colonisation? The outward urge? Sowing the seed of humanity across the cosmos? Not a chance. Such grand visions never come to pass. No one is prepared to pony up the trillions necessary to fund that kind of dream-scale project. No one has the vision. Governments are irredeemably short-termist. They plan five years ahead, if that. This is why I don't write space opera. To me it isn't SF, it's pure fantasy.

Things to come are things to dread. My two sons will grow up in a world where the best is past and where our present era will seem like a golden age – unlimited travel, plentiful food, material affluence, technological superabundance. They will look back on my generation with envious amazement, wondering how we could have been so reckless, so lacking in foresight, so wilfully vandalistic, so damn *lucky*. And all I'll be able to do, if I'm still around, is apologise and say we couldn't help ourselves. We tried but we just couldn't break the habits of greed and squandering. We recycled our bottles and newspapers, but we knew it was a drop in the ocean. We installed low-energy lightbulbs, but our immense flatscreen TVs made up the difference in electricity consumption. We wanted to go veggie, but the lure of a fat juicy steak was too great.

I was in the dentist's chair the other day, having a checkup. The dentist enquired about an article I'd written in the paper, prognosticating dire times ahead for planet Earth. She told me, with a grim chuckle, that I was about to have a very uncomfortable experience at her hands if I genuinely believed everything was as dark as I'd stated in that piece. She would show her disapproval as only a dentist knows how.

With scenes from *Marathon Man* playing in my head, I desperately racked my brains to recall whether anything I'd submitted to the *FT* lately matched what she was describing. Some book review where I'd blithely let slip that I reckoned civilisation was screwed? Then, light dawned. There'd been a case of mistaken identity.

"Oh, you mean James Love*lock*," I said. "The great prophet of eco-catastrophe. That's not me. Definitely not. You can put away your rather enormous drill now. I disagree with everything the man says."

I don't, though.

Political Teen Reads – *Guantanamo Boy* by Anna Perera, *Message In A Bottle* by Valérie Zenatti, *Torn Pages* by Sally Grindley, *The Carbon Diaries 2015* by Saci Lloyd, *Journey Of Dreams* by Marge Pellegrino (2009)

British-born Khalid is visiting relatives in Pakistan, shortly after 9/11, when he's taken captive. Faster than you can say 'extraordinary rendition', he's whisked off to Kandahar and from there into detention at Guantanamo Bay, Cuba. His only crime, apart from being a young male Muslim, is that he played an online game with the unfortunate name 'Bomber One'.

This may sound like a news story or the plot of a thriller. It's not. In fact, Khalid is the 15-year-old protagonist of Anna Perera's *Guantanamo Boy*, a novel aimed at teenage readers.

We've heard a lot about teen fiction ever since the first Harry Potter appeared in 1997. Teen reads now frequently ride high in the bestseller charts. In J. K. Rowling's wake the market is dominated by fantasy and wannabe wizards, as well as the hard-edged spy thrills of the Young Bond and Alex Rider series, and the dewy-eyed high-school vampire romance of Stephenie Meyer's *Twilight* saga.

There's nothing wrong with escapism, of course. And fantasy can often be a vehicle for exploring important, pertinent subjects. It certainly isn't new to write fiction with a 'message' of some kind. Most fairy stories were intended as cautionary tales, after all – warnings about human predators couched in terms of wolves and witches, or parables of greed or selfishness.

More recently, the CS Lewis' *Chronicles Of Narnia* (1950-1956) embedded a Christian message in an otherworldly saga of battle and betrayal. Philip Pullman's *His Dark Materials* (1995-2000), was the anti-*Narnia*, which used the same trick to different ends: railing against religion in general and Catholicism in particular.

Teen fiction, though, need not dress up in magical robes or equip itself with high-tech gadgets to reach a wide audience – or to get across a serious point.

In contrast to the fantasy boom, five recent teen novels, among them *Guantanamo Boy*, address some of the most vexed social and political questions of our age with a straightforward approach. All are distinct from adult fiction partly because each centres on a teen protagonist. In each of these books, however, there is no 'backgrounding' of the subject matter – it isn't smuggled into a readers' consciousness disguised in allegory or metaphor. All five are boldly and baldly *about* something.

That makes them interesting. But does it make them a good read? Isn't there a danger that novels of this kind may campaign rather than entertain, dictate rather than elucidate, provoke yawns rather than thought?

In many ways these novels demonstrate that the themes of fiction – the overcoming of obstacles, triumph in adversity – are as suited to contemporary traumas as they are to the classic settings or fantasy worlds of teen books. But by considering which of these books make strong novels – which are good fiction whatever their setting – we can also see that the more 'difficult' the subject matter, the more important it is not to turn plot into propaganda, characterisation into cartoon simplifications.

In *Guantanamo Boy*, London-born Perera's first work for teenagers, Khalid's experiences of torture at the hands of his CIA interrogators are a savage, Kafkaesque nightmare. The louder he proclaims his innocence, the less he is believed.

At first glance it may seem that the War on Terror is a convenient hook on which to hang a classic 'unjustly imprisoned victim' plotline. But readers will be disappointed if they expect Khalid to perform some kind of miraculous, Count of Monte Cristo–style escape. His predicament is bleakly realistic and relentlessly ineluctable. Perera is also careful to depict him as an ordinary boy, interested in girls and football, not some paragon, a devout martyr who represents all Islam. Similarly, the Americans in her book aren't all bad, and Pakistanis are shown as complicit in the identification and capture of terror suspects in their country. The argument is as well balanced as the moral outrage is palpable.

The problem with a novel so topical, however, is that the news moves on. Guantanamo Boy's appeal may be more limited now that Barack Obama has promised to close down the Cuba detention camps.

Some issues, however, dominate the headlines for longer. French author Valérie Zenatti's *Message In A Bottle* is set amid the Middle East conflict – one that will continues to dominate the headlines for some time.

When Naïm, a Palestinian boy, finds a note in a bottle thrown into the sea by Tal, an Israeli girl, the two strike up an email correspondence. What starts out as a spiky verbal joust ends as a warm not-quite-love-affair as the two come to appreciate their similarities and differences. In some ways this is a traditional love story – though at one point Naïm states hotly that he and Tal are 'not Romeo and Juliet', *Message In A Bottle* is superficially an update of Shakespeare's teen tragedy; religion is the source of division rather than family feuds.

Ultimately, however, the novel is less about impossible romance than the absurdity of young people growing up in an environment where war and sudden death are commonplace. Zenatti spent her own teen years in Israel. She has direct experience of daily life threatened by rocket attack and suicide bombing, and it shows. Naïm describes with wonder a friend's experience of life in London: "There's a park where people [...] read or chat or kiss, living their lives without worrying that some missile's going to land on them..."

Zenatti sketches the history of the Middle East crisis as succinctly as possible without oversimplification. Yet her novel never trivialises or cheapens the grim, intractable situation by using it as the context for a 'will they, won't they?' love story.

Not all the troubles of the world today can be blamed on politics or religion, however. If there's a rising trend for international fiction led by social issues, Sally Grindley is definitely part of it – her previous novels include one about girls in China sold into domestic servitude (*Spilled Water*), and one on Indian children who scavenge on rubbish tips for a living (*Broken Glass*). Her latest offering, *Torn Pages*, is about a trio of African siblings orphaned by AIDS.

Lydia, the eldest of the three, is struggling to bring up her brother Joe and sister Kesi. She works so that they can go to school – foregoing an education herself. Her sole source of comfort is a journal left by her mother, a 'memory book' to guide her through the bad times and remind her of the good.

The spectre of AIDS hovers over the story, all the more sinister since the disease isn't mentioned by name until more than 100 pages in.

What Grindley doesn't address, however, are questions about safe sex and condoms. The only references to sex comes are the extramarital affair conducted by the children's father, which brought the disease into their household.

In that respect, *Torn Pages* is perhaps less pertinent to Western teens than it could be. In Africa, AIDS is a widespread, terrifying scourge. In the West it's something that can be avoided, with the right precautions, and treated. Few in the developed world have to live like Kesi, born after her father's affair, who may have inherited HIV. Equally, few could read this book and not be struck by the iniquity of a world in the disease's effects are so different between regions.

The underlying message of *Torn Pages* is the effect of inequality, a theme that is prevalent also throughout much adult fiction, in novels about immigration and racism. The same sense of global interconnectedness is implicit in another teen novel, Saci Lloyd's *The Carbon Diaries 2015*.

Britain is blighted by environmental catastrophe in this novel: epidemics, lack of clean water, food shortages – many of the ills, in other words, that currently bedevil the developing world. Through a year's diary entries, narrator Laura Brown describes how she and her family are coping with newly introduced 'carbon rationing' and learn to limit their use of 'luxuries' such as electricity and petrol.

The book's overall tone is satirical. As blizzards threaten to sweep in from the continent, she describes a trip to the supermarket, where "all the nice middle-class people" pretend that they aren't panic buying "and that it was completely normal for them to be pushing six trolleys around... My mother nearly had a fight with this other woman over a multi-pack of garlic and basil passata."

This humour sweetens what would otherwise be a bitter story. Lloyd has plainly thought carefully about how Britain might work in the near-future might work – or indeed how it might fail to work. The acutely observant, occasionally angst-ridden Laura is an easy point of identification for her readership. The threat she is telling us about is not only credible but immediate.

As with most examples of the future-dystopia genre, *The Carbon Diaries 2015* flags up where our society seems to be headed. The tone is less a rallying cry, more a gloomy, stoic shrug, however. The novel doesn't sermonise. The same cannot be said for Marge Pellegrino's

Journey Of Dreams, which, of all these books, comes closest to being a work of propaganda, labouring under the weight of its own worthiness.

In mid-1980s Guatemala, the government carried out a 'slash and burn' campaign against the indigenous people. *Journey of Dreams* tells of a family ousted from their home by soldiers and forced to make a desperate, dangerous journey to the US. The viewpoint is that of 13-year-old Tomasa, whose fantastical, symbolic dreams are a counterpoint to the slog of the family's trek to freedom.

The US is regarded as a magical destination, the Emerald City at the end of the Yellow Brick Road. Once there, Pellegrino implies, your story ends and your troubles are over. She does not show us how well, or how badly, Tomasa and family adjust to their new home. As we well know, not all refugees acclimatise in the Promised Land.

Journey Of Dreams is involving read, strong in its celebration of Mayan-inflected folklore and culture. But it fails to argue from an unbiased standpoint. Teenagers are apt to see the world in terms of polar opposites – something is wrong or right, uncool or cool, bad or 'bad'. If a teen novel is to open their eyes to a difficult, nuanced subject, it needs to explore the grey areas between the different views. Authors who credit teen readers with the willingness to be brought nose-to-nose with harsh truths should also credit them with the intelligence to decide for themselves how they feel about them. Don't moralise. That's the moral of the story.

Colin Wilson: The Search For The Extraordinary (2011)

An appreciation written a couple of years before its subject's death.

Few living writers have applied themselves to the subject of the paranormal with the same level of seriousness and intellectual rigour as Colin Wilson. In a career spanning more than fifty years he has penned nearly 200 books, and of those a significant proportion concern occult matters, from ghosts and magic to Atlantis and aliens. His work combines readability with a remarkable breadth of research, and even if one may not always agree with his conclusions, one has to admire the logic of the argument by which he reaches them and the persuasive, good-natured style in which they're conveyed.

Wilson was born in 1931 in Leicester, and at an early age fled to London to escape what he feared would be a life of working-class drudgery. He was a precocious, bookish young man, and digging trenches for the local electricity board – his first proper job – was clearly not for him. As he puts it in his autobiography *Dreaming To Some Purpose*, "I didn't want to do other people's work; I wanted to get on with my own."

In the capital, he slept rough on Hampstead Heath and spend his days in the Reading Room of the British Museum, where he wrote what was to become his first publication and his signature work. *The Outsider* appeared in 1956 and was an instant, spectacular success both with the critics and in terms of sales. It propelled its 25-year-old author into the limelight and almost as quickly drove him into self-imposed exile in the wilds of Cornwall.

The Outsider is an absorbing and erudite study of great men – thinkers, artists, doers – who have thrived outside the limits of societal norms. They are those who are impelled by their creativity, their Nietzschean 'will to power', to follow their own visions and remake reality in their own image, whether it's T. E. Lawrence fighting on the side of the Arabs as a kind of messianic warrior-preacher or Nijinsky striving through intense discipline and abnegation of the ego to create ballet of a complexity and sublimeness never seen before.

The book was a sharp riposte to the prevailing philosophical tenor of the times: the existential pessimism of the post-war austerity years. It asserts that humans can achieve great things, even superhuman feats, by the simple application of positivity and concentration. Lawrence, Nijinsky and other geniuses such as Van Gogh and T. S. Eliot, each an Outsider in his own way, pushed the boundaries of thought and self-expression and thereby changed the world.

Almost all of them, however, ended up defeated, disillusioned, even mad. Wilson contends that this fate could have been avoided had they not allowed themselves to succumb to an overwhelming sense of futility. These Outsiders lost sight of the big picture. Though extraordinary individuals, they failed to grasp that the everyday life which they surpassed is extraordinary too. Having excelled, they came to the conclusion that there was nothing else, nothing more. They gave in.

After *The Outsider*'s considerable impact there came, inevitably, a backlash. Wilson's next few books were either viciously mauled and derided in the review columns or, perhaps worse, roundly ignored. In part this was because he had the misfortune to become tangentially associated with the Angry Young Men movement of the 1950s, that loose agglomeration of authors and playwrights such as John Osborne and John Braine who kicked against the pricks of the British establishment and then found establishment pricks kicking them back. But also, it seemed that the public was unable to digest, or lacked the appetite for, further helpings of Wilson's message of logical positivism. Nor did his immodesty help. Rather like Oscar Wilde, but without the irony, Wilson was fond of declaring his own genius.

He retreated with his wife and family to the West Country, where he still lives and where he has continued to write prolifically and productively but by and large in obscurity. There have been novels, many of them SF, for instance the Spider World series and *The Space Vampires*, which was turned into the trashy but oddly enjoyable movie *Lifeforce* by director Tobe Hooper in 1985. There have been further volumes in the 'Outsider cycle', notably *The Age Of Defeat* and *The Strength To Dream*, alongside books on a whole host of topics – literature, astronomy, deviant sexuality, wine, true crime. Eminent among these are a fascinating study of the Fred and Rose West serial killings, *A Plague Of Murder*, and a valuable appraisal of the author David Lindsay, best known for the beguiling, phantasmagoric Edwardian fantasy masterpiece *A Voyage To Arcturus*.

Further *Outsider*-level success has eluded Wilson, but he came close with *The Occult* (1971) and its follow-ups *Mysteries* (1978) and *Beyond The Occult* (1988). This trio of investigations into the paranormal constitutes as grounded and penetrating a survey of the subject as one could hope for. The books also espouse a core belief of Wilson's that humans are far too prone to blinkeredness – to a wilful obliviousness of the extraordinary – and would achieve greater fulfilment in life and perhaps even gnostic revelation if they would only open their minds to the range of amazing phenomena that the universe has to offer. It is as if we are at the circus but have turned round in our seats and are looking the other way. In the ring the clowns, acrobats, lion tamers and other performers are putting on a wonderful show, and we're sitting there paying no attention and having a hard time fathoming why we're so bored.

The Occult opens with Wilson stating that magic and mysticism are not the sole province of neurotics and madmen, nor should they be. He says they first became of interest to him personally because "they confirmed my intuition of another order of reality, *an intenser and more powerful form of consciousness*" (his italics). He goes on to argue that supranormal abilities such as telepathy, premonition and thaumaturgy (the power to heal) are innate and part of our cultural heritage as a race. Our tendency now to dismiss their existence or ignore evidence of them is the fault of modern rationalism, an erroneous worldview that divides everything up into that which can be empirically proven and that which can't. Anything in the latter category, by our strict, over-reductive standards, must be untrue, and therefore worthless.

The entire book seeks to refute this, drawing together numerous diverse examples to build a very plausible case. Wilson discusses how the *I-Ching* and the Kabbalah can bring insights by stirring up dormant regions of the mind. He talks of the psychologist Abraham Maslow, who identified 'peak experiences', the moments when the self breaks free from its prison of doubt and grasps objectively the essential meaningfulness of reality. He scrutinises famous exponents of spiritualism, among them the Fox sisters and Daniel Dunglas Home, and acknowledges that fraud may have played a part in some of the phenomena such people produced but suggests, too, that in many instances genuine communication with the dead did occur – the facts allow for no other interpretation.

An impressive array of sources are marshalled to reinforce Wilson's claims. Bertrand Russell, Robert Graves, W. B. Yeats, the Russian philosopher P. D. Ouspensky, Carl Jung, William James, Arthur Koestler and many others are cited. The passages the book devotes to Rasputin, the 'Great Beast' himself Aleister Crowley, and Wilhelm Reich – he, you'll remember, postulated the existence of a field of 'orgone energy' that interpenetrates all living matter, rather like the Force in *Star Wars* – are particularly compelling.

Key to *The Occult*, and to a lesser extent its two successors, is Wilson's notion of something he calls 'Faculty X', which he summarises as "that latent power that human beings possess *to reach beyond the present*" (again, his italics). Faculty X, he avers, lies behind all poetic and mystical experience. It is the moment when the conscious mind relaxes, lets go, and an intense, dazzling focus of our energies is possible. Trivialities fall away. We break through to some kind of deeper understanding, and from there creativity and inner power may flow, in abundance. Athletes and musicians are apt to refer to this state of calm brilliance as being 'in the zone'. They find themselves performing better than they have before, better than they perhaps thought possible.

One might infer that all of Wilson's Outsiders share the ability to access Faculty X, whether knowingly or not. The same goes for anyone who has had direct contact with the supernatural, anyone who is born with some uncanny knack such as the gift for dowsing for water or the capacity to pluck multiple-digit primes from the air, and anyone who is touched by genius or by genius' dark twin insanity – they are able to tap into a bottomless reservoir of mental power which is common to us all. We all possess Faculty X, but the mundanity of our material lives prevents the majority of us from taking advantage of it.

With effort, goes Wilson's argument, the situation can be reversed. Indeed, he suggests that mankind's next collective evolutionary leap will be backwards not forwards, a break away from pure intellect towards instinct again, feeling making a resurgence over thought, left brain rising up to challenge the dominance of right brain.

We see Wilson expanding on this point in more recent works, books which purport to be one thing but are in fact another. *From Atlantis To The Sphinx* (1996), for example, is ostensibly a distillation of the theses of archaeological 'heretics' such as Graham Hancock, Robert Bauval and Robert Temple, all of whom are convinced that ancient civilisations were far more advanced, and for that matter far more ancient, than is generally reckoned. But in fact *From Atlantis...* is a restatement of Wilson's contention that modern man has lost or forgotten valuable knowledge and skills which our distant ancestors took for granted.

Similarly *Alien Dawn* (1998) seems to have been commissioned and written solely in order to cash in on the late-nineties fever for all things esoteric and extraterrestrial that was sparked by the huge popularity of *The X-Files*. Actually, though, the book recasts the long and often bizarre history of UFO sightings, contact and abduction as a modern gloss on a pre-existing set of psychological phenomena. That is to say, Wilson treats 'close encounters' as inner events rather than outer, instances of altered states of consciousness rather than genuine realworld occurrences. Our imaginations, cloistered by too much materiality, are rebelling and trying to make themselves heard, and they're doing so dressed up in the pop-culture paraphernalia of aliens and spaceships.

For Colin Wilson, his life's goal seems to have been exhorting people to liberate themselves from the grey valleys of laziness, anxiety and depression where they spend too much of their lives. Through sheer willpower alone, he says, one can elevate oneself to sunlit uplands where the views are broad and breathtaking.

It isn't a very fashionable stance to adopt but it has earned him a hardcore following of admirers, among them David Bowie. Wilson tells us over and over again that the world is weirder than we realise but that we need not be frightened or intimidated by this. We should instead, as the lyric of Bowie's song "Changes" tells us, "turn and face the strange", for by embracing what we don't understand we can unlock our own true potential. We can all, chrysalis into butterfly, transform into Outsiders and soar.

Apocalyptic And Post-Apocalyptic Science Fiction (2012)

Part of the brief for this treatise on an SF subgenre was for the author to include one of his/her own books and discuss it in the context of the tradition to which it belongs. Hence, the intrusion of my own Untied Kingdom *into the argument towards the end is not some act of monstrous egotism but prescribed by editorial fiat.*

Every major religion has a tradition of apocalypse. In Judaeo-Christianity there are the prophesied 'end times', a period of extreme tribulation for humankind culminating in a final conflict between the forces of good and evil, Armageddon. The Earth will be purged, the righteous saved.

Islam has Yawm al-Qiyamah, detailed in the Qur'an as a last judgement where Muslim and non-Muslim alike will be held to account before God for their actions. According to Hindu scripture, meanwhile, we are currently living in the Kali Yuga, an 'age of vice', the last of four stages the world must go through over and over in an eternal cycle of decay and renewal which parallels the four seasons of the year. Similarly, the Mesoamerican Long Count calendar, devised by the Mayan priesthood, states that we are coming to the end of a thirteenth *b'ak'tun* (a period of 144,000 days), which coincides with the end of a fourth and final phase of creation. Time is running out. December 2012 is when the fun begins – or, rather, stops.

The Norse canon has its Ragnarök, the 'final destiny of the gods'. Three icy years of Fimbulwinter will precede the destruction of Midgard, the Earth, and its subsequent rebirth. Going back further we find the flood myth of the ancient Babylonians, a precursor of the Biblical flood of Noah. The Babylonian myth depicts the rising waters as a divine punishment, bringing about the demise of corrupt civilisation. The gods encourage one man, Uta-Napishtim, a favourite of theirs, to build a boat in order to save himself, his family and specimens of each living creature. Uta-Napishtim then becomes the founding father of a new, improved human race. Zoroastrianism combines these two elements – snow and survivalism – in the myth of long-lived Yima, whom God, Ahura Mazda, instructs to build a subterranean sanctuary for the best individuals from all species in order to escape the effects of a series of terrible, destructive winters.

In each instance cited, the tropes are more or less the same. The world is in a sorry state. People are sinful. Divine reckoning will come to sweep away everything that is old and decadent. An almighty cataclysm will punish the wicked but spare (and perhaps even exalt) the righteous.

There is, it seems, a basic human need to believe that the world is coming to an end or has done so in the past and that, through immersion in the crucible of global catastrophe, humankind is tested and purified and bettered. Not all can survive the apocalypse, but those that do will be deserving inheritors of a golden age, a perfect new world.

Apocalyptic and post-apocalyptic science fiction takes this religious doctrine and, almost without exception, secularises and satirises it. For the reader, the appeal of this subgenre is that it affords the cathartic thrill of experiencing and surviving the end of the world. He or she joins the last of the race, however few they might be, in their desperate fight to keep the spark of civilisation alight. For the author, it's a chance to raise the stakes as high as they will possibly go. There can be no bigger crisis, surely, and no more dramatic milieu, than doomsday.

The Beginning Of The End

It is perhaps no coincidence that the first major work of apocalyptic and post-apocalyptic science fiction – which I shall from now on abbreviate to A&PASF – arrived as the white-hot glow of the Enlightenment had just started to fade. Mary Shelley's *The Last Man* was published in 1826 and may be considered as a riposte to, even a rejection of, a synonymous poem of two years earlier, Thomas Campbell's "The Last Man". Campbell writes of a lone man, in the aftermath of a time of plague and famine, watching the sun sicken and grow cold and pale. This "last of Adam's race" proclaims himself undaunted, however. His faith in God and the immortality of the soul remains unquenchable.

Shelley's novel features all the portents and devastation you might find in a Christian eschatology, but there is no optimistic message at the end, no sense of redemption, no covenanting rainbow, not so much as a glimpse of a New Jerusalem.

For its first third *The Last Man* tells of Lionel Verney and his relationships with Adrian, Earl of Windsor, and Lord Raymond, two characters who are thinly disguised analogues of, respectively, Shelley's husband, Percy Shelley, and Lord Byron (both of whom had died not long before the book was written). Not much happens in these early passages; nor, although the action is set in the late 21st century, is there much of an effort at future-building. Verney takes a trip on a commercial passenger balloon and there is a passing mention of machines which "supply with facility every want of the population" when it comes to food[1]. Otherwise, Shelley's imagined future is barely distinguishable from her Romantic-period now.

Then a plague strikes, a virulent pandemic of unspecified origin and nature, so lethal that it eradicates humankind almost entirely in the space of a few years. At this point the novel picks up pace, and Shelley's depictions of a dwindling population, corpse-strewn streets and abandoned capitals are vigorous, often haunting. By the end, there are only four people left alive: Verney, Adrian, and Verney's daughter and son Clara and Evelyn. The last three die of natural causes, leaving Verney to wander Switzerland and Italy alone, half-maddened by solitude but finding some consolation, as a good Romantic ought, in the wonders of landscape and the beauties of art.

The Last Man is nowhere near as memorable or as influential as Shelley's earlier *Frankenstein* (1818). It is in many respects a clumsily executed piece of work. For instance, the text purports to be a translation of various scraps of prophetic writing found littering the cave of the Sibyl at Cumae near Naples – yet the prophecy takes the form of a first-person memoir being written for the benefit of posterity (not that anyone remains to read it). This fictive structure does not hold up to scrutiny.

That said, the book has moments of undoubted power, and it is the godfather of all A&PASF. Whatever directions later novels took the subgenre, their roots lie in this one. *The Last Man* came first.

---

[1] p. 84, *The Last Man*, Wordsworth, 2004.

Pastoral Cares

In pastoral A&PASF, the apocalypse is a disaster but also an opportunity. It allows humankind to make a fresh start by rediscovering old ways. We can dispense with the machinery and industrialisation which have put us at odds with the demands and rhythms of Nature and embrace a simpler, purer form of existence.

The first true pastoral A&PASF novel is Richard Jeffries' *After London* (1884). Jeffries was a Wiltshire-born naturalist who wrote several books about rural life, and *After London*'s opening chapters – which relate how England becomes greened and forested anew after rising sea levels inundate the capital and cause it to sink into a swampy morass – show the eye of an author who has observed Nature closely and keenly. Roads disappear, once-managed brooks seep over their banks to form marshes, and wild-roaming packs of dogs haunt the woods. Although these introductory passages serve merely to set the scene, they are the book's high point, an evocative and authoritative vision of countryside running to seed.

The story itself concerns Felix, son of a noble, a young man with plenty of ambition but no fixed aim, no focus for his dreams. In search of purpose he sets out in a homemade dugout canoe to explore the Lake, the freshwater inland sea that has been created by the silting up of the Thames. Before leaving, however, he pledges his love to a baron's daughter, Aurora. His journey is as much an attempt to prove worthy of her as it is a voyage of self-discovery. Eventually, by aiding a group of shepherds in battle against their 'gipsy' enemies, Felix becomes the warrior-leader he always knew he could be, and returns to Aurora head held high.

The post-apocalyptic, ersatz medieval-feudal setting of *After London* is really just a backdrop for an adventure tale about courtly love. The novel harks nostalgically back to the idealised certainties of a bygone age, celebrating the power and eternal resilience of Nature but also the manly, chivalric virtues – hunting, weaponcraft, courage in combat, worshipful adoration of woman. These, Jeffries seems to be saying, are in danger of being lost, eroded by the effete urbanities of modern civilisation.

George R. Stewart's *Earth Abides* (1949) advances a not dissimilar argument. Set in mid-20th-century America after an airborne virus has wiped out almost all humankind, it shows Nature swiftly claiming ascendancy over the relics of Progress. This is envisaged as a kind of slow blurring of boundaries:

The smaller houses looked as if they were shrinking back shyly and beginning to hide in the woods. Fences also were being obscured. There was no longer a sharp line between the road and the surrounding country. [2]

The plot revolves around on the efforts of one man, biologist Isherwood Williams, to repopulate the Earth and keep the flames of civilisation and culture alight. Increasingly, however, the children of his small tribe of survivors grow more feral, better suited to their untamed, overgrown environment. In the end Ish, as he is known, has to accept reluctantly that a primitive lifestyle is preferable if it means that ensuing generations will coexist in harmony with the natural world. He and his wife Em, progenitors of a new race of people, have become a second Adam and Eve; fallen America, a second Eden.

It's a beautiful, meditative novel. For a more extreme but no less eloquently realised example of pastoral A&PASF, we can look to J. G. Ballard's *The Drowned World* (1962), part of the quartet of catastrophe-themed novels with which the author launched his career. [3] In *The Drowned World*, increased solar activity has raised the planet's temperature and melted the polar icecaps. Cities are now under water, riddled with lagoons and sweltering in tropical heat. Jungles fester where buildings once held sway; alligators crawl through the shells of ruined houses.

The focus of the novel, however, is not the physical changes the catastrophe has wrought on the planet so much as its effect on the human psyche – the interior apocalypses it generates. The central character, Robert Kerans, is part of a group of soldiers and scientists studying submerged London. The novel sees him grappling with his own responses to the way the postdiluvian environment is regressing around him and devolving into a version of the Triassic period. He

---

[2] p. 54, *Earth Abides* (SF Masterworks #12), Millennium, 1999.

[3] The others are *The Wind From Nowhere* (1961), set in a world devastated by hurricanes, *The Burning World* (1964), where toxic waste precipitates a global drought, and *The Crystal World* (1966), where some kind of virus is transforming everything to, well, crystal.

finds primitive feelings welling up within, his id coming to the fore and revelling in the chaos and entropy all around.

This altered world is no paradise, no lush, idyllic nursery in which infant-new humankind may take its first toddling steps. Quite the opposite:

Many of the smaller lakes were now filled by the silt, yellow discs of fungus-covered sludge from which a profuse tangle of competing plant forms emerged, *walled gardens in an insane Eden.* [4] [my italics]

At the novel's close, Kerans makes the decision to travel, not north to where pockets of civilisation (and safety) reside, but south, deeper into the heat and the 'phantasmagoric forest', alone. He is 'a second Adam' but a solitary, Eve-less one, and the goal of his quest is not to start anything new but to lose himself completely, to merge with the steaming wilderness and in all probability die. The novel's message is a parodic echo of that of *After London* and *Earth Abides*: under the pressure of Nature unbound, too much Nature, we do not see the human spirit rising to the challenge, we see the human mind fragmenting and collapsing in on itself. *The Drowned World* is pastoral A&PASF phase-shifted into a rationalist, neurotic nightmare.

A similar note of despairing acceptance of the new natural order can be found in another novel published the same year as Ballard's, Brian Aldiss' *Hothouse*. Here, we're taken to the far future where the Earth has halted in its rotation and now constantly faces the sun, which is huge and swollen and on the brink of going nova. Half the planet is haywire forest. Vegetation rules all. Some plants have grown as high as the moon, holding it fast in its orbit with gigantic tendrils. Others have developed locomotion and sentience. Of the animal kingdom only a few insect species remain, alongside a shrunken, attenuated form of *Homo sapiens*, childlike in thought as well as stature.

Hothouse is apocalyptic in the sense that it depicts a world long past the mitigating influence of human civilisation, wild in every aspect. Not only that: at the conclusion we learn that the sun is on the point of exploding. Spores of life are being projected out into space, like thistledown on the wind, to find other planets to alight on and inseminate. Some of the humans join them on their journey.

---

[4]p. 53, *The Drowned World* (SF Masterworks #17), Millennium, 1999.

Aldiss' vision is that of Ballard's in *The Drowned World* extrapolated to the nth degree. Humankind and Nature have become so intertwined, so fused together, that there is hardly a distinction between the two any longer. If Ballard's Kerans had lived on for several millennia, he'd have found the world of *Hothouse* a fiercely comforting place.

So, over the course of a century pastoral A&PASF changed from an expression of love of landscape into a vector for eco-age anxieties. The 'green' apocalypse, so welcomed in *After London* and *Earth Abides*, had by the 1960s become a source of existential dread. It's significant that a book seminal to the environmentalist movement, Rachel Carson's *Silent Spring*, came out in the same year as *The Drowned World* and *Hothouse*. All at once humankind was becoming conscious of the damage its activities, particularly its industry, were doing to the biosphere, and of course science fiction, being very much a bellwether of the zeitgeist, reflected this.

Mutationally Assured Destruction

While the Cold War was in full spate between the 1950s and the 1980s, terror of nuclear annihilation was the prevailing concern articulated by a great number of A&PASF works.

In a crowded field, one of the frontrunners, quick out of the starting gate, is *Star Man's Son* (1952)[5]. Andre Norton's novel is set in America some 200 years on from 'the Great Blow-up', a nuclear exchange perpetrated by the 'Old Ones' whose descendants now live in scattered tribal communities which view one another with suspicion and hostility. Some of the continent's cities remain intact enough to be scavenged for supplies. Others are too hot with radiation to enter.

Thanks to radiation-derived genetic mutation, our hero, Fors, possesses super-hearing and the ability to see in the dark, talents which make him an outcast among his tribe, if useful too as a forager. He has a feline sidekick, Lura, with whom he shares a form of psychic rapport. [6]Lura also is a mutant – she is tiger-sized but with the markings of a Siamese cat. Radiation, in fact, has worked all kinds of unlikely

---

[5]Also published under the title *Daybreak 2250 AD*.
[6]We find a similar relationship in Harlan Ellison's 1969 post-holocaust novella *A Boy And His Dog*, in which Vic and Blood, the title characters, converse telepathically.

evolutionary wonders over the course of a mere two centuries, fashioning creatures such as the Beast Things (gibbering human/rat hybrids) and some large, tool-using, pack-mentality lizards.

Realism, then, is not *Star Man's Son*'s strong suit. In fact, the book is essentially a sword-and-sorcery fantasy saga transplanted from the murky dawn of pre-history to the gaudy twilight of a post-holocaust future. The effects of radioactivity are even referred to as though something a wizard might have conjured up out of a cauldron:

"Radiation." Fors played with the hilt of his short sword. "Radiation mutations – but sometimes it worked well. Lura's kind was born of such magic."[7]

The plot is a breathless concatenation of captures and narrow escapes, flights and fights, but when it's all over Norton offers an upbeat conclusion. Conflict, she suggests, is part and parcel of the human condition but not inevitable. Fors manages to foster peace among the various tribes, and it is mooted that generations hence humankind will, through renewed co-operation, resume its aborted voyage to the stars. The pattern which resulted in the Great Blow-up has been broken.

Walter M. Miller's *A Canticle For Leibowitz* (1960) takes a less sanguine view. The novel charts a thousand years of post-holocaust future history, beginning 600 years after the war, known as the 'Flame Deluge'. There has been an anti-technological backlash, and now books and learning are preserved and jealously guarded by monastic orders.

The novel's first section, "Fiat Lux", hinges on the discovery of 'relics' – including a handwritten shopping list – in an old fallout shelter in Texas near an abbey that was founded by Isaac Leibowitz, a survivor of the war. The second part, "Fiat Homo", takes us 500 years onward as technology is gradually being rediscovered and, at the same time, a schism appears within the all-powerful Church. The final part, "Fiat Voluntas Tua", hops forward another half-millennium to find a world where nuclear weapons are once again in play and a new Cold War has arisen between two global superpowers, the Asian Coalition and the Atlantic Confederacy. History repeats itself, Armageddon recurs, but a fortunate few lift off in a Church-built rocket to colonise space.

Originally published as three self-contained novellas in *The Magazine Of Fantasy And Science Fiction*, *A Canticle For Leibowitz* makes a virtue of

---

[7]p. 79, *Star Man's Son*, Gollancz, 1987

its tripartite structure, balancing and counterpointing themes from one segment to the next. For instance, each part ends with a few paragraphs describing how the animal kingdom responds to the carnage which humans wreak. The first two times, after a murder and then after a battle, buzzards feast well on corpses. The third time, however, the devastation is so absolute, not even carrion birds can survive, let alone thrive.

Miller gives us a brooding, complex meditation on the human inability to learn from past mistakes and the failure of religion to influence people's behaviour for the better. There is just a glimmer of hope in the closing chapter. For a lighter, pulpier take on the nuclear A&PASF subgenre one may look to Roger Zelazny's *Damnation Alley* (1969), a lean, grimy action novel that envisions a radiation-blasted wasteland as a kind of future Wild West where men can be men and gunfire solves most problems.

Hell Tanner – yes, that's his given name – is an ex-biker shanghaied by the Californian authorities into transporting crates of vaccine across the US to Boston, where bubonic plague has broken out. The East and West Coasts of America are all that remain after cobalt bombs rained down in what is referred to as the 'Big Raid' (implying a pre-emptive strike by those no-good Commies against an innocent democracy). Everything that lies between these two slivers of civilisation is the titular Damnation Alley. Tanner leads a convoy of three heavily armed and armoured vehicles across this almost uninhabitable nightmare zone, encountering many lurid hazards along the way: swarms of giant bats, dinosaur-sized Gila monsters, wild dogs, marauding bison, vicious hailstorms, lethal sandstorms...

The novel is, in its unashamedly trashy B-movie way, terrific fun. Tanner is a classic counterculture antihero, a nihilist with a well-buried streak of morality, who embarks on his mission for reasons of sheer self-interest – he'll be granted a pardon for all his crimes, past and future, if he makes it to Boston – but ultimately stumbles upon the value of altruism. And while for the most part Zelazny is content to keep the prose stripped down and the plot incident-packed, he does pause for brief, lyrical interludes.

A far cry from Zelazny's romp is Russell Hoban's *Riddley Walker* (1980), the most compelling and oddball of all the novels under discussion in this section. The book is both pastoral and post-holocaust

A&PASF. South-east England is the location – Kent, to be precise – some three centuries after Armageddon, the 'Bad Time'. Not only has society broken down, reverting to the level of Iron Age civilisation, but language has broken down as well. The first-person narrative, delivered by the eponymous 12-year-old Riddley, is a crude dialectical stew of English in which swirl scraps of pre-holocaust catchphrases and jargon. 'Surprise' becomes 'sir prize', 'galaxies' become 'gallack seas', and so on. Punning and densely allusive, the prose is hard for the reader to grasp at first but, with persistence, becomes familiar and decipherable.

The story turns on attempts by the Mincery, the secretive fusion of church and state that forms the ruling government, to reinvent the lost, dimly remembered 'clevverness' of the past. Specifically it is after the knowledge of how to split the atom – the "Littl Shining Man" – the means by which a country known as Eusa brought about the annihilation of the world all those centuries ago. Riddley is tricked into freeing from prison a boy whom the Mincery is convinced knows the secret of the 'yeller-boy stoan' (sulphur), an ingredient of gunpowder. Reinventing gunpowder is the first step back down the same disastrous road that led to atomic fission and the apocalyptic '1 Big 1'.

This mirrors the argument of *A Canticle For Leibowitz*: that history is cyclical, that humankind is too inquisitive for its own good, and that science, in corrupt hands, is a surefire recipe for doom. Though the two novels, Miller's and Hoban's, were written 20 years apart, one can correctly infer from them that the prevailing geopolitical situation had not improved much during that time. The USA and the USSR indeed remained intractably at loggerheads, and the mushroom cloud bore down pressingly on novelists' imaginations, an emblem of everything that could possibly go wrong. The imminence of Armageddon proved fertile grounds for SF novels bemoaning human folly and our race's collective lack of moral compass.

Mother Nature's Ruin

We don't necessarily have to destroy ourselves. The universe might just do it for us.

The Purple Cloud (1901) is the most purely bonkers of any A&PASF novel, featuring as it does a 'last man' protagonist who roams the ruined planet setting fire to cities as he goes. M. P. Shiel's book can best be described as a solipsistic fever-dream, tracing the descent of an already fragile mind into out-and-out insanity and back up again to a state of queasy equilibrium.

Our narrator Adam Jeffson embarks on an expedition to the North Pole, but before he has even got there he has managed to murder two of his colleagues. Reaching his destination alone, he discovers a weird lake and a column in the middle of it inscribed with unreadable runes. He has transgressed, set foot where no man should, and it gradually becomes clear that this act of trespass – a tasting of the forbidden, the sin of a second Adam – has somehow caused a number of South Pacific volcanoes to erupt, releasing a deadly purple cloud from the bowels of the Earth. The cloud, spreading slowly to blanket the planet, smells of peach blossom and almonds – it contains cyanide. Almost every air-breathing creature dies except Jeffson.

Monarch of all he surveys (and what he surveys is nothing), Jeffson sets about immolating the great cities so as to give himself something to do but also to show his defiance of a God whom he perceives as unjust and arbitrarily cruel. Then, bored of arson, he spends 17 years building an immense palace. Then, grown dissatisfied with that, he happens upon another living soul, a wild, mute Arabic girl as immune to the poisoned atmosphere as he is. Tempted to kill and eat her, Jeffson thinks better of it and clothes and educates her instead, although he does whip her now and then (for her own good, you understand). Having read the Bible, the girl elects to call herself Eve, and by the novel's close Jeffson has accepted the inevitability of fate's, or God's, plan for him, and dons the mantle of the new Adam.

Engrossing in its strangeness, and with plenty of hard fact to offset its more outlandish moments, *The Purple Cloud* is religious A&PASF for a sceptical age. Jeffson is a thoroughly disagreeable person in whose company to spend 300 pages. But this is surely Shiel's point. If as miserable and damned a wretch as this can be spared for a higher purpose, either by God or by Nature, then why not any of us?

There are no deep theological musings in *When Worlds Collide* (1932) by Philip Wylie and Edwin Balmer. This is a novel that depicts a mechanistic universe doing its very worst to our home planet: throwing another planet at it, like one cosmic snooker ball being rolled against another.

Actually there are two rogue planets hurtling Earth's way in *When Worlds Collide*, and they're dubbed Bronson Alpha and Bronson Beta. Alpha near-misses on its first pass, but its gravitational influence causes tidal chaos, earth tremors, volcanic eruptions, and cyclones, which together put paid to a fifth of humankind. Then it swings around the sun and comes back for a head-on crash.

Beta, though, which Alpha has been dragging along in its wake, proves to have land, vegetation, oceans and a breathable atmosphere and, better yet, will remain in stable solar orbit once Alpha has obliterated our world. So atomic-powered rockets are built, chosen representatives of our race are gathered, and these lucky few escape in the nick of time to colonise the new home so providentially provided.

Entertaining as it undoubtedly is, in places the novel will make the contemporary reader squirm. Enjoyment of it depends on one's tolerance for high-flown dialogue such as:

"The world is going to be destroyed. Tony, oh Tony, the world is going to be most thoroughly destroyed; yet some of us here on this world, which most surely will come to an end, some of us will not die!"[8]

There's also quite a bit of casual racism, not to mention the uncomfortable fact that those selected for survival are exclusively well-heeled WASPs. Eugenics even rears its ugly head, when one character proposes that future sexual liaisons on Bronson Beta will be determined by scientific methods, so as to create the most propitious reproductive matches. Happily, love (rather than genetic compatibility) wins out between our dashing hero Tony and his 'girl' – a woman who goes by the name of, wait for it, Eve.

A more modern take on the cataclysm-from-outer-space tale is Larry Niven and Jerry Pournelle's 1977 blockbuster *Lucifer's Hammer*. Here it's a comet that spells our doom, rather than another planet, and the novel painstakingly depicts the build-up to the impact and its long-term consequences. The comet hits, epic earthquakes and tsunamis ensue, and the world – which in this US-centric book equates to mainland America – shrugs off the veneer of civilisation pretty swiftly, lapsing into anarchy, violence and cannibalism. The action focuses on two main survivor enclaves, one presided over by an astronomer, the other

---

[8] p. 24, *When Worlds Collide*, Bison Books, 1999

by a religious zealot. A final pitched battle between the two factions sees the forces of rationality routing the forces of crazed spirituality, and thereafter a level of technological capability is re-established. The comet, then, is no Act of God – it's a wake-up call, to remind us that we humans are small and insignificant in the eye of the universe, but we are clever too, and that may be our one saving grace.

England Endures

'Cosy catastrophe' is the somewhat derogatory label coined by Brian Aldiss in his encyclopaedic overview of SF, *Billion Year Spree*, to give to that niche of A&PASF principally occupied by John Wyndham and John Christopher. Aldiss' opinion is that the extinction-level threat in a 'cosy catastrophe' novel never impinges too deeply on the hero. He "should have a pretty good time [...] while everyone is dying off".

The accusation hardly holds up before the evidence, though. Bill Masen, in Wyndham's *The Day Of The Triffids* (1951), starts the book in hospital having been temporarily blinded by the venomous sting of a triffid, a man-sized, intelligent, ambulatory plant. Subsequently, when almost everyone else loses their sight courtesy of a strange meteor shower, Masen is taken captive, struggles to locate his surrogate daughter, attempts to establish a safe haven in a farmhouse surrounded by triffids, and is menaced by rogue soldiers, before he finally finds refuge with others on the Isle of Wight. By no stretch of the imagination can he be said to have an easy time of it.

Likewise the protagonists of Christopher's trio of disaster novels – *The Death Of Grass* (1956), *The World In Winter* (1962) and *A Wrinkle In The Skin* (1965) – embark on quests which don't necessarily have happy outcomes and which, moreover, force them to make difficult, sometimes repugnant choices along the way. For instance, in *The Death Of Grass*, where a virus wipes out all forms of grass including crops and sparks worldwide famine, the hero must kill in order to stave off starvation and survive.

Wyndham's and Christopher's apocalypses are no less dire than those in any other A&PASF novels. If there is 'cosiness' at all in these books, it is in their stoic, comfortingly British-middle-class belief that societal order can and must be maintained whatever the circumstances.

The Not So Nervous Noughties

A&PASF in its traditional forms has become less prevalent and popular in the first decade of the 21st century. Perhaps we feel that the ICBMs are sleeping more soundly in their silos these days. Perhaps, with global warming high on the political agenda, we sense that moves are being made, if only tentatively, to tackle environmental degradation before it is too late. Perhaps, rightly or wrongly, we are a touch more confident about the future than we were. We no longer have the urge to experience apocalypse vicariously, in fiction, and exorcise our terror of it that way.

Or perhaps we've simply grown complacent.

Consider the recent glut of zombie novels. Zombie apocalypse symbolises many things: fear of loss of identity, fear of pandemic, fear of the rise of a moronic consumer underclass, fear of a massively overcrowded world in which we are metaphorically savaging and eating one another, frantic as caged rats.

Max Brooks' *World War Z* (2006) is far and away the pre-eminent work in this field. Shaped as an oral history of a globe-spanning zombie plague, it traces events from initial outbreak through efforts to contain and combat the growing hordes of ravenous undead to the final uneasy aftermath when the zombies have mostly been eradicated. 'Interviewees' provide first-person accounts that are skilled acts of literary ventriloquism by Brooks, and some lovely ironies crop up along the way, such as Israel walling itself off from the world, effectively becoming a Gaza Strip of its own.

Away from zombies, there's Adam Roberts' *The Snow* (2004), an altogether more Ballardian piece of A&PASF. Snow falls all over the Earth, forming a layer three miles deep. All but a few thousand people perish. It turns out, though, that this silent white apocalypse isn't just some freak of extreme weather. It's the precursor of an invasion by alien imperialists who've engineered our planet's climate to make it hospitable for themselves – extraterrestrial terraforming. Glacially cool throughout, Roberts' novel ends on a surprisingly warm note, with a truce declared and human population numbers on the rise. Coexistence with the aliens is found to be possible, and even acceptable.

The Road (2006), by Cormac McCarthy, is A&PASF of almost intolerable pathos and bleakness. It takes place in an unending grey twilight, beneath a perpetually overcast sky that rains down ash. The cloud cover is either a 'nuclear winter' or the product of dust thrown up by a vast meteor strike. The only clue we get to the nature of the apocalyptic event itself is a gnomic one-line description: "A long shear of light and then a series of low concussions." Now, some years afterwards, a father and son trudge through the wasteland, pushing a shopping cart filled with their belongings and hunting for food. The father is dying of lung disease. The only thing driving him on is the idea of keeping his boy, who to him embodies a thinly flickering flame of hope, alive. And there are plenty who would want them both dead, including roving bands of cannibals.

The prose is pared down, without frippery; even apostrophes and inverted commas have no place in so denuded a world. In all it's a gruelling read, and the glimmer of light at the end of the tunnel is so faint it may as well not exist. *The Road* is an amazing piece of fiction nonetheless.

My own *Untied Kingdom* (2002) was an attempt to reconfigure the 'cosy catastrophe' in a form relevant to the concerns of the new millennium. The initial inspiration came from the Balkan conflict of the 1990s. In a spirit of satiric inversion I asked myself, Suppose it happened here, in Great Britain? What I didn't want to write, however, was a story about militias committing atrocities and carrying out ethnic cleansing, which might trivialise such true-life horrors. I was more interested in exploring the nature of leadership – why it is always corrupt and inefficient on a macro scale, why Big Government achieves so little, how governance works best in small communities, how situations like the Balkan crisis occur.

The trigger for Britain's meltdown in the novel is a so-called Unlucky Gamble, a disastrous parliamentary fiscal policy which I leave unidentified so as to imbue it with a numinous, quasi-mythical heft, like the Great Blow-ups and Flame Deluges of other A&PASF. The result is economic collapse, social upheaval, and pariah status. Our islands are now blockaded by the navies of the 'International Community' (a buzzphrase at the time). Missiles get lobbed in every so often from afar, to remind people to behave.

Fen Morris, a schoolteacher in a small Sussex town, sets out to find his wife, who along with several other women has been abducted by a gang of London thugs. His journey takes him, like Odysseus, through a series of episodic encounters with strangers, some of whom are benign, some mad, and some downright dangerous. His nation is not what it was, and may never be again. But the point of the novel is that an apocalypse doesn't axiomatically have to be a bad thing. 'Apocalypse', after all, in Greek literally means 'lifting of the veil', 'revelation'. Those who live through catastrophe can learn. As a forest fire is sometimes necessary to get rid of the dead wood and encourage new growth, so a purging conflagration might benefit humankind, refine us, sharpen us.

Not that I would want such a thing to happen. I was just wondering out loud, in *Untied Kingdom*, if maybe we shouldn't dread the end of civilisation as much as we do.

That, I submit, is the grimly grinning message of the new A&PASF, such as it is. Don't panic. Look on the bright side. It's only the end of the world.

Recommended Further Reading:

A Boy And His Dog – Harlan Ellison
The Chrysalids – John Wyndham
Cloud Atlas – David Mitchell
Down To A Sunless Sea – David Graham
I Am Legend – Richard Matheson
The Kraken Wakes – John Wyndham
On The Beach – Nevil Shute
The Stand – Stephen King
This Is The Way The World Ends – James Morrow

Radley Revisited (2013)

This FT *feature was written to coincide with the airing of* A Very English Education, *a BBC documentary in which I featured and which gathered together alumni of a previous documentary thirty years earlier in which I also featured.*

For my first week as a new boy at Radley College in the summer of 1979, I was followed around by a film crew. This was not supposed to happen.

I'd known in advance that the BBC were making a fly-on-the-wall documentary series about Radley, called *Public School.* The producer, Richard Denton, had visited my parents' house and explained that I would feature in the opening programme but only peripherally. The spotlight would be on Donald Payne, who was the top scholar in that year's intake. Donald and I were both going to be 'stigs' (new boys) together in the same 'social' (house) and the same 'shell' (class), so I could expect to be in shot some of the time while the cameras followed his every move.

On the very first day of term, however, my mother and I were greeted at the front door of the social by a somewhat sheepish-looking Denton. Donald had fallen ill, he told us. The 'flu. He was still at home. Would it be all right if they filmed me instead?

I was an eager-to-please 13-year-old. It seemed rude to say no, especially as I thought Denton, with his purple corduroy jacket, collar-length hair and tinted peardrop spectacles, pretty cool.

So I became, by default, the focus of the episode, which aired the following January on BBC2 under the title "The Right Habits For Life". A further nine half-hour weekly episodes followed, together painting a portrait of life at one of Britain's second-tier independent schools: the rituals and slang, the day-to-day running, the eccentric masters, the duties of the Warden (headmaster).

For the demographic of the British population with no experience of fee-paying boarding education – the vast majority – it was a peek behind the curtain into a strange, even arcane world. The first episode opens with the Warden performing the time-honoured induction ceremony for the new term's 'pups' (house prefects). It takes place in a linenfold-panelled dining hall hung with gloomy oil portraits. Everyone is wearing black academic gowns. A few carry mortar boards. The Warden is speaking in Latin. But for the lack of floating candles and a Sorting Hat, it could be the Great Hall at Hogwarts.

The voiceover throughout the series, by Denton himself, was the kind of deadpan commentary typical of TV documentaries at the time, laced with insinuating irony and sardonic understatement. What became apparent as the episodes unfurled – and even as a somewhat naive teenager I could see it – was that this charming, intelligent filmmaker had an agenda. *Public School* revealed itself to be a sly, subliminal hatchet job, an attempt to depict the British boarding school as a hidebound, reactionary, deeply conservative institution, entrenched in the past, emblematic of all that was wrong with the just-dawning Thatcher era.

His plan backfired, in as much as applications for pupil places at Radley tripled in the wake of the broadcast.

The show attracted a respectable two million viewers, 4% of the British public, and critics gave it a Marmite reception, either loving it or hating it. Some howled in outrage, like the *Guardian* writer who spluttered over the way girls were bussed in like cattle for a school dance. Others were pleasantly surprised, such as Peter Davalle in the *Times* who called it "an unqualified success". Also in the *Times*, a bewitched Joan Bakewell wondered why the portrayal of the school wasn't darker – "I can't deny the delights of lingering in its alien pastures, but doesn't such golden sunshine cast any shadows?" – while *The Listener*'s John Sayer made paradoxical comparisons with another very popular series about an educational establishment, saying, "Ask viewers about Grange Hill and they will tell you it is real. Ask about Radley, and they think of it as purest fiction." In 1999 the *TES* listed the documentary as a key event in its timeline of *1000 Years Of Education*.

The series reignited, once more, the controversy about independent schools, single-sex boarding and the old boy network. The Callaghan government, in its death throes, had been considering revoking public schools' charitable status in order to make them even less affordable and thus drive them out of business. Thatcher's election to office put paid to that idea, but her first Cabinet was heavily weighted in favour of public school alumni; her Secretary of State for Education, Mark Carlisle, had himself been to Radley. In this heavily politicised atmosphere a post-mortem TV debate, aired the night after the last episode of the series was shown, saw the Warden, Dennis Silk, having to defend Radley vigorously against accusations of elitism and irrelevance from the then Shadow Education spokesman, Neil Kinnock.

Before filming began there had been arguments among the school staff about the wisdom of letting the cameras in, and Denton, in an interview in the *Radleian* magazine conducted after the filming was complete, said: "I could number the members of Common Room who have really understood what the series is trying to do on one hand, and I find that depressing. But I hope that we will get the right things across." Radley had no right of veto about the programme's content. Consequently, it could hardly cry foul if Denton failed to show, say, much in the way of actual teaching happening and instead focused on the antics of some of the more theatrical personalities he found. His stated aim, after all, was to entertain and "flatter the audience", so why not devote an entire episode to Mr Goldsmith, a florid-complexioned maths teacher with his own private vocabulary and a temperament linked to the fortunes of his beloved Ipswich Town FC? Why not follow the shenanigans of an anguished adolescent called Hugo who was entirely at odds with the system or, in perhaps the most memorable of all the ten episodes, depict the desperate *Inbetweeners*-style efforts of sixth-formers to score with girls at a school disco?

I felt largely sheltered from all of this fuss. Being at boarding school in the pre-internet era, especially a boarding school tucked away in the Oxfordshire countryside, was like being in a cocoon. You had your own life; world events happened elsewhere. But also, once the series was over Radley itself seemed content to move on, an ocean liner too large to be thrown off-course by any squall. Christopher Hibbert's history of the school published in 1997, *No Ordinary Place*, devotes no more than half a page, out of 400, to the documentary – an act of magnificently lofty disdain.

The process of being filmed was, I found, peculiar but not discomfiting. At 13, you are malleable, adaptable, better able to take the unusual in your stride. Initially I felt self-conscious about having a five-person crew – cameraman, soundman, production assistant, Denton himself and executive producer Roger Mills – shadowing me as I attended my first meal in the dining hall and my first lesson with my form teacher (the abovementioned Mr Goldsmith), as I padlocked my tuck box and scrambled into my creakily-sprung dormitory bed, all those awkward settling-in moments. Once the initial novelty wore off, though, the crew's presence became a fact of life, slightly irksome but something you could overlook or swat away – much like that proverbial fly on the wall.

Observational documentaries were fairly new at the time, and fairly rare. The *Up* series – still going, of course – had started dipping in and out of the lives of its subjects at seven-yearly intervals back in 1964, creating an anthropological snapshot of the nation. Franc Roddam's *The Family* (1974) emphasised the down-to-earth ordinariness of its participants, the Wilkins family of Reading. Two years later came Denton's own *Sailor*, tracing the ups and downs of life aboard the aircraft carrier HMS *Ark Royal*.

There was certainly no expectation back then that a slot on primetime telly might earn you a free pass into the gilded world of celebrity. 'Reality TV' was still a couple of decades in the future. All an appearance on this sort of programme asked of you was that you did your thing, keeping calm and carrying on while the cameras peered inquisitively for the benefit of others. It was less prurient and intrusive than, say, *Big Brother*, and less artificially structured than something like *The Only Way Is Essex*. The aim wasn't to create stars, just to present characters and situations as realistically as possible, with the merest sketch of a storyline imposed on top. The culture didn't yet exist that nowadays entitles someone like *Pineapple Dance Studios*' Louis Spence to parlay urgent bottom waggling into a full-time career as a fixture on panel games and chat shows.

My public exposure on *Public School* garnered a smattering of fan mail from girls, which was good, and letters from mothers saying I was the sort of boy they'd like their daughters to go out with, which was not quite as good. In no way did I become the centre of media attention, subject to national scrutiny, as might happen today. There was no lasting fame, just a sense of having been involved in an interesting experiment. At the school itself, my main problem was becoming known overnight to all of my 600 fellow Radleians. I would cringe as senior boys yelled my name across the clock tower quad and parroted my own blithe, impromptu remarks from the documentary back at me. Had I anticipated that this would happen, I might have made some effort to be wittier and pithier onscreen.

That aside, the fallout was minimal, and because I own a copy of the programme – a VHS recording, later transferred to DVD – I have what many do not, which is a formal visual souvenir of their first days at senior school. I can show it to my sons. That's me, wide-eyed, rosy-cheeked, bad haircut, feigning fascination as my 'tutor' (housemaster) rabbits on about the virtues of being a 'wet bob' – someone who elects to do rowing as a sport during spring and summer, as opposed to a 'dry bob' hockey player and cricketer. That's me in my pyjamas, blissfully unaware of a rogue splodge of toothpaste stuck to the corner of my mouth. That's me deliberately failing to hold a tune so that I wouldn't be selected for the dreaded chapel choir.

Over the next few years I didn't think much about *Public School* again. While at university I took part in a perfunctory follow-up programme made by Denton to accompany a daytime repeat of the series, but that was it. Time closed over the memory. I got my degree, had a debut novel published, evolved into an author. Life marched on.

Then last autumn I received an email out of the blue from Hannah Berryman, a documentarian best known for her contributions to the BBC's *Wonderland* strand. Berryman's forte is assembling groups of people who share a single event or experience in common and examining how their lives have turned out subsequently. Her topics have included former beauty pageant queens, women who were photographed in their youth for *Country Life*'s 'girls in pearls' frontispiece page, and the chorus of children who sang on Pink Floyd's single "Another Brick In The Wall".

Her latest wheeze was to trace the lives of some of the boys from *Public School*. She would explore their backgrounds, their present circumstances, how they had grown up into the men they had become, what effect public school – and *Public School* – had had on them.

She and I spoke at length on the phone. We met in person. She sent me discs of her previous work. Her style as a documentarian struck me as impartial and non-judgemental. She allowed her subjects to tell their own stories. There was little in the way of editorial interference, barely any voiceover commentary – a far cry from the Richard Denton approach.

Pretty soon I'd agreed to be involved, with a few low-level misgivings. This is the age of social media, after all, and the thorny briar thickets of Facebook and Twitter are out there, haunted by trolls and weirdoes. I knew I could be opening myself up to far more public scrutiny than back in 1980, some of it likely to be negative.

In fact, as I watch the current Sky series *Harrow: A Very British School*, I wonder how the boys in that programme are coping with the exposure. It's a markedly friendlier show than *Public School* ever was, right down to the plummy, jovial voiceover by posh comedian Miles Jupp. The young Harrovians are still being treated like animals behind glass, but they're portrayed as cuddlier creatures than we Radleians were – meerkats rather than exotic reptiles. Since they're probably already used to revealing their own lives online in some depth, perhaps it won't make any difference to them to be on television. Undoubtedly they'll be better equipped to handle the attention than I was at their age.

That said, I am old enough and thick-skinned enough to take whatever's thrown at me. I've also been a published author for twenty-five years, meaning that I have developed something of a public persona separate from my private life.

Being in my late forties, I am also at an age when many people begin to assess (and reassess) their lives. Hence I decided, on balance, that revisiting my time at Radley might be a valuable exercise. Enough time had passed. I had perspective, distance. How had a writer of SF emerged from an environment where genre fiction of any sort was frowned on as 'trash'? How had someone who during his formative teenage years had been cloistered away from the opposite sex evolved into a happily married husband and father? I had a sense of things coming full circle. Possibly I was looking for that American pop-psychology concept, closure.

The filming took place over the course of one very long day in February at my house. Berryman is a bespectacled blonde whose deceptively scatty demeanour hides a shrewd, incisive mind. I discovered that her interviewing technique was a process of slowly and patiently teasing out information, with the odd ambush here and there. A string of easy questions would be interrupted by a sudden left-field surprise poser. Had I resented my parents sending me away from home from the age of eight onwards? How did I feel about being a relatively academic sort in an institution where sporting prowess seemed to be prized above all else? She was like a boxer softening up her opponent with light jabs before delivering a haymaker out of nowhere. She was good cop and bad cop rolled into one.

She also had developed the habit of mirroring her interviewee's body language, perhaps unconsciously, so that if I crossed or uncrossed my legs, she did too. Clearly she somehow managed to win my trust with this cunning behaviourist voodoo, because at one point she had me reading through my school reports and letters home, next to my mother. It was fairly embarrassing to discover that I hadn't been the all-round genius I remembered myself as being and to read again, for the first time in thirty-odd years, my petty complaints about teachers and my plaintive pleas for extra spending money. Then Berryman got me leafing through some old satirical comics I had drawn, as scurrilous and scatological as anything in *Viz*. That, in many ways, was worse. In the strips, I skewered – sometimes literally – my fellow pupils and members of staff. Had I really been that vindictive? That obsessed with bodily functions? Apparently I had.

Berryman's crew was smaller and more lightly equipped than Denton's had been: a cameraman and an assistant producer, plus someone to wrangle lenses and take rostrum shots of my academic memorabilia. A streamlined modern commando unit for the digital age, they brought chaos to our well-ordered household for precisely twelve hours, from eight 'til eight, then disappeared. If the *Public School* filming had been a long drawn-out campaign, this was a guerrilla raid.

Five other Old Radleians from the original series – including Donald Payne, who eventually featured in an episode about scholarships – will also be appearing in Berryman's one-off documentary, due to air on BBC2 this November and titled *A Very English Education*. The final edit has been locked but I have not yet seen the programme. It is corporation policy, I've been told, not to preview shows until at most a fortnight before broadcast, and often not even then.

From conversations with Berryman I gather she has interwoven the six old boys' stories. Wives and children, and the odd parent, will feature. Talking-head monologues will form the backbone. Donald is now a doctor in Australia, and while he and I were reasonably good friends at Radley, we haven't kept in touch since. I'm curious to see how much he's changed and how much I will recognise of the boy I knew. Will the years have been kinder to him than me, or vice versa?

The theme of my own strand, as I understand it, is that I was a schoolboy geek who, during the long weeks away from home, found solace and inspiration in the books of Ray Bradbury, Robert E.

Howard, Michael Moorcock and Stephen King and in American superhero comics, and who went on to forge a more or less successful career in SF. There may be some truth in this.

What sticks in my mind about the day's filming was an incident at the end, when my two sons, age 9 and 6, were getting ready for bed. They had just had a bath but were still buzzing from all the unaccustomed activity in the house. While Berryman and her crew were busy packing up their kit, the boys got the notion into their heads that it would be hilarious to run round up and down the stairs stark naked. My younger son shouted out from the hallway, "Dad, this is fun! You should do it!" And all I could think was that, in a manner of speaking, I just had.

Tove Jansson – *The Moomins And The Great Flood* by Tove Jansson, *Tove Jansson – Life, Art, Words* by Boel Westin, *Sculptor's Daughter* by Tove Jansson (2014)

In the autumn of 1945, as an exhausted Europe emerged from almost six years of war, young Finns and Swedes were introduced to a family they would come to know very well. Tove Jansson's first book, *The Moomins and the Great Flood*, follows Moominmamma and her son Moomintroll in their search for Moominpappa, who is lost, feared dead. They travel through a dark forest, drawn beautifully by Jansson in pen and tinted wash, using a Primitivist style reminiscent of Henri Rousseau. Near the end of their quest, the weather turns strange: "It had become very hot late in the afternoon. Everywhere the plants drooped, and the sun shone down with a creepy red light." This presages a rainstorm so powerful that the land is submerged. Moominpappa is eventually discovered alive and well, perched high above the waters in the branches of a tree.

The Great Flood was not a commercial success and attracted little attention, which perhaps explains why it took more than 60 years for an English version to be published. It was only when the third volume in the series, *Finn Family Moomintroll*, came out three years later that the Moomins began their ascent to international fame. By the 1960s Jansson's creation was manifesting as TV cartoons, stage plays and a bewildering range of licensed merchandise. There were picture books and also a widely syndicated newspaper strip, which Jansson wrote and drew herself before handing over responsibility to her younger brother Lars.

The Moomins remain big business. All the books are in print and sell healthily. The Finnish city of Turku boasts a theme park, Moomin World, where you can visit the characters' houses and have your photograph taken with actors in costume. There is even a shop in London's Covent Garden peddling nothing but what one might call 'Moominery'.

The stories have also exerted an influence on many modern writers, for adults as well as children. Ali Smith, Jeanette Winterson and Maggie O'Farrell are self-professed Moomin fans. Philip Pullman has called

Jansson a 'genius', while Frank Cottrell Boyce drew important life lessons from the Moomins at an impressionable age. "Jansson valorised coffee and pancakes and reticence and the mystery of others," he wrote in a review of Moomin picture book *The Dangerous Journey*. "But more to the point she showed me how it might be just those small pleasures that keep us together when we start to grow apart."

The young Boyce, however, was also drawn to the Moomins because he sensed an existential darkness at the heart of the books. Jansson wrote in the dominant mode of 20th century children's literature, fantasy, but hers was fantasy shot through with a quiet anguish. Apocalypse through natural disaster – flood, volcano, potentially Earth-shattering comet – looms in the background of her stories. Characters are solitary, lonely, sometimes on the brink of despair, and acknowledge the fragility of things with an accommodating liberal shrug.

Boel Westin's biography of the author, *Tove Jansson: Life, Art, Words*, arrives in English translation in time for the centenary of its subject's birth (the Swedish edition came out in 2007, the Finnish in 2008). Westin is at pains to show that, although the Moomins are Jansson's lasting legacy and a significant body of work in their own right, there was more to her. The book gives equal weight to her achievements as a painter, a cartoonist, a muralist, a memoirist and a writer of fiction for adults.

Jansson grew up in Helsinki, the eldest of three children. Her parents, Finnish sculptor Viktor Jansson and Swedish illustrator Signe Hammarsten, maintained a bohemian household in which love and art were valued above all else, but the family's existence was financially precarious. By her mid-teens young Tove was already helping top up the Jansson coffers by providing illustrations and comic strips for children's periodicals. Studying fine art in Stockholm, Helsinki and Paris, she saw her future as a painter, with commercial illustration an income-generating sideline. During the war she contributed frequently to the magazine *Garm*, including several cartoons lampooning Hitler and Stalin. Soon she had begun accompanying her signature on the pictures with a drawing of a cute little hippopotamus-like creature with big guileless eyes, which she called a 'Snork' – the prototype for Moomintroll.

Once the Moomin bandwagon began rolling in earnest, Jansson – almost to her own surprise – proved to be a shrewd businesswoman.

She personally supervised contracts for merchandising spin-offs and berated licensees when their product failed to meet her exacting standards. On one occasion, she lambasted the makers of a Japanese animated series that depicted the Moomins (normally plain white) in various colours and featured them boozing and carousing, something they never did in the books. She also nixed, on grounds of good taste, a proposal from a tampon company to manufacture sanitary towels for young girls printed with the image of Moomins' adopted daughter Little My.

Although Jansson had had affairs with men and nearly married a leftwing intellectual called Atos Wirtanen, it was with a graphic artist called Tuulikki Pietilä that she found contentment. From the 1950s the two women lived together, travelled extensively and collaborated professionally. Jansson's lesbianism upset her mother but, if Westin's account is anything to go by, seems not to have scandalised Scandinavia or raised any eyebrows in the wider world.

Westin shows how the Moomin phenomenon became a millstone for Jansson. As the cash and contracts kept rolling in, the author found herself longing increasingly for space and solitude, the freedom to work uninterrupted by business demands and by the promotional duties that were stressful to someone so solitary and self-contained. She built a house on a tiny, remote island in the Gulf of Finland but still Moomin aficionados trooped to her front door and begged her time. She dutifully, if grudgingly, replied to fan mail, which came in by the sackful. Her mother had drilled into her the importance of not leaving correspondence unanswered.

After the ninth and final Moomin book, *Moominvalley in November*, Jansson concentrated on writing for adults, mostly in the form of short stories. By then, the Moomins had in any case become victims of their own success, at least as far as the critics were concerned. Reviews of the later books found the stories and settings too cosy, too conservative. "Ideology and class were more important on the agenda of the age," Westin writes, "and the Moomins' superficially gender-determined way of life was an easy target in the socially aware 1960s."

Here we come to a problem with *Tove Jansson: Life, Art, Words*, namely that Westin is a professor of comparative literature at Stockholm University, specialising in children's fiction, and her own criticism of the texts carries a deadening whiff of academe. When discussing Jansson's picture book *Who Will Comfort Toffle?* , for example, Westin says:

> The story is in fact constructed from holes, openings and grottoes combined with phallus-shaped environments and objects [...] The oblong milk can links mother and child (though the milk goes sour) and is transformed into a symbol of incipient (male) independence.

Yes, or it could just be a charming, inventive little fable for toddlers.

Parts of the book read like a doctoral thesis, and at times the tone seems to straitjacket its subject matter. We get precious little sense of the whimsicality that's to be found in the Moomin stories, nor the underlying sombreness. Westin could afford to lighten her analysis, to relax and let her evident love for all things Moomin shine through.

That said, her biography – translated smoothly and unobtrusively by Silvester Mazzarella – is never less than engaging. It is also copiously illustrated with photos and reproductions of Jansson's artwork, which is appropriate for a book about a woman for whom word and image were of equal significance and who did her utmost to find a harmonious balance between the two in her creative output.

Jansson, a habitual self-portraitist, left several prose snapshots of her life in the form of novels and short-story collections that are so autobiographical they may as well be called memoir. One, *Sculptor's Daughter*, first published in 1968, has recently been reprinted, and it's an unusual, haunting re-creation of Jansson's childhood, told impressionistically as a series of discrete episodes.

"The Bays", for instance, is a tour of five deserted rocky inlets that Jansson loved to explore in her youth. It opens with the line: "The house is grey, the sky and sea are grey, and the field is grey with dew. " The girl in the story is herself 'light grey', almost invisibly a part of the landscape. It is an affecting evocation of a pure, unquestioning relationship with nature, the kind that we can only really have as children.

Elsewhere there are glimpses of life in the freewheeling Jansson family household, where mishaps are greeted with a phlegmatic, Moomin-like acceptance. When the narrator's father's pet monkey knocks over a couple of his works-in-progress in the studio, ruining them, he speaks consolingly to it. When the narrator hides under the Christmas tree and accidentally breaks one of the baubles, her mother says, "Actually that ball has always been the wrong colour." Similarly, when Moominpappa drops a vegetable dish on the floor in *Comet In Moominland*, Moominmamma calmly says, "Never mind. It's really a good thing it's broken – it was so ugly."

Sculptor's Daughter tells us as much about Jansson's formative years and the genesis of her most famous creation as any biography could, in succinct, dreamlike prose shot through with striking images and turns of phrase. Its themes are the consolations of home, the certainties of family relationships, the contentments of childhood – the same things that have kept the Moomins forging stoically on.

Comics

Sandman: The Kindly Ones – Neil Gaiman, Marc Hempel and others (1996)

The latest (and thickest) collection of Neil Gaiman's award-winning *Sandman* comic, *The Kindly Ones*, brings to a conclusion the epic begun five years and sixty-odd issues ago, as Morpheus – the King of Dreams and one of the Endless, seven godlike embodiments of abstract human concepts – meets his Nemesis in the shape of Lyta Hall, a former superheroine known as the Fury and the widow of the Silver Age superhero version of the Sandman. Lyta, tricked into believing that her infant son has been kidnapped and killed by Morpheus, goes in search of vengeance, and finds it in the form of her namesakes, the Furies of classical Greek tradition, who descend on the Dreaming and start slaughtering the inhabitants one by one, working their way slowly up to the lord of the realm, Dream himself. Does Morpheus stage a valiant last-ditch battle to save his kingdom? If you think that's going to happen, you've been reading the wrong comic. Can an immortal die? For the answer to that question, you'll just have to read *The Kindly Ones* and see.

For anyone new to the world of *Sandman*, *The Kindly Ones* is not a good place to start. Dozens of characters from previous story arcs return to play their parts in the unwinding tale. Events from as far back as the first issue are referred to, and sometimes developed on (one can only marvel at the deftness with which Gaiman has managed to draw together every single previous plot-strand into a tight, cohesive whole; why, it's almost as if he *planned* it this way). Without some kind of score-card to help keep track of who's who, the neophyte is going to be hopelessly bewildered.

But for anyone who so much as has dipped a toe in *Sandman* before, *The Kindly Ones* offers delights by the bucketload. Foremost among them is the art by Marc Hempel that graces almost every chapter. His style would at first glance seem to be too cartoony for the portentous subject-matter, but its beauty is in its apt simplicity. His solid, energetic layouts reflect the elemental forces being deployed in the story; his thick ragged lines are the impending tragedy in ink-form; moods and facial expressions he delivers with a few, swift, accurate brushstrokes. In the fourth chapter, as the grieving Lyta's grip on reality gradually crumbles, the breakdown in her ability to distinguish between the actual and the imagined is conveyed in a series of stunning visual shifts that culminate in a page where the full-colour panels (fantasy) are set against a monotone background composition (reality) that cunningly incorporates aspects of their layout into its own. Stunning stuff.

Then there is Gaiman's bold and brilliant use of world mythology. A whole smorgasbord of gods and beings from fable exist side by side and interact throughout the book. There is an unholy alliance between Loki and Puck (Together Again For The First Time!), the angel Remiel pays the exiled Lucifer a visit in his earthly nightclub, Odin drops in on Morpheus, and the triple-goddess manifests herself in dozens of different aspects, from the Furies themselves to trios of female characters in TV sitcoms. The dialogue, too, is clever and spicy. The gods talk just how you'd imagine them to talk; the human characters talk just like people you know. And though it is shot through with a sense of doom right from the start, *The Kindly Ones* never becomes oppressive, merely melancholy. Fatalism, Gaiman seems to be telling us, is in the natural order of things, and there is no harm in resigning yourself to death, especially when Death, as *Sandman* readers know, is a cute Goth-rock babe in black.

As a feat of knowledge and imaginative daring, *The Kindly Ones*, and indeed the entire run of *Sandman*, is without peer, which makes it all the more regrettable that only one more collected volume remains to be published after this one.

Comics (2002)

I don't think there's been a better time to be a fan of comics.

This may seem a contentious view, particularly to those who maintain that the medium's heyday lies long in the past. How can anything that's put out nowadays (these traditionalists ask) hope to rival the early Marvel stuff from Stan Lee, Jack Kirby and Steve Ditko? The Golden Age of DC Comics, when heroes calmly did the impossible and never forgot to address one another as 'old chum'? The industry's pioneering wonders such as *Little Nemo in Slumberland*, now a century old? The debased rags that presently clutter up the shelves of comic shops (and of few other retail premises) are as nothing before these hallowed greats. Even to consider comparing the two – heresy!

Well, maybe. Comics today are not comics as they used to be, that's for sure. They're not simple – some might say simplistic – morality tales any more. They're not gaudy four-colour power fantasies designed to soothe the hearts of aggrieved adolescent males. They're no longer toiling in the shadow of the Saturday morning serial and the pulp paperback. These days they're a richer, stranger creature, and stronger for it.

Take Alan Moore's *Promethea*. A study of myth and magic, it dovetails didacticism and elegant fantasy in a way that's never been done before, with the accompaniment of gorgeous artwork from J. H. Williams III, Mick Gray and Jeromy Cox.

Or take *The Ultimates*, Marvel's re-imagining of its mainstay superhero team the Avengers. Mark Millar's sly, scabrous script is as good an example of the modern trend for updating and downgrading old icons as you will ever find, while the widescreen visuals from Bryan Hitch and Andrew Currie manage to be realistic and at the same time inspire a sense of awe.

Or take *New X-Men* by Grant Morrison and Frank Quitely, and *X-Factor* by Peter Milligan and Mike Allred. You thought the X-seam was tapped out? The work of these restlessly inventive minds will make you think again.

Or take Mike Mignola's *Hellboy*, a bizarre black cocktail of superheroics and supernatural investigation, tricked out with deadpan wit and dense, dark, Gothic illustration.

Or take self-published gems like Jeff Smith's *Bone* and David Lapham's *Stray Bullets*. One is high fantasy, the other low-rent crime drama. Both demonstrate the diversity, the sheer range of genres, available now to comics creators as never before.

Or take...

Never mind. You get what I'm driving at.

Comics these days are good-looking artefacts, too. Top-quality paper, exciting lettering, vibrant computer-aided colouring and special effects. Really, they are things it is a treat to hold and behold. And the content, by and large, matches up to the superficial beauty. Some of the most talented artistic individuals in the world are pouring their hearts into the work they do for this once ubiquitous, now sidelined and backwatered pop-culture art form. The comic book isn't popular any more, and it's thriving as a result, thank you very much.

Take a look.

Keep an open mind.

You'll see.

Superman: Birthright by Mark Waid, Leinil Francis Yu and Gerry Alanguilan (2004)

Another reboot of Superman's origin? Well, it was probably due. The last time DC did one was back in the mid-80s, when John Byrne took the Man of Steel and decluttered his backstory. It was necessary then because Superman had become too powerful. He needed taking down a peg or two in order to prevent him becoming boring. Omnipotence, after all, does not easily lend itself to drama. So Byrne redesigned Krypton, pared away a lot of the excess continuity that had accreted over the course of five decades (bye-bye, Superboy), and scaled back Supes' power level (which has crept up a few notches since, returning almost to its former height). He even gave him a cape that got tattered in battle. This was at the dawning of the grim'n'gritty era, remember, when heroes had to look like they were getting their butts kicked before they in turn kicked butt.

Now writer Mark Waid has been given the job of conceptualising a Superman for (cliché alert) the New Millennium. It's a tough assignment, in that there now exists a generation for whom the character is as antiquated and irrelevant as Popeye or Betty Boop. As Waid himself puts it in the afterword to this book, there are kids to whom "white picket fences are suspect because they hide dark things – and [...] that's the world Superman *represents* and the status quo he *defends*." He's no longer the champion of the weak and oppressed, as Siegel and Schuster envisioned. He's whitebread America with a cape. He's a corn-fed totem of might-makes-right. He's the alternate-universe Republican monster of Frank Miller's *Dark Knight Returns* become reality. And with the US currently jumping at shadows and on the verge of national hysteria, that image is one that you can't believe will fly any more.

So, what to do?

First off, Waid turns the Superman mythos into a quest for identity, which is something that all of us, Gen-Xers included, can empathise with. *Birthright* is as much about why Superman becomes Superman as it is about how. To that end, Waid plays up Clark Kent's awareness of his extraterrestrial heritage. He is the ultimate immigrant, who has assimilated himself invisibly into his adoptive culture yet still remains an outsider. How can he fit in? With the abilities he possesses, what does he have to do to be accepted as a citizen of this world?

Next, Waid offers a plausible and persuasive set of reasons for the established Superman tropes – costume, S symbol, secret identity, et al. In essence, it boils down to standing for something, being a part of something. The S symbol, it turns out, is the emblem of Krypton, the rallying-point of a unified civilisation. Therefore, to Superman, it's the equivalent of wearing the Stars and Stripes on his chest, or perhaps an old family photograph. His powers have been slightly recalibrated, too, although not reduced. He's man plus, every human attribute enhanced and improved to an awesome degree.

Finally, to generate drama and conflict, Waid has Lex Luthor exploit Superman's alien-ness (and some brand new capabilities of kryptonite) in an attempt to scupper Superman's nascent efforts at becoming a hero. Luthor sows fear and panic, in true neo-Con fashion, by engineering a fake invasion of Metropolis. Fear of the outsider is translated into fear of Superman. It nearly succeeds, too, and Luthor nearly gets to reap the financial benefits, à la Bush/Cheney and the 'War on Terror'.

That's the thesis behind the refit. Does it succeed as entertainment? After all, this is very familiar territory. Yawningly familiar. Do we really need to have all these concepts served up to us once again? Is there any surprise here?

Surprisingly, there is. *Birthright* is a fantastic piece of work, managing to combine old and new seamlessly, using familiarity to highlight variation and vice versa. Waid synthesises almost every extant iteration of the Superman saga, even inserting elements from the *Smallville* TV series (Clark Kent and Luthor knew each other as kids). There's a crashing-helicopter sequence reminiscent of the first Christopher Reeve movie. The famous descriptive stock-epithets – faster than a speeding bullet, etc. – are cleverly referenced. The supporting cast is brought up to date without any glaring sacrifice of tradition. Perry White, for example, is still wont to exclaim, "Great Caesar's ghost!" and still gets apoplectic when Jimmy Olsen calls him 'chief', but he is also depicted as a credible newspaper editor, constantly at loggerheads with the *Daily Planet*'s manipulative, Rupert-Murdoch-esque proprietor. Good use is made of the marvels of the modern electronic age such as email and online reportage. *Birthright* is about a Superman who exists right now rather than in some halcyon Golden Age, a Man of Tomorrow in a world where Tomorrow has actually arrived.

The Filipino art team of Yu and Alanguilan turn in an impressively consistent and consistently impressive job. At times their combined style is reminiscent of Mike Mignola and Kevin Nowlan, but that's hardly to its detriment. Storytelling clarity is to the fore. The intermittent splash pages are thrillingly epic, and the use of panels is a master class in placement and pacing. Super-feats, for instance, are frequently implied rather than shown. The gutter between panels serves as a jump-cut, one image succeeding another at eye-blink speed. This is how writing and art *should* blend.

Above all, what started life as a twelve-issue miniseries reads, in collected form, like a novel. No obvious chapter beaks, no cliffhangers, just a controlled plot sweep running across some 290 pages, telling a rounded, character-driven, action-packed tale. Waid – an uneven writer who can produce great stuff, such as his initial *Fantastic Four* issues, and dire nonsense, such as *Ruse* – has excelled himself here. *Birthright*, even as a twenty-five quid hardback, is a worthy purchase. Whether you regard Superman as a longstanding acquaintance or as an arcane figure from bygone times, there is something in this book for you. You will see him and his world with fresh eyes.

Batman: Hong Kong by Doug Moench and Tony Wong (2004)

Late one night in Gotham City, a computer hacker stumbles across a snuff site. A live feed shows a man suspended upside down, getting fatally bitten by a snake. The crime is reported, but Commissioner Gordon can do nothing about it. There is no evidence of a misdeed other than the hacker's word. So the youth takes it upon himself to investigate ... and winds up as the killer's next victim. Batman, learning just too late about these events, races across the Gotham rooftops in order to save the hapless hacker. He fails to make it in time, and vows to avenge the murder.

Two weeks later, in Hong Kong, reformed street gangster Benny Lo finds his one-time partner in crime Johnny Chang dead – executed in the same manner as the murder victims in Gotham, hung upside down and killed by snakebite. Lo, too, vows vengeance.

The obvious connection between the crimes persuades Batman to act as a go-between for Commissioner Gordon, couriering a set of files to Gordon's Hong Kong counterpart, Police Chief Yee. This, of course, is merely a pretext so that he can track the murderer in that city.

The sight of Batman on the case inspires Benny Lo to don a similar, dramatic, criminal-scaring guise. He becomes a Chinese Batman-analogue, calling himself Night-Dragon. The two dark, obsessed heroes meet, join forces, and begin unravelling an intricate mystery involving a Triad boss, Tiger One-Eye, and various murky past doings.

The point of this graphic novel, principally, is to provide an English-language showcase for Tony Wong (a.k.a. Wong Yuk-long, a manga artist of some repute, best known for chronicling the long-running exploits of his kung-fu-fighting, monster-mashing hero Ultraman Tiga). The story itself is very much Batman-by-numbers. Other than the Oriental setting and the absence of any of the rogues' gallery of Bat-villains, there is little here that is new or unusual. It's the kind of tale that veteran comics writer Doug Moench could put together in his sleep, and probably did. The eastern flavour reflects his famous run on *Shang-Chi, Master of Kung Fu*, as does the young Night-Dragon's attempt to find a path between good and evil, between passivity and violence. In short, plot-wise Moench has been here before, and so have we.

That leaves the artwork, then, as the book's USP – and if you like manga, you should like Wong's stuff. It's none more manga. It's manga turned up to eleven. Kinetic, hyper-realistic, shot through with whiz-lines, panels zigzagging everywhere, big eyes, gurning facial expressions…

It's also rather odd. Anatomy is not Wong's strong suit, and everywhere you look there are tiny heads perched atop huge, ungainly bodies. Most of the panels utilise ink linework, but every now and then, for no fathomable reason, a fully painted panel appears. It isn't as if the two different media are being used to distinguish, say, flashback from main narrative. It's as if Wong just felt like using his brushes for a while, before returning to his pens. An artistic whim.

The stylisation extends to Wong's rendition of Batman himself. When Bats is in action, his cape sprawls in all directions with tendrils like a tarantula's legs. This doesn't, however, look as dynamic and cool as it sounds. It just looks implausible and misjudged.

And that seems to sum up *Batman: Hong Kong* – implausible and misjudged. The juxtaposition of a standard Batman plot and Asian milieu is an uneasy one, as unedifying as attempts at fusion cuisine often are. Had Moench pushed the envelope a bit and Wong reined in his excesses, this might have been an interesting slice of hardboiled superhero noir. But garish art and lacklustre scripting do not a happy marriage make. The book is at once different and not different enough. The Hong Kong shown here is just like Gotham, only with a tad more neon. Unfamiliar, and yet not unfamiliar enough. Night-Dragon is a pale imitation of Batman. Dark-Knightish, but not Dark-Knightish enough. Somewhere midway across the Pacific, a decent premise was fumbled and dropped into the drink. With another writer and another artist, *Batman: Hong Kong* might have been a triumph. Instead, we must file it in that dusty and capacious drawer marked Misfires.

Comics: An Overview (2004)

It can be claimed that comics is a medium which ought to have grown up long ago but continues to exist in a state of retarded adolescence, much like its readership.

All parts of this statement are false but the statement as a whole contains some truth and conforms to the general public perception – at least in the US and the UK – that comics are the exclusive home of superheroes, with all the concomitant negative associations of teenage power fantasy, sublimated body-builder homoeroticism, and soap-opera-with-spandex literary standards. Such a view is reinforced by the global success of the *Batman*, *Spider-Man* and *X-Men* movies, which, for all their sophistication and intelligence, perpetuate the myth that comics have little else to offer but muscleman butt-kicking with a dash of added angst. The adjective 'comic-book' is still, in certain quarters, pejorative, denoting trashiness and superficiality.

Comics themselves, however, are evolving and have for years been trying to broaden their appeal beyond their core fan base, which would seem to consist, these days, predominantly of twenty- and thirty-something males who have grown up loving the medium and continue to cherish it even when, perhaps, there is less for them in those dynamically drawn pages than once there was.

Inarguably, the majority of comics exhibit higher standards of craft and artistry than they ever did, with very little hackwork in evidence and even those titles not designated 'For Mature Readers' delivering a level of characterisation, subtlety and conceptual freedom which their forerunners could only have dreamed of. Nevertheless, they remain predominantly about superheroes. A good 80% of comics being published today in the English-speaking world are about superheroes. Superheroes are like a gravity well from which the medium, despite the huge impetus given it by some top-notch creative minds, has yet to break free.

Nor does it need to break free entirely. Superheroes, after all, are the medium's *ur*-genre. Comics thrived and flourished in Depression-era America thanks to Superman and Batman, and although the medium in general went into recession in the immediate post-war era, it and superheroes were reborn to live again in the mid-50s when then DC

Comics editor Julius Schwartz decided to revamp an old character, The Flash, and in so doing inadvertently ushered in comics' Silver Age. The success of The Flash in turn inspired Stan Lee's so-called Marvel Revolution in the early sixties, since which time caped and cowled do-gooders have been an industry mainstay.

Without superheroes the world of comics would (literally) be a less colourful place. The genre is the medium's default setting and continues – even after *Watchmen* and *The Dark Knight Returns*, which, when they appeared in the late eighties, looked like being the final word on the subject – to be what the medium does best. In the words of Spider-Man co-creator Steve Ditko: "The costumed hero is what the comic book is all about ... a costumed hero in action."

There is, all the same, much more going on. In recent years, through self-publishing and independent small presses, not to mention specialist imprints set up by the Big Two companies, Marvel and DC, other genres have budded and grown in the superhero shade. Out-and-out fantasy has been given a huge boost by the bestselling success of Neil Gaiman's *Sandman* series and by other hits such as Jeff Smith's *Bone* and Dave Sim's *Cerebus the Aardvark*. Horror has surged back into the greasy yellow flicker of the limelight, mainly due to Mike Mignola's inimitable *Hellboy* series. There have been attempts to resurrect SF, sword-and-sorcery and Western comics, with mixed results (we shall gloss over the absurd gay-cowboy campness of Marvel's recent *Rawhide Kid* miniseries).

The confessional, slice-of-life cartoon, which in collected form has long been a steady seller in 'proper' bookshops, looks set to achieve even more widespread renown on the back of the *American Splendor* movie. Serious socio-political work is now commonplace, following in the footsteps of Art Spiegelman's *Maus* and Joe Sacco's *Palestine*. Something as eccentric and unclassifiable as Chris Ware's *Jimmy Corrigan, The Smartest Boy In The World* has been a highbrow, broadsheet *succès d'estime*.

Then there is manga, translated reprints of which have seen a phenomenal growth in popularity in the West lately and have the additional virtue of appealing to and attracting a female readership. In Japan, and also in mainland Europe, comics have long been diverse, catering for every taste (not least that of porn fanatics), and if this is now being reflected in the Anglophone world, all well and good.

Comics should be a broad church, welcoming all denominations.

Another encouraging development is the readiness and consistency with which publishers have taken to reissuing old and new comics in collected form. Trade paperback editions of notable runs of titles are superior to the 'floppy' originals on many counts: they are bookshop- and bookshelf-friendly, they are blessedly advert-free, they are usually better value for money, and they present in a single volume what was previously published in instalments at monthly (or longer) intervals, allowing the creators' over-all intent to be better appreciated.

In all, it genuinely does seem as if the comics medium is lurching towards belated maturity and a general acceptance, while happily still clinging to the traditions on which it was founded. In creators such as Mignola and Gaiman, Frank Miller and Will Eisner, Jean 'Möebius' Giraud and Alan Moore, it boasts some of the most brilliant and fertile imaginations at work in any field of the arts today.

If the medium truly desires respectability, it will gain it. If, on the other hand, it wishes to remain a serious minority interest, adored and coveted by a partisan cognoscenti, a cult in-crowd, it will achieve that too, and no harm done.

There currently exist two books on the subject which are all but indispensable to the casual and the serious enquirer. One is Scott McCloud's *Understanding Comics*, a broad-ranging introduction to the whys and hows of the art-form, wittily conveyed in strip format. The other is Frank Plowright's *The Slings and Arrows Comic Guide*, an encyclopaedic assessment of virtually every comics title ever published. Each in its way is an ideal atlas for the novice, for the long-time aficionado, indeed for anyone interested in discovering, or deepening his knowledge of, the mazy metropolises and backwater byways of Comicsland.

The Originals by Dave Gibbons (2005)

It's about belonging. And let's face it, who doesn't want to belong?

Dave Gibbons certainly did. When he was young, he was a Mod. He adopted all the accoutrements of Mod culture – the clothes, the haircut, the music, the Vespas. He was passionate about these things.

That passion shows on every page of *The Originals*, but it's a passion tempered by time and filtered through the dimming, distancing lens of adulthood – passion recalled from the perspective of someone wiser now, someone who understands that you can no longer feel things as fervently in middle age as you did in your green and salad days. Profound emotions are youth's privilege and at the same time youth's downfall, because invariably they lead to, at best, disappointment; at worst, disaster. We see this exemplified in *The Originals*, which is as much a re-imagining of Gibbon's own teen years as it is a near-future gang warfare thriller.

The story's narrator-cum-hero, Lel, and his best-mate-cum-sidekick Bok, have no other goal in life than to join the Originals. The Originals are the coolest gang in town, with their Hovers (think antigravity Vespas), their Parka-like 'Mantles' and porkpie-hat crash helmets, and their appetite for a wide range of uppers and downers with names such as Degs, Emms and Zebs. They live hard and party hard, and there's nothing they hate more than their main rivals, the Dirt, and there's nothing they like more than a good rumble with said Rocker-alike foes.

So far, so sixties. But Gibbons wisely sets the action of the book in a non-specified day-after-tomorrow city, one that appears to be (but isn't) post-war London with its bomb craters and absent buildings. I say 'wisely' because this renders his tale universal rather than limiting it to a specific time and location, although there may also have been commercial considerations involved. Would a comics editor, even one at edgy, allegedly experimental DC Vertigo, agree to commission a standalone graphic novel, even one from a lauded veteran like Gibbons, if it was an historical, autobiographical artefact rather than a work of slipstream SF?

Be that as it may, the point is that the Originals might resemble Mods but they could be any gang; similarly the Dirt. What counts, what Gibbons is exploring, is the tribal antagonism between the two – the mutual opposition, and the identification that each kind of gang member find in that opposition. Each gang believes implicitly in its ethical and stylistic superiority over the other. Each side defines itself by what its counterpart isn't: right and wrong, Yin and Yang, yadda yadda yadda.

As the story develops we see Lel, and to a lesser degree Bok, fall under the sway of the Originals' charismatic leader Ronnie. Both also fall for the same girl, Viv, although Lel achieves greater success there than his friend. The two of them have a further thing in common, and are equal in that respect at least: they both despise middle-class Original-wannabe Warren, whom they tell to fuck off and leave them alone with monotonous regularity.

These plot strands are drawn together during a weekend trip by the Originals to Brighton-analogue 'the Water', where a fight with the Dirt is a definite fixture on the itinerary – one might indeed call it a seaside attraction – but where unexpected tragedy also awaits.

The art is black-and-white with a range of grey tones. This not only gives *The Originals* the look of a grainy British kitchen-sink movie but underscores, paradoxically, the book's principal theme of duality. We're in a world where the main characters would all like to feel that every situation can be considered in straightforward, polar black-and-white terms but where, of course, there are actually innumerable shades and nuances in between. (Warren illustrates this perfectly. Even when he becomes an Original, Lel and Bok still can't bring themselves to like him or accept him. They find such a compromise incompatible with their Manichean, either/or worldview, and yet the irony of this is lost on them.) The duality conceit extends to the opening and closing double-page spreads, respectively solid black with a small box of white text and solid white with a small box of black text, signifying a shift from occlusion to expansion, innocence to experience, certainty to uncertainty, youth to maturity. Lel's journey from one state to the other is not easily achieved, and just because everything ends in pure, dazzling whiteness doesn't mean he's any happier or more contented than he was to start with.

In all, it's a tough tale with a tough message delivered in tough terms. Indeed, if I told you that the dialogue's 'fuck' quotient wouldn't shame either of those notorious comics swear-*meisters* Garth Ennis and Mark Millar, you'll understand that Gibbons isn't sentimentalising or idealising anything here. Likewise, the violence, though sporadic, is unflinchingly depicted (and all the more shocking for its sparing use).

There has always been a restraint in Gibbons' artwork – and to a less meaningful extent his writing – indicative of iron self-discipline, of creative wildness controlled. Who but he could have so successfully interpreted Alan Moore's manically detailed scripting on *Watchmen* or channelled Frank Miller's iconoclastic exuberance on the Martha Washington series?

This restraint lends itself perfectly to the material here. Having said which, *The Originals* is also a story with heart, compassionately and feelingly told. Gibbons has long been acknowledged as one of the foremost illustrators working in the comics field today, but this is the first time the quality of his writing has paralleled the quality of his draughtsmanship.

A one-man *tour de force*, *The Originals* is a graphic novel that draws the reader in and absorbs him/her utterly. And you owe it to yourself to join in by buying a copy. Because, you see? Like I said at the start, it's about belonging.

Four-Colour Freak (2005)

Back in the era of Ted Heath and the Three Day Week, five newly decimalised pennies could buy you quite a lot. To wit: *Spider-Man Comics Weekly* issue number 2, in which Spidey took on the Enforcers, that trio of non-powered mob thugs going by the names Montana, Fancy Dan and the Ox, while in the half-length back-up feature the mighty Thor battled the Executioner (not the axe-wielding Asgardian warrior baddie but a South American military dictator also going by that name).

As printed artefacts go, it was hardly high-quality; by today's glossy, computer-coloured standards it was downright primitive. The paper had the consistency of council-issue toilet roll and the strips were reproduced in blurry black and white with added Letratone texturing. But that hardly mattered. I knew, the moment I lifted that comic off the newsagent's shelf and opened it up and began to read, that this was Great. This was Exciting. This *mattered*.

I have no idea what possessed my father to buy it for me. Well, no, of course I do. Five pence was a small price to pay to stop his seven-year-old son embarrassing him in a public place with pestering which, if unchecked, would graduate to impassioned pleading and then no doubt to a full-blown tantrum. But we are talking about a circuit court judge here, a man married to a woman who taught piano and sang with the Bach Choir. He must have had hopes that his only son would grow up cultured, sophisticated, steeped in the classics, able to hold his brow high in highbrow company. *Spider-Man Comics Weekly*? What could he have been thinking?

Because thirty-three years on I am still, in certain respects, that seven-year-old boy. Nowadays I purchase my 'graphic literature' from comic shops rather than the local newsagent's, and five pence will get me perhaps one fortieth of the current issue of *Spider-Man*, but the behavioural pattern of acquiring and reading and loving comics is well ingrained, an indelible ink-mark in my psyche.

How come?

Well, first off, let's not forget that comics back then, particularly Marvel comics, were superb. Stan Lee with his larger-than-life characterisation and his love of verbiage, Jack Kirby with his rough-edged dynamism and his epic sense of scale, Steve Ditko's quirkiness,

John Buscema's impeccable draughtsmanship – what kid couldn't fall in love with all that?

But there was more to it. Comics, to a small boy living in a small South Downs town, were another world. They were reports from a distant frontline of hyperbole and angst and muscularity and grandiosity. They were, in the most literal sense of the word, extraordinary. They were everything that someone like me *wasn't* brought up to respect and cherish. They existed wholly outside the realm of convention, beyond the pale of middle-class orthodoxy. They were not the Jennings books. They were not the Friday 'cello lesson. They were not *Peter and the Wolf* and *Blue Peter*. Much though I enjoyed those things, comics emanated from a glorious elsewhere, a place that abounded in arcane Americanisms, clashes of titans, skyscrapers, soul-searching and head-pounding and innumerable exclamation marks. A place it seemed only I knew about.

For a while I assiduously collected and read *Spider-Man Comics Weekly* and all the other hebdomadal British Marvel reprints, but then one day, at another local newsagent's, I stumbled upon imported copies of the actual monthly US originals, kept in a small, unsorted stack on the floor. Of course I had been aware that these originals existed, but I'd had no idea they could be bought anywhere other than the States. To find them on my very doorstep…! This was the next level. This, if such a thing were possible, was a step up from Cloud Nine.

I had only enough cash on me for one of them, so I chose *The Defenders* issue 23, for reasons of value for money – it contained lots of superheroes rather than just a few or one. I got it home and read it avidly and then reread it even more avidly. It had so many virtues. It was in colour – excuse me, *color*. It had a thoroughly seventies sensibility (until then the UK reprints had kept me, without my realising it, in a sixties timewarp; one hip-talking, raised-consciousness script by Steve Gerber was all it took to bring me slam bang up to date). Perhaps best of all, it had advertisements, page upon page of them interleaved with the story. That remarkable range of unattainable consumables: sea monkeys and Charles Atlas courses and Hostess Twinkies. How I envied those American kids, with their dollars and their zip codes. How I longed to be able, as they were, to send off for a wooden chest full of plastic Civil War soldiers for 99¢ and to earn 'amazing' prizes selling American Seeds or something called *Grit*.

It wasn't long afterwards that I discovered comic shops. Comic shops! Savour that concept. Shops that sell nothing but comics. Dark They Were And Golden Eyed was the first I ever visited. I wangled half an hour to myself on a family trip to London and, using the *A to Z*, intrepidly found my way to the Soho side-alley where it was located. There was an honest-to-gosh prostitute's flat opposite, with a red light above the doorbell and everything. The mean streets.

The sweetly pungent aroma of processed woodpulp hit me as soon as I entered the shop. So did the size, the fullness of the place. Two storeys brimming with four-colour wonder. There wasn't enough pocket money in the world.

Almost every other comic shop I've been to since has, like Dark They Were And Golden Eyed, been situated in a somewhat insalubrious urban area, be it the darker crevices of the West End, Oxford's Cowley Road, the North Side of Chicago, North Laine in Brighton. This, for me, has been an integral part of the perverse glamour of comics. From the very start they had that aura of subversiveness, and this only intensified when, aged nearly nine, I was packed off to boarding school. There, comics were strictly *verboten* (as indeed was anything that carried the least whiff of popular culture) and like the good little pupils we were, we all went along meekly with this edict. We affected to despise comics. We called them 'trash mags' and believed they had no place in our well-educated lives.

Except that I knew better. So I had to go cold turkey for weeks at a stretch. I had to leave the comics at home, lest they be discovered and torn up by some well-intentioned teacher bent on keeping my mind an unsullied haven of learning. I could handle this. I was strong. I quietly kept the faith.

I kept it through preparatory school and then through public school. Comics were my secret, indulged in only during the holidays and on those precious exeat weekends. I couldn't share my love of them with anyone except a couple of close friends because I knew I would be derided for it. There is an unctuous consensus among the great mass of the middle-class young. *We must be grown-up at all times. We must act like the important adults we are predestined to become.* I played along, poker-faced among my peers. And this, for what it's worth, has been one of the ancillary benefits of my love affair with comics. It has taught me the art of passing as normal. I'm a geek with the ability to move through polite society without prompting a single raised eyebrow, without rippling the surface of the Chablis. In a way, you could say I have a secret identity. By day, ordinary person. By night, comics enthusiast. It's like a double life, like some kinky but harmless vice. Better than "I wear rubber underwear". Better than "I snort cocaine". "I read comics".

And, like so many a young man who has developed a vice, I have my father to blame. It was all his fault. If only he had kept that five pence in his pocket.

What *could* he have been thinking?

Action and Starlord (2006)

My friend Johnny's house was the place to go. His mum would feed us burgers and rum-and-raisin ice cream – you know, the *good* stuff – and we were allowed to stay up late to watch the Hammer double bill on Saturday nights.

My friend Johnny also knew about the best comics before I did. He was the one who told me about *Action*, coming to school with lascivious tales about the gore and violence this new 7p weekly contained.

He wasn't wrong either. *Action*, by the standards of the mid-70s, was absurdly graphic and nasty, and its cynicism and its downbeat antiheroes were a million miles from the square-jawed derring-do of Dan Dare and the soldiers in *Battle Picture Library*, not to mention the angst-ridden positivism of my beloved Marvel superheroes.

Action also offered a thrilling taste of the forbidden, since the majority of its strips were swiped, shamelessly, from then-popular movies that its core readership hankered after but was too young to see. Thus, *Dredger* was *Dirty Harry* in all but name, *Death Game 1999* was *Rollerball* with pinball add-ons, and *Hookjaw* was *Jaws* with a social conscience, the eponymous shark acting as a kind of ethical nemesis, usually sparing the good and eating only the criminals and eco-vandals.

Even more subversive was *Kids Rule OK*, which imagined a future where a plague had wiped out all adults, leaving the juveniles to run riot.

It was this last strip above all that prompted the National Viewers and Listeners Association to act. Mary Whitehouse's band of purse-lipped, professional killjoys wagged their fingers in outrage and saw to it that *Action* had to emasculate itself or face being boycotted by the major newsagent chains. The comic did soften its tone, readers deserted in droves, and cancellation soon followed.

But its begetter and editor, Pat Mills, learned his lesson well, and when he launched *2000AD* a year later, he knew how to pitch the tone just right. The new comic was edgy but not offensively so, safe but not blandly so, and has, of course, survived for nearly 30 years now. *Action*'s legacy, other than fond memories, is *2000AD*'s longevity.

My friend Johnny picked up on *Starlord*, *2000AD*'s glossy offshoot, long before I did. With evangelistic glee he extolled its high production values and cool new characters such as Strontium Dog, the mutant bounty hunter, and the Ro-Busters, *Thunderbirds* with robots. *Starlord* was to *2000AD* what colour telly was to black and white, he said.

Once again, he wasn't wrong. *Starlord* used a larger format and was printed on quality paper rather than the cheap, Izal-alike stuff used for *2000AD*. It employed the better *2000AD* artists, such as Kevin O'Neill, Dave Gibbons and Carlos Ezquerra, and gave their full-colour artwork a chance to shine. It was classy, ambitious... and doomed to fail.

It wasn't dissimilar enough from its sister comic to be distinctive and it was too expensive (12p!) for the average pre-teen pocket. After 22 issues and one summer special it suffered the fate of many an ailing weekly and was subsumed into another comic, which in this case, naturally, was *2000AD*. The merger saw *Starlord's* best strips being kept by the older, more successful title and everything else ruthlessly discarded. Asset-stripping indeed.

For me, *Action* and *Starlord* are the two finest weeklies of my boyhood, precisely because, unlike *2000AD*, they didn't last. Time has not tarnished their lustre. They had their heyday and then were gone. There was no lingering, interminable afterlife. Their Golden Age was brief but, by God, it was golden.

My friend Johnny now works in legal insurance, while I am a grifting author. He always seemed to know something I didn't, and he was seldom wrong. Perhaps that's still the case.

The Rainbow Orchid by Garen Ewing (2009)

Originally a much-lauded webcomic, *The Rainbow Orchid* is unashamedly indebted to the work of that most famous of Belgians, Georges Remi, a.k.a. Hergé, the creator of Tintin. Garen Ewing has mastered the *ligne claire* style which Hergé and his 'Brussels school' pioneered and perfected back in the 1950s. This means strong, clean visuals, lines of a uniform size, no stippling or cross-hatching, the artful use of colour to separate foreground from background, cartoonish figures set against realistic backdrops, and often very wordy captions.

Ewing also follows the Tintin template in having a plucky, wholesome, if somewhat anodyne central character who acts as anchor to a supporting cast of eccentrics.

Said central character, Julius Chancer, is the youthful assistant to historical researcher and collector of antiquities Sir Alfred Catesby-Grey. They are approached by Lord Reginald Lawrence, who's wagered a priceless heirloom – and his family honour – in a drunken bet with businessman Urkaz Grope. Grope, a classic shifty-European type, looks set to walk away with the upcoming national orchid competition at the Wembley Exhibition, thanks to his impossibly rare 'black pearl' orchid. If Lord Lawrence can't win the competition, his estate is forfeit.

Luckily, Sir Alfred knows of an extraordinary iridescent orchid, considered a fable but, he believes, still extant in northern India. Julius hares off in search of it, accompanied by Lord Lawrence's Hollywood starlet daughter Lily and her hucksterish publicist Nathaniel Crumpole. Grope, however, has an ulterior motive for wanting his lordship's land and will stop at nothing to ensure our hero's quest fails...

Like Hergé, Ewing has taken great care over research and plotting. The between-the-wars period setting is meticulously rendered, the story intricate and engrossing. There is also room for broad comedy, such as a very low-speed traction engine chase and a slapstick inebriation scene that recalls Captain Haddock at his least continent.

In all, *The Rainbow Orchid* rises above its roots. It's no mere homage. Ewing has crafted something at once reverential and joyous that has a life of its own and an all-ages appeal. With the UK publishing industry so notoriously graphic-novel-phobic, it's heartening that someone has given a book like this a chance. Readers should too.

The Horror! The Horror! and Four Color Fear (2011)

Horror comics were huge in the early 1950s. Up to a hundred different titles were appearing every month, not just from the usual suspects like EC and Charlton but obscurer outfits like Ace and Ziff-Davis and even from publishers better known for their family-friendly fare such as Fawcett and Harvey. Sales of an individual issue could reach a million copies. Newsstands throbbed with garish, gruesome cover images designed to shock and entice in equal measure. Then, in the manner of a violently impaled eyeball, the bubble burst.

The sharp implement in this case was, of course, *Seduction Of The Innocent*, published in 1954. The book, by crusading psychoanalyst Dr Fredric Wertham, blamed all the ills of society on comics and singled out horror and crime comics as especially responsible for depraving the youth of America. There followed the Senator Kefauver hearings and the comic-book industry's craven, self-imposed institution of a strict set of rules and regulations, the Comics Code Authority – and that was that. Horror comics' gore-soaked, Brothers-Grimm-esque morality tales were censored out of existence. All those rotting revenants, melted corpses and brain-eating ghouls were replaced by far timider, emasculated fare.

The Horror! The Horror! recounts this tragedy superbly. Author Jim Trombetta fixes the fifties horror boom firmly as a product of its era and draws fascinating parallels between the various genre tropes used in the stories and the prevailing cultural mores and obsessions. For instance, he sees in the recurrent theme of necrophilia – characters finding themselves betrothed, willingly or otherwise, to corpses – an implicit satire on monogamy as the romantic orthodoxy of its day.

Trombetta's text is copiously illustrated. Whole strips and single pages and panels are reproduced complete with misregistered colouring, smeary blacks, and age-browned paper. Covers sport creases, tears and bumped edges. It's delicious, timewarp eye candy.

Four Color Fear is best enjoyed in tandem with *The Horror! The Horror!* , as its editor Greg Sadowski offers little in the way of contextualising or scene-setting. There are useful, thorough notes at the back, but the value of the book lies its assemblage of around 40 cherry-picked strips. Writers and artists are credited, a courtesy not always extended in the original comics, and here we can marvel at the sheer breadth and depth of talent on display.

The plots may be a little creaky, the twist endings at times frankly bonkers, but the pictures carry the day, be it the intricate stylings of Frank Frazetta or the creepily smooth detail of Basil Wolverton (a man who could give Charles Burns the willies). Easily the standout is the Bob-Powell-drawn 'Colorama', a much-feted strip that puts the psycho in psychedelic, but all of them have plenty more to offer than simple kitsch retro appeal.

Bronze Age Marvel (2011)

In the history of comicbooks there have been several distinct epochs, known as Ages. The Golden Age refers to the comics industry's crude but vibrant early days just before and after the Second World War. The Silver Age covers the mid-50s to 1970, when a greater sophistication and hipness entered the medium. The Bronze Age extends into the mid-80s and is characterised by the social relevance and seriousness that permeated storylines. Since then, we've had what some call the Image Age (named after the publishing imprint which at that time specialised in dumb, overwrought superheroics) and others the Dark Age; for many the two terms are synonymous. And now? Well, eras tend to be defined only in retrospect, but I suspect posterity will look very fondly on comics' modern age.

The Marvel Comics Revolution, which kicked off in November 1961 with the first issue of *Fantastic Four*, had begun to lose momentum by the dawn of the 1970s. Stan Lee's innovation of superheroes with real-world problems had boosted the company to the forefront and allowed it to outshine its Distinguished Competition for a decade, but the creative well was running dry. The contrast of godlike powers with all-too-human angst was in danger of becoming clichéd. The House of Ideas was looking increasingly like the House of Idea.

In 1972, Marvel publisher Martin Goodman retired and Lee took over the job, relinquishing his editorial and scripting duties. The next generation of creators seized the reins, foremost among them Roy Thomas, who remained a core writer while also assuming the mantle of editor-in-chief. Thomas was the Trotsky to Lee's Lenin. Under his leadership a second wave of revolution got under way, as Marvel began to experiment and diversify as never before.

At the time, the comics industry was in the financial doldrums. The US economy was on the downturn. The counterculture was on the rise, and there was a readership of teens and adults, weaned on superheroes, who were looking for something more, something different, comics that reflected their maturer tastes and more cynical worldview. Marvel, desperately seeking a wider audience, responded to these stimuli with a risk-taking, nothing-to-lose strategy. The company's early-70s output represents, arguably, the most varied and fecund phase in its history.

It was a period when anything and everything was tried, the

buckshot approach to making a buck. Some ventures succeeded spectacularly, others failed spectacularly, but the overall results, from a reader's point of view, were seldom less than interesting. All at once Marvelites were being given an unprecedented level of choice, and the spandex crowd faced a serious challenge to their supremacy.

Of all the several genres Marvel branched out into, horror was the one it pursued with the greatest vigour and enthusiasm. Its biggest hit on this front was *Tomb Of Dracula*, which debuted in 1972 and lasted an impressive 70 issues.

Marv Wolfman wrote almost the entire run and Gene Colan drew every single page, his flowing pencils never better than when graced with the inks of Tom Palmer. Together this creative team depicted the Lord of Vampires as cruel and ruthless but not without honour and even capable of love. They pitted him against enemies that numbered Rachel Van Helsing, a descendant of his one-time foe from the Stoker novel, and Blade, the half-vampiric vampire slayer. These were nominally the good guys, but Dracula himself was so compelling an antihero that most of the time you were rooting for him.

Such was *Tomb Of Dracula*'s popularity that other classic horror icons inevitably received the Marvel treatment. The Frankenstein Monster shambled through 18 issues of his own title, mainly drawn by Mike Ploog, whose artwork can best be described as sinisterly ploppy (and that's a compliment). There was *Werewolf By Night*, in which jaded teen Jack Russell – yes, that was his name – got wild and shaggy three nights a month. There was the Living Mummy, who enlivened several issues of *Supernatural Thrillers*. He was an African slave, N'Kantu, who was mummified alive by an evil Egyptian priest 3,000 years ago and finally escaped from his tomb in the present day. His lumbering, linen-wrapped adventures were sharply illustrated by Val Mayerik in best Neal Adams mode.

There were also original, whole-cloth creations that fused trad superheroics with offbeat eldritch concepts, in wonderfully loopy fashion. Ghost Rider was stunt motorcyclist Johnny Blaze who sold his soul to Marvel's very own Lucifer-lite, Mephisto, and would turn into a flaming-skulled demon astride a burning-wheeled bike whenever danger loomed or the plot demanded – Evel Knievel transformed by evil. The Son of Satan was Daimon Hellstrom, who rejected Dad's devilish ways in favour of becoming a consulting exorcist. When on the job he wielded a hellfire-spouting trident and rode an airborne chariot pulled by three demonic horses. Then there was Brother Voodoo. Psychologist and arch-rationalist Jericho Drumm got infused with the soul of his dying houngan brother Daniel and, if need be, could manifest vaguely voodoo-esque powers, surrounded by clouds of smoke and the pulse of beating drums. Brilliantly batty.

And, lest we forget, there was the Man-Thing. This "muck-encrusted mockery of a man", product of a super-soldier serum experiment gone awry, roamed the Florida Everglades and acted more or less as guest star in his own book. Steve Gerber's excellent stories were human-interest tales where the Man-Thing would usually turn up near the end to mete out natural justice. His role as mindless agent of nemesis was encapsulated in the pungent tag-line "Whatever knows fear – burns at the Man-Thing's touch!"

Science fiction was another genre Marvel turned its attention to, although ironically the two features that served it best in this regard fell victim to premature cancellation and neither would earn itself its own title, at least not until a couple of decades later.

Deathlok The Demolisher occupied 11 issues of *Astonishing Tales* and was plotter/penciller Rich Buckler's finest hour. In the dystopian future year of 1990, soldier Luther Manning was blown up on the battlefield and resurrected as a cyborg with a talkative guidance computer installed in his brain. Deathlok was ugly, angry, suicidal and conflicted, out for revenge on the authorities who'd made a monster of him and also seeking to regain his humanity. *Robocop* and *Terminator* fans need look no further than here for the forerunner of those characters.

Killraven, who headlined a dozen issues of *Amazing Adventures*, was a gladiator-turned-freedom-fighter. In the year 2001, H. G. Wells' Martians had returned for a second invasion, a century after their first attempt in *The War Of The Worlds*. This time they'd had more luck. Earth was now theirs, with humankind subjugated, but Killraven and his band of assorted scrappy rebels were determined to change all that. What made the series stand out wasn't the scripting of Don McGregor, a writer famous for the quantity and verbosity of his captions; it was the art by P. Craig Russell, which was delicate, dynamic and, when he provided the colouring himself, jewel-like.

The future worlds of both Deathlok and Killraven lay outside established Marvel continuity (although time-travel team-ups with

Spider-Man did occur). Within the Marvel Universe proper, SF elements infused the ongoing adventures of Captain Marvel and Adam Warlock.

Both of these cosmic-hero characters benefited hugely from the attentions of writer/artist Jim Starlin. Captain Marvel was a Stan-Lee-created alien soldier, a Kree warrior-spy who, in Starlin's hands, underwent a change of philosophy and became an enlightened, pacifist superbeing. Trapped in the Negative Zone, he was obliged to swap bodies with Marvel's all-purpose teenager Rick Jones, via the Nega-Bands on their wrists, if ever he wanted to manifest himself in our plane of existence. His antagonist was Thanos, the so-called 'mad god' who wished to destroy all life in order to prove his love to his mistress Death.

Thanos was also an opponent of Adam Warlock. Warlock first appeared in 1967 as the FF foe known only as Him, but gradually over the years he evolved into a schizophrenic golden boy with messianic leanings. During Starlin's tenure he sported a green Soul Gem on his forehead – a two-edged weapon like Elric's sword Stormbringer, as dangerous to user as victim – and waged war with his dark side, embodied as the mauve-skinned, perm-haired Magus.

The galaxy-spanning sagas of both Captain Marvel and Warlock allowed Starlin to indulge his love of eccentric panel layouts and images of bizarre planetscapes and elaborate spaceships hurtling against effervescent starry backdrops – and also his unfortunate propensity for self-absorbed, agonised soliloquising. Ultimately the two heroes' fates intertwined as they and the Avengers joined forces to take down Thanos once and for all, in a multi-issue crossover widely hailed as a 70s classic.

Warlock ended up inside the Soul Gem, in a kind of bucolic nirvana, at one with everything. Captain Marvel would subsequently die, prosaically but poignantly, of cancer. Thanos? Well, he's been back several times. You can't keep a good baddie down.

Roy Thomas was an ardent admirer of the pulp fiction of Robert E. Howard, and in 1970 Marvel started turning out comics adaptations of Howard's Conan stories and elaborating on the existing mythos of the Hyborean Age.

Conan The Barbarian was written by Thomas and initially drawn by British artist Barry Windsor-Smith, whose meticulous attention to detail and use of pioneering graphic effects (for instance, sequences of repeating panels to show time passing) won him plaudits and industry awards. From #25 on, John Buscema assumed the art chores and, with his classical, fine-line style, established the now canonical image of Conan as beetle-browed brute in a furry loincloth.

The comic went on to notch up nearly 300 issues in all, not counting sister title *King Conan* and black-and-white magazine spinoff *Savage Sword Of Conan.* Another Howard hero, King Kull, got his own title too, as did Conan supporting character Red Sonja, she of the flame-red hair and impractical chainmail bikini. Sword and sorcery, it seems, was the one truly bankable genre of the era.

Never slow to jump on bandwagons, 70s Marvel capitalised on pop-culture trends that were then booming. Luke Cage, who was a Hero For Hire first, then the more emancipated Power Man, surfed the wave of blaxploitation cinema that broke with action movies such as *Shaft* and *Sweet Sweetback's Baadasssss Song.* Ex-con Cage was a streetwise hero, perpetually at odds with The Man, using his enhanced strength and unbreakable skin to help the little people. His dialogue was a middle-class white writer's idea of jive talk, salted with PG-rated swearing along the lines of "Sweet Christmas!" and "Holy freakin' spit!" Among his enemies were shotgun-toting pimp-alike the Cockroach and massively overweight big mama Black Mariah. If not beautifully drawn, the stories were still good undemanding fun, particularly if you imagined an Isaac Hayes wacka-wacka guitar soundtrack while reading.

The martial arts craze, fanned to a frenzy by the worldwide popularity of Bruce Lee films, found its Marvel incarnation in *Shang Chi, Master Of Kung Fu.* Shang Chi was the son of Fu Manchu, the 'yellow peril' villain from the pulp novels by Sax Rohmer, and was forever thwarting his father's nefarious schemes, although given a choice he would have preferred not to fight at all. This comic was one of the undisputed gems of the era, thanks to scripts by Doug Moench that took a silly idea seriously and, better yet, to a series of terrific photorealistic artists – in chronological order, Paul Gulacy, Mike Zeck, Gene Day – working at the top of their game.

Another martial arts hero, Iron Fist, was more conventionally Marvel, in that unlike Shang Chi he was masked and costumed, but at least he had an interesting and unusual back-story. Caucasian Danny Rand trained as a boy at the mystic Himalayan city of K'un L'un – a kind of chopsocky Shangri-La – and gained the ability to channel his chi into his fist until it glowed and became "like unto a thing of iron!"

Later, his title and Luke Cage's were merged together as *Power Man And Iron Fist* in the apparent hope that, with their respective fads on the wane, combining them might still yield results. In the event, the odd-couple dynamic between blueblood plutocrat Rand and ghetto groover Cage proved to be a winning one, and *Power/Fist*, as the series title was sometimes shortened to, endured well into the 1980s.

The 1970s also saw Marvel move into newsstand magazine publishing under the Curtis Magazines imprint. These larger-sized black-and-white monthlies and bimonthlies were designed to attract older readers who might have abandoned the four-colour format as too juvenile. Mainly they were horror anthologies – *Vampire Tales*, *Monsters Unleashed*, *Tales Of The Zombie* – but there was interesting tryout series *Marvel Preview* and the laudable *Unknown Worlds Of Science Fiction*, which focused on adaptations of classic SF works, including *The Day Of The Triffids*.

There were also movie tie-ins such as *Doc Savage* and *Planet Of The Apes*, both of which bore material that improved on their progenitors, and the martial arts showcase *Deadly Hands Of Kung Fu*. In Marvel's Curtis magazines, themed articles appeared alongside the strips, the majority of which were drawn by a stable of talented Filipino artists such as Rudy Nebres and Tony De Zuniga. Their alluring, sophisticated artwork was wholly in keeping with the line's high-end, aspirational aims.

Without a doubt, though, the very best series to emerge from this period, in any format, was *Howard The Duck*. Across 30-odd issues, the cigar-chomping, irascible, dwarf-size water fowl stomped through stories satirising everything from the political process to capitalist conformity to self-improvement gurus. Howard was an everyman – sorry, every mallard – railing against the inanities he saw around him, his temper tempered by his well-meaning and very understanding human girlfriend Beverly Switzler.

With *Howard The Duck*, writer Steve Gerber hit the mark every time, even in the notorious fill-in issue #16, an illustrated text story wherein he moaned about deadline pressures and the hardships of the creative life and still somehow managed to be funny. Howard could have been a one-note joke but, in Gerber's hands, he became a fully-fledged individual, a duck island of sanity in an insane world. The art by the indefatigably prolific Gene Colan complemented the scripts cleanly and perfectly.

Characters from early 70s Marvel are still around. Some have been refurbished, rehabilitated, and reinstalled in the modern Marvel Universe, not least by current *Avengers* scribe Brian Michael Bendis, who seems to have a penchant for trashy oddballs like Luke Cage and Brother Voodoo. Others – Howard the Duck, to name but one – haven't fared so well and languish in relative obscurity, very much products of their times.

They're still fondly remembered, though, emblematic of an age of remarkable, even reckless boundary-pushing – perhaps the most sustained and extraordinary creative flowering a mainstream comics publisher has ever known.

Addendum

Six Ways You Know You're Reading A 70s Marvel Comic

1) Bad Clothes
Characters' casual wear included mountainous bellbottoms and jacket lapels the size of an aircraft carrier flightdeck. But for a truly wince-inducing superhero costume look no further than the pre-disco fashion disaster that is Luke Cage. Steel headband? Tight-fitting satin trousers? A chain for a belt? Really?

2) Enlightened Politics
Killraven and his sidekick M'Shulla shared a homoerotic interracial bond. Elsewhere, black power was acknowledged in the number of heroes 'of colour' coming to the fore, among them Luke Cage, the Falcon, the Black Panther and, ahem, Black Goliath. This last, who had his own series for 5 lacklustre issues, wasn't much more than an African-American Giant-Man knockoff. Clue's in the name.

3) Hippy-Dippy Philosophising
Cosmic heroes such as Captain Marvel and Adam Warlock turned on, tuned in and dropped out, undergoing spiritual and psychological

transformations accompanied by sequences of mind-bending art and weirdo panel shapes. Heavy, man, but like, beautiful.

4) Psychedelic Colours
They seemed to melt beyond the confines of the black lines. Oh no, wait, that was just bad printing on cheap paper stock.

5) Marvel Value Stamps
What were they for? Why were we supposed to collect them? No idea. But clipping one out, as advised, would reduce the resale price of your comic to zero. Not so much 'value', then.

6) Hostess Adverts
Each month, baked-goods conglomerate Hostess would take out a full-page promotion in comic-strip form. A Marvel hero would catch bad guys using a combination of guile and moreish dough-based comestible. Fruit pies, cupcakes, Twinkies™ – mmm, they looked delicious all right, and in no way laden with toxic levels of sugar and preservative.

Dynamic Duos – Batman Team-Ups (2012)

Batman. The Caped Crusader. The Dark Knight. One-man scourge of evildoers. A lone figure perched atop a Gotham skyscraper, peering out keenly over the city he has sworn to protect. A vigilante detective waging a private war against scum and villainy.

That's the image we most commonly have of him. Batman's solitariness is an integral part of his mystique. It appeals to the loner in all of us that here is someone so damaged, so driven, that he has forsaken the consolations of society and transformed himself into a creature apart, a human machine of justice. He operates solo because there is nobody else like him, nobody who can match his prowess.

It's not entirely so, of course. Batman, for such an aloof, alienated character, is surprisingly gregarious. For starters, there's his extensive 'Bat-family'. Since 1940, barely a year after Batman first appeared, he has had a more or less permanent companion in the form of Robin. Several youngsters have worn the Boy Wonder's domino mask and dodgy shorts: Dick Grayson, the ill-fated Jason Todd, Tim Drake, and most recently Bruce Wayne's own son Damian.

Then there's the plethora of distaff Bat-people: at least three Batgirls, two Batwomen, and the Huntress, a Bat-lady in all but name. All have assisted Batman is some capacity or other down through the years. Catwoman may be considered an honorary Bat-associate, having plagued Batman's life initially as an out-and-out villainess and latterly as a morally ambiguous love-interest-cum-sparring-partner. Mention should also be made of Alfred Pennyworth, loyal butler; Lucius Fox, business manager; Commissioner Gordon, rule-bending cop; and not forgetting faithful Bat-pet, Ace the Bat-hound.

This is one Lone Ranger who sure has a lot of Tontos.

Batman has also interacted continually with characters from the wider DC Universe and beyond. He's a fully paid-up member of the Justice League, and has headed up a super-squad of his own, the Outsiders. Not only that, he has been a stalwart of the team-up scene since the early 1950s, regularly forging alliances with the good, the bad, the ugly, and the just plain weird.

It all began with *World's Finest Comics*. Debuting in 1941, the title was a 96-page quarterly anthology, every issue of which featured one adventure starring Superman and another starring Batman, with both heroes shown consorting merrily on the cover. The format was a sound commercial decision – DC's two big names in a single comic, backed up by a variety of other strips featuring lesser luminaries – but when in 1954 the company was forced to reduce page counts on economic grounds, the decision was made to amalgamate the Superman and Batman stories. So, from issue #71 onward, the pair became inseparable, romping through a series of gimmicky escapades most often involving aliens, time travel, magic, and 'imaginary' scenarios.

Batman here is very much the larky, gadget-mad Batman of the times, with Superman as his well-muscled, chisel-chinned foil. Batman does rudimentary detecting while Superman can always be relied on to perform some feat of Kryptonian might as and when required. Characters from both heroes' supporting casts pop their heads round the door frequently, but perhaps the most interesting and enjoyable episodes are the 'imaginary' tales (what we would now call 'Elseworld' or 'What if?' stories) which muck around with the status quo for fun. In one of these, young Bruce Wayne is adopted by Ma and Pa Kent, so that Batman and Superman grow up as stepbrothers. In another, the two heroes have sons.

World's Finest Comics, which ran for 323 issues until cancellation in 1986, did all it could to erase the differences between the two superheroes. There was minimal tension between the grudge-nursing detective and the world's biggest boy scout. The 1990 prestige-format miniseries *World's Finest*, on the other hand, plays wonderfully on the characters' dissimilarities. Written by Dave Gibbons and drawn by Steve Rude, it's both a homage to the Silver Age Bats/Supes strips and a witty and engaging study in contrasts. Rude, channelling Dick Sprang as well as the usual Jack Kirby, depicts Gotham City as a seedy Gothic hell and Metropolis as an Apollonian Art Deco heaven. Gibbons, for his part, pulls off a neat trick by having the two heroes swap locations in order to save both cities from the depredations of their arch-nemeses, Lex Luthor and the Joker.

Mention must also be made of *World's Funnest*. This one-shot, which came out in 2000, sees other-dimensional imps Bat-Mite and Mr Mxyzptlk go on a rampage of violent mischief and mayhem, during which they manage to eradicate just about everyone on all of DC's multiple Earths. A host of artistic greats supply the visuals for Evan

Dorkin's hilariously irreverent, nose-thumbing script. *World's Funnest* takes the Batman/Superman partnership to its logical extreme and then beyond, way beyond, into glorious absurdity.

Batman gained his very own team-up book in 1965. For its first 24 issues, *The Brave And The Bold* had been an anthology title spotlighting historical adventure characters such as Viking Prince and Silent Knight. With #25 it became a try-out book, and then, with #50, a venue for team-ups between established DC superhero characters. Batman took his first lead role in #59, and from #74 until its demise with #200, *The Brave And The Bold* was exclusively a Batman team-up title.

The early Batman issues rank among the best Bat-comics ever produced. In large parts this is because Neal Adams is supplying the art, and Bob Haney, as writer, raises his game to match the superb visuals. Batman joins forces with top DC names such as The Flash, Aquaman and Wonder Woman, as well as offbeat second-stringers like Deadman, the Creeper and, in a flashback to World War II, Sgt. Rock and Easy Company. Issue #85 is an acknowledged classic, as it introduces Green Arrow's new, tougher-looking costume.

From #98, Jim Aparo took over as main penciller, with Nick Cardy filling in here and there, and *The Brave And The Bold* remained a solid, entertaining read with the occasional outstanding issue. The one in which the Atom shrinks down to microscopic size and commandeers a comatose Batman's body in order to save a hostage (#115) is as crazy as it sounds but terrific fun nonetheless, and #150 is a strong story with a surprise mystery guest star (hint: think *World's Finest*). Batman meeting international air aces the Blackhawks in #167 is memorable, as is his encounter with Hawk and Dove in #181. The final issue of the run is enlivened by art from Gibbons, among others, and has an interesting twist in that the two characters billed as teaming up – Batman and his Earth-1 counterpart – don't actually meet.

The main thrill of reading *The Brave And The Bold* month after month, as with any team-up book, was the sheer range of the guest stars. You were never sure who was going to turn up next. It could be someone predictable like Hawkman, Green Lantern or Black Canary, or someone you'd perhaps barely heard of, such as Kamandi, Rose and the Thorn, or Richard Dragon, Kung Fu Fighter. Yet at the same time Batman was a constant, anchoring the title, giving it consistency and stability.

This combination of familiarity and the unexpected allowed the title to remain fresh. It didn't seem to matter how temperamentally compatible Batman was with his ally. In fact, placing the dour, deadpan Batman of the Bronze Age alongside characters as light-hearted and absurd as Plastic Man, Metamorpho and the Metal Men, and even forcing him into a brief, uneasy alliance with one of his madcap antagonists like the Joker or the Riddler, often yielded the best results. Batman would then become the straight man in a comedy double act, the anvil off which sparks could be struck.

Batman has strayed outside the DC Universe a number of times to co-star with other publishers' characters. The first recorded instance of this is the Batman/Hulk one-shot in the early 80s, following on from the successful *Superman Vs. Spider-Man* treasury edition of 1976 and its 1981 sequel *Superman And Spider-Man*. Though graced with crisp art by the perennially underrated José Luis García-López, *Batman Vs. The Incredible Hulk* is an odd, incongruous affair. Batman, more brains than brawn, and the Hulk, more brawn than brains, really don't have much in common, and in spite of the best efforts of the creators involved, nothing gels. There's a nice scene, though, where the Hulk throws a car at Batman, and Batman, rather than get out of the way, leaps to safety by hurling himself head-first through its windows.

Better Batman/Marvel outings were to follow. Batman seemed to mesh more comfortably with Marvel's 'street-level' heroes such as Spider-Man, Daredevil and the Punisher. It was a more natural fit. *Spider-Man And Batman: Disordered Minds*, for instance, makes much of the fact that both heroes have utterly unhinged foes to face (namely Carnage and the Joker), even if the plot fails to give Spidey much to do.

Surpassing them all is the 1996 prestige-format one-shot teaming Batman with Captain America. John Byrne pulls out all the stops as writer-artist, telling a World War II tale with the Joker and the Red Skull as the baddies *du jour*. Throw in a sidekick swap – Robin and Bucky exchanging their adult partners, and snarking at each other in the meantime, as only teenagers can – plus an atom bomb and a genuine, honest-to-gosh death trap, and you have a nostalgia-laced treat.

Outside Marvel, there is the mid-90s double threat of *Batman/Spawn* and *Spawn/Batman*. These two comics deserve to pass without mention, except to say that the former is just dull while the latter sees Frank Miller (script) and Todd McFarlane (art) at their laziest and most cynical – it's basically one long stupid fight scene.

Far more noteworthy are the brace of encounters between Batman and Matt Wagner's Grendel. These two microseries benefit from having Wagner himself solidly at the helm and also from being set firmly within the established Grendel continuity. The first sees the psychopathic Hunter Rose daring the Batman to catch him, in a kind of, if you will, bat-and-mouse game. The original Grendel proves a worthy opponent for the Dark Knight. The second has the Grendel-Prime cyborg travel back in time from the future to kill thousands of Gothamites in a 'blood sacrifice' intended to summon the soul of Hunter Rose. Basically it's Batman versus the Terminator, not subtle but a rip-roaring read nonetheless.

Batman has butted heads with über-cop of the future Judge Dredd on no fewer than four occasions, between 1991 and 1998. It's one of those concepts that shouldn't work but somehow does. The plots play up the black humour of having two such stony-faced arbiters of justice clash. Mega-City One, after all, is just Gotham amped up to the max, and Dredd a version of Batman with the reason and accountability removed.

Batman has tackled Hollywood sci-fi icons too – Aliens and Predators – but the problem with these crossovers is that they satisfy neither as Batman tales nor as extensions of the movie franchises. In an Alien or Predator film, part of the fun lies in watching a cast of actors get picked off one by one in various gory ways. Batman, however, is hardly likely to wind up incubating a chest-burster or impaled fatally on the wrong end of a double-pronged set of wrist-mounted claws. So what's the point?

Batman/Tarzan: Claws Of The Cat-Woman defies expectations by being really rather good, drawing parallels between the pulpy origins of both characters – orphaned scions of great wealth who have adapted to their environments and trained themselves to excel. Conversely the Batman/Hellboy/Starman three-way disappoints, in spite of the usual inkily evocative art job by Mike Mignola.

Finally, how about a couple of just plain bonkers Batman team-ups? The first is *The Devil's Workshop*, in which an early-twentieth-century Batman unites with none other than Harry Houdini in order to combat a child-abducting albino known as the Joker and his master, who's a vampire. The script by Howard Chaykin and John Francis Moore gets pretty much everything about Houdini wrong – for instance, it has him fluent in Yiddish, when in reality he didn't speak it at all despite his Jewish background – but at least makes nice use of his escapology skills, and the watercolour art by Mark Chiarello is outstanding.

Then there's the fiftieth anniversary issue of *Detective Comics* (#572) in which the Dark Knight Detective solves a case in tandem with the greatest fictional sleuth of all, Sherlock Holmes. Never mind that Holmes is 135 years old, kept in health "thanks to a proper diet, a certain distillation of royal jelly, developed in my beekeeping days, and the rarefied atmosphere of Tibet, where I keep my primary residence". Few could argue that this was a literary mash-up just waiting to happen, and indeed it's proof that, whoever Batman is teamed with, no matter the sheer unlikeliness of the coalition, there's always a way of making it happen.

Building Stories by Chris Ware (2012)

Building Stories is more a multifaceted artefact than a mere graphic novel. Inside a sturdy cardboard box sit fourteen separate comic-strip sections of wildly varying size. Some are as small as a leaflet, others large as a broadsheet newspaper. Two are hardbacks with thick card covers, like children's books, and there is also a schematic which unfolds like a boardgame board.

They can be read in any order and, together, tell of a brownstone apartment block in suburban Chicago and its three sets of tenants: an angst-ridden mother with a weak heart and a prosthetic leg, an embittered bickering couple, and an elderly lady increasingly withdrawing into her memories.

Their stories overlap and interlock. Ware reveals vignettes of lives that are adrift, yearning, melancholy, lost. He spares us no detail of his characters' day-to-day existence, however intimate or sordid. Oral sex, dirty underpants, muffin tops, leg-shaving – we see it all, until we begin to feel almost voyeuristic. Moreover, we're privy to these people's innermost thoughts, which are as humdrum, self-doubting and vainglorious as our own.

Yet we are invited to share, too, in little domestic joys and triumphs: a cute remark from a child, a backhanded compliment from a spouse. There is also a fourth strand to the narrative, featuring Branford the Best Bee in the World, an anthropomorphised insect whose adventures provide an ironic counterpoint. Branford is an anxious, hard-working drone who has moments of existential crisis and entertains hopeless fantasies of mating with his queen. In other words, for all that his days are spent hopping around flowers and lapping up nectar, he is no happier than any of the humans.

If all this sounds somewhat depressing, rest assured that it is not. Ware writes and draws with immense compassion. He isn't prying or judging, only showing. On several occasions he has the building itself deliver wistful monologues about the many inhabitants who have lived under its roof over the decades. Here is the bigger picture, the long-term view. The vista opens out, and it is made clear that, in the grand scheme of things, everyday worries do not matter. This too shall pass.

Ware illustrates in the *ligne claire* style, whose most famous exponent is Tintin creator Hergé. This means simple, solid lines, fields of flat colour, and a strong overarching sense of design. He is an exquisite miniaturist, and his use of multiple panels to convey time passing, whether slowly or swiftly, is nothing short of masterful. Excerpts from *Building Stories* have appeared in numerous American publications over the past ten years, but they cohere beautifully in this book, which is much more than a thing simply to be read. It is a thing to be experienced.

The Man-Thing (2012)

"Whatever knows fear – burns at the touch of the Man-Thing!"

As taglines go, they don't get much better than that. Those ten words sum up everything you need to know about Man-Thing. Even if you were unfamiliar with the character, you'd grasp the essential premise in a flash, and you'd be intrigued to find out more.

Man-Thing first shambled his way into the Marvel Universe in 1971, in a black-and-white short tucked away in the pages of *Strange Tales* #1. He was co-conceived by Stan Lee and Roy Thomas, based (in Thomas' own words) on "the notion of a guy working on some experimental drug or something for the government, his being accosted by spies, and getting fused with the swamp so that he becomes this creature".

The scientist's name is Ted Sallis, and he is attempting to create a chemical solution that will turn men into super-soldiers, for a scheme called Project: Gladiator. When his own wife sells him out to an unidentified enemy agency (later retconned as tech-terrorists AIM), Sallis injects himself with the formula and, fleeing, crashes his car into the Florida swamps. A combination of science and, we learn in due course, mystical forces brings him back to life as a seven-foot-tall mass of sentient vegetation, super-strong and all but indestructible, his body wreathed in twisted roots and stems, his face sporting a lumpy carrot-like nose and brow and doleful crimson eyes.

There must have been something in the Manhattan air back then, beside the usual pigeons and carcinogens, because over at DC, more or less contemporaneously and entirely coincidentally, Len Wein and Berni Wrightson were dreaming up their very own human-swamp-chemicals-interface entity, Swamp Thing. Both monsters, in turn, owed a debt to Golden Age comics muck-beast The Heap, who himself was resurrected in his own title by Skywald Comics that very same year. Typical. You wait ages for a swamp monster to come along, then three turn up at once.

At any rate Man-Thing, after a guest appearance in the Ka-Zar feature in *Astonishing Tales* #12-13, was finally granted a strip of his own in October 1972, when he commandeered horror-reprint anthology *Adventure Into Fear*, beginning with #10. Gerry Conway scripted that issue, but Steve Gerber took over with #11, and it's here that Man-

Thing's story really starts.

Gerber, a Missourian newly installed on the Marvel staff and already disenchanted with writing cookie-cutter superheroics, realised that a series centred solely on a creature who can neither speak nor think, only respond empathically to the emotions of others, was going to be a tall order, not to mention a hard sell. Readers were unlikely to come back month after month to follow the adventures of a mindless, personality-free cipher who wanders around the Everglades, clashing now and then with the local wildlife and moonshine-sodden hillbillies.

Instead, the strip became a vehicle for human-interest stories and Gerber's unique brand of outsider satire. Man-Thing remained the nominal star, the mossy nucleus around which the plots orbited, but what counted were the people whose paths crossed his, a dramatis personae of angry losers, frazzled outcasts, dangerous crazies, and well-meaning but ineffectual hippies.

Nothing escaped Gerber's writerly wrath and bile. He criticised rapacious land developers, embodied in the form of the unsubtly-named businessman F.A. Schist. He tackled racism, somewhat heavy-handedly but with balance, showing flawed individuals on both sides of the black/white divide. He tweaked DC's nose with his Superman parody character Wundarr (Marvel was nearly sued by its rival over the story, and Gerber came close to being sacked by Lee). He introduced the messianic Foolkiller, a religious nut-bar prone to slaying anyone who does not meet up to his lofty moral code, using a 'ray of purity' gun. And of course he brought us the wise-quacking Howard the Duck, who debuted – along with Korrek, a barbarian who manifests out of a jar of peanut butter – in *Adventure Into Fear* #19.

Great acclaim and popularity meant that Man-Thing graduated to his own title in 1974, by which time Gerber had really hit his stride. By this point he had established that the Everglades, or rather the particular region of it centred around the town of Citrusville, was a 'Nexus of All Realities', a point of intersection between Earth and countless otherworldly dimensions. It was a masterstroke, meaning he could write in almost any genre he felt like, from high fantasy to horror to SF, simply by broaching a portal to another alternate plane and bringing in a crew of ghostly pirates, say, or a demon, or a cone-hatted, wand-wielding magician. Recurring characters, such as radio DJ Richard Rory and reincarnated sorceress Jennifer Kale, flitted in and out of the comic. Although stories were usually one-and-done, with the occasional two-parter, there was still a rare sense of ongoing continuity and inner cohesion.

The captions could sometimes be florid and overcooked, in that seventies Marvel style. A certain amount of repetition set in, too. Every issue, Man-Thing could be relied on to turn up like a misshapen *deus ex machina* and mete out moral justice by means of his incinerating fear-triggered touch, and almost invariably there would be a scene where he encounters alligators or giant snakes and flails them around like reptilian bullwhips.

For all that, the individual tales were never less than enjoyable and often nothing short of brilliant. "The Kids' Night Out!" in *Giant-Size Man-Thing* #4 is a haunting, no-holds-barred study of the deadly consequences of high-school bullying. "A Candle For Sainte-Cloud" in *Man-Thing* #15 is a powerful and moving tale of love, self-loathing and hallucination. And issues #17-18 neatly excoriate right-wing censorship and the so-called 'moral majority'.

Moreover, Gerber was a whiz when it came to dreaming up story titles. "Day Of The Killer, Night Of The Fool!", "Night Of The Laughing Dead!", "How Will We Keep Warm When The Last Flame Dies?", "A Lunatic On Every Corner!", "Pop Goes The Cosmos!" When you saw one of those in the blurb box advertising the next issue, how could you not want to buy it?

He was also blessed when it came to artists. Most of his Man-Thing scripts were graced with pencils by Val Mayerik and Mike Ploog, both of whom, if they sometimes fell short of absolute accuracy when depicting the human anatomy, could nonetheless conjure up a beautifully oozy, drippy, moody sense of place and portrayed Man-Thing himself with a glorious shaggy solidity. The same, alas, can't be said of Jim Mooney, who did the art duties on Gerber's final few issues. His stiff, romance-comics style did not suit the material, although his self-inked #20 is impressive.

Man-Thing has always been firmly a part of Marvel continuity, yet Gerber included superhero guest stars only sparingly and on his own terms: a comical two-panel 'just swinging by' cameo from Daredevil and the Black Widow, for instance, or a group of demons briefly masquerading as Spider-Man and Shang-Chi, among others. *Man-Thing* was very much Gerber's baby, his pocket universe within the Marvel

Universe.

It was fitting, then, that his swansong story, which came when the title was cancelled in #22, features himself as a character, tying up various narrative loose ends and reflecting on his creation. "Do you realise how many lives we touched – how many deaths we've recorded – how much agony and love we've split open and dissected and exposed for the world's inspection?" this fictional Steve Gerber muses, before delivering a slightly barbed signoff: "It's been fun. Honest. I'll miss it. But I really can't go on... it says here." Twenty years before Grant Morrison injected himself personally into *Animal Man*, Gerber was playing metatextual games with a comic, breaking down the fourth wall in the 'ninth art'.

Even at a time when Marvel was as renegade and undisciplined as it would ever be, the comic was trippy, head-spinny stuff (although, according to contemporary Bullpenner Steve Englehart, no drugs were involved – "Gerber's weirdness came directly from his id"). When Man-Thing was given a second crack at his own book in 1979, under the aegis of writer Chris Claremont, the results were competent enough but could not recreate the intrinsic oddity and humaneness of the earlier version.

Since then, Man-Thing has bumbled through various titles such as *Marvel Comics Presents*, *Legion Of Monsters*, *Dark Avengers* and *Thunderbolts*, and also a third series of his own. He has been possessed by an otherworldly entity, bleached white, fought zombies as a member of the Midnight Sons, used as a kind of glorified teleportation device by the Thunderbolts, identified by Satana as something called "the Vogornus Koth", and gifted with the power of speech. All in all, it seems that lots of writers love him but no one has any real idea what to do with him.

That may be because Gerber's stamp is indelibly all over the character, and always will be. The care and love he expended on Man-Thing was evident throughout his run, right down to the lengthy text pages that betrayed his ambition to be a 'proper' author, the kind who does prose not funnybooks.

Gerber died in 2008 of complications arising from pulmonary fibrosis, aged sixty. His final, unpublished Man-Thing script appeared posthumously this year as a three-issue miniseries, *The Infernal Man-Thing*, with painted art by Kevin Nowlan. Titled "Screenplay Of The Living Dead Man!" it's a sequel to 1974's memorable "Song-Cry... Of

The Living Dead Man!". In the earlier story, a writer, Brian Lazarus, is seen slowly cracking up in an abandoned insane asylum, driven mad by selling out his art in order to eke a living as an advertising copywriter. "Screenplay..." picks up his story thirty years on, after he has made a hollow success of his life writing scripts for crappy TV cartoons and Hollywood potboilers.

Lazarus seems very much a mouthpiece for Gerber, an on-the-page alter ego, railing against conformity, commercialism, the blandness of modern society, and the emptiness of lowest-common-denominator entertainment. Gerber himself did his level best not to compromise or short-change his readership. He had an integrity and an honesty that may at times have been the despair of his employers but resulted in some damn fine comics, of which *Man-Thing* is probably the prime example, along with *Howard The Duck*.

"We promise not to bog down, not to take the easy route," Gerber wrote in an editorial in *Giant-Size Man-Thing* #1. "We pledge to make each issue a *new experience*, for you and for us." It was a vow he amply fulfilled.

James Bond Comics (2013)

This is the first of three features written for Comic Heroes *under the umbrella title "Meet The Prose", in which I discuss how well-known characters from prose fiction have made the transition to the comics medium. The other two follow directly hereafter. I had intended to continue the series with pieces on Dracula, Tarzan, Conan, Zorro and others, but alas, the magazine's untimely cancellation put paid to that plan.*

He's the secret agent whose name the whole world knows: Commander James Bond of MI6. The suave super-spy who has saved the planet countless times and goes by the codename 007. The man whose gun in his pocket *does* mean he's pleased to see you.

Beginning in 1953, Ian Fleming turned out a dozen novels and eight short stories featuring the character before his death from heart disease in 1964. Since then, thanks to an extraordinarily successful movie franchise and a series of follow-up novels penned by such diverse hands as John Gardner, Raymond Benson, Charlie Higson, Sebastian Faulks and William Boyd, James Bond continues to be one of the highest-profile literary properties around.

007's fortunes in the world of comics, however, have been as mixed as a dry martini. Some of his sequential-art adventures have struck gold(finger) while others have been very much a case of (Doctor) No.

The *Daily Express* was first to hit on the idea of a James Bond comic strip. When the newspaper approached Fleming with a view to buying cartoon serialisation rights in 1957, the author was sceptical, fearing the transition to an illustrated medium would cheapen his work. "I have grave doubts about the desirability of this," he said. "Unless the standard of these books is maintained they will lose their point."

Nonetheless he overcame his misgivings, and the following year the *Express* began adapting the novels in chronological order, starting with *Casino Royale*. Anthony Hern provided the script for that strip, but Henry Gammidge then became writer for the next twelve entries in the series, apart from *Doctor No* which was written by Peter O'Donnell of *Modesty Blaise* fame.

For the most part the adaptations were faithful, and the art by John McLusky was tidy, gritty and intensively textured. The *Thunderball* strip was cut short owing to a contractual dispute between Fleming and *Express* proprietor Lord Beaverbrook, but was later concluded for syndication to other newspapers.

In 1966 writer Jim Lawrence and Czech-Russian artist Yaroslav Horak took over the job, and the quality rose several notches. Their first effort was *The Man With The Golden Gun*, based on the final Fleming novel, published posthumously in 1964. In Lawrence and Horak's version, Bond is given a greater, more personal motivation for going after Scaramanga – it is shown that the master assassin has very nearly killed a friend of his. The creators' take on *The Spy Who Loved Me* adds even more to the original. A lengthy opening sequence, in which Bond foils a SPECTRE blackmail plot in Canada, supplies story detail that the novel only sketches out in flashback.

Thereafter – aside from an adaptation of the 1968 novel *Colonel Sun*, the first ever Bond continuation, written by literary lion Kingsley Amis under the pseudonym Robert Markham – Lawrence and Horak generated all-new material. Lawrence, whose only other comics credits are scripts for issues of the UK weekly *Super Spider-Man And Captain Britain*, certainly knew his way around a great Bondian title: *Double Jeopardy*, *Sea Dragon*, *Death Wing*, *Nightbird*. But he could lapse into pulpiness, both in titling and plotting, as in *The Golden Ghost*, *The Black Ruby Caper*, *The Xanadu Connection* and *The Phoenix Project*.

The stories adhere to the Fleming formula of exotic locations, alluring females, bizarre villains, world-imperilling schemes and casual sadism. There are cool gadgets and inventions, such as a bullet-firing briefcase, a cigarette lighter that issues a jet of a knock-out gas, a watch radio, an all-terrain car equipped with a hot-air balloon, and a backpack fitted with helicopter-style rotor blades. Recurring characters from the canonical novels appear: M, Miss Moneypenny, M's Chief of Staff Bill Tanner, and Bond's CIA pal Felix Leiter. The villainous Doctor No even crops up in *Hot-Shot*, having survived his apparent death-by-a-buttload-of-guano and assumed the new identity of tiger-loving Indian businessman Huliraya.

As the strips progressed and the 1960s gave way to the 1970s, wackier fantastical themes began to creep in. There's a remote-controlled death-dealing automaton in *Fear Face*, an eerie fireball of doom in *Starfire*, space-alien kidnappers in *Nightbird*, and a vampire cult in *League Of Vampires*. Everything has a rational, mundane explanation, nothing veers off into the realm of the genuinely supernatural, but still these elements would seem more at home in the world of Steed and Mrs Peel, or indeed Scooby-Doo, than Bond.

Lawrence's dialogue has its fair share of clunky moments. Bond is forever calling women 'luv' and men 'mate', entirely out of keeping for a former naval officer and an alumnus of Eton and Fettes. He talks of a new club drug that can "groove you out of this world on absolutely cosmic highs" (*Die With My Boots On*) and defends a moment of cautiousness with the line "I never did dig that Light Brigade jive" (*The Girl Machine*). Really, 007?

Horak's art, though, is consistently impressive. His Bond has the forelock so often mentioned by Fleming, and isn't a slavish representation of either Sean Connery or Roger Moore. If anything, the character here resembles Hoagy Carmichael, the American singer whom Fleming himself felt Bond should look like.

Horak uses cross-hatching and jagged, slaloming brushstrokes beautifully, packing the panels with detail while still leaving plenty of white space to make things visually comprehensible. He also seems very happy to draw nubile females in their scanties or else entirely, if decorously, nude, whether or not this state of undress is appropriate to the surroundings or the weather. Though the choppy, episodic nature of the daily newspaper strip format can become tiresome when the stories are read in collected form, they're still hugely entertaining and on occasion are an improvement on some of the non-Fleming novels (we're looking particularly at you, Jeffery Deaver, and your *Carte Blanche*).

A couple of dozen further Bond strips continued to come out in Sweden well into the 1980s. There have also been Spanish, Dutch, Hungarian, Chilean and Japanese manga incarnations. None has yet been translated into English.

Comics adaptations of the Bond films have appeared sporadically over the years. The first was *Doctor No* in *DC Showcase* #43 (1963) by Norman J. Nodel, which was published in the UK as an issue of *Classics Illustrated*. It includes a scene cut from the movie, where a manacled Honey Rider is menaced by crabs, and No himself is killed by electrocution rather than drowned in bird poop – an altogether less sticky end. Marvel did *For Your Eyes Only* and *Octopussy* in the early eighties, the former boasting Howard Chaykin pencils utterly ruined by

Vince Colletta's inks, the latter not a bad effort from Steve Moore and Paul Neary.

Eclipse Comics then produced *Licence To Kill* in 1988, which saw Mike Grell on writing and art duties. This was a good fit of creator and material, not least since Grell had already produced the very Bondian *Jon Sable, Freelance* earlier in the decade.

Permission To Die, an all-new three-issue prestige format Bond miniseries from Grell, followed a year later, and it's far and away the best comics 007 tale there has been. Grell cleaves to the Fleming originals in plot structure and tone, while at the same time acknowledging the influence of the movies. There's a 'pre-credit sequence' which gets Bond into a dinner jacket and kilt, followed by a double-page spread which offers a montage of images from the films.

The story then sees Bond, having been provided with the latest sidearm by Q Branch, travel to Hungary and rendezvous with Luludi, gypsy daughter of Kerim Bey from *From Russia With Love*. The mission is to extract the niece of a former Soviet rocket scientist across the border into Austria and thence to Idaho, where said rocket scientist, Erik Wiziado, has fashioned himself a high-tech lair inside a former US Navy training base. Disfigured by torture, Wiziado covers half his face in a featureless mask and plays a huge, elaborate pipe organ, much like the Phantom of the Opera – and yes, he's a nutjob who intends to frighten the world into total nuclear disarmament by lobbing an atomic warhead at Victoria, capital of British Columbia.

It's a serious story with a moral message but it doesn't stint on the softcore sex and hardcore violence. The art in the middle issue is a letdown, Grell relying heavily on assistants, but overall the quality remains high. Best of all, Wiziado, unlike other Bond villains, has a conscience about his heinous acts, and is more misguided philanthropist than raving megalomaniac. You're left wondering, as Bond does, if the world might not have been a better place had his plan succeeded: "Sacrifice a few to save the many. Who knows, it might have worked... and I'd be out of a job."

In 1992 Dark Horse picked up the Bond baton and commissioned *Serpent's Tooth* from Doug Moench and Paul Gulacy. It must have seemed like a good idea – a dead cert, even – since these two were the writer/artist team that had had such a hit with their mid-70s run on Marvel's *Shang Chi, Master Of Kung Fu*. They had drawn on Bond extensively for that comic, even to the point of including a supporting character who claimed to be 007's son.

Serpent's Tooth, alas, is a bit rubbish. Moench has Bond investigating the disappearance of agent 009, who was sent to Peru to track down nuclear missiles stolen from a British submarine. The baddie is Indigo, a biogeneticist who has tried to cure himself of a rare blood disease via injections of reptilian DNA results have left him with serpentine features and a desire to set off earthquakes which will wipe out 83% of the Earth's population; what parts of the planet remain intact will be his to rule and repopulate using girls kidnapped from local native Indian villages. Oh, and he has a pair of albino henchmen and a bunch of genetically re-created extinct animals too.

Moench shoots for arched-eyebrow one-liners in the Roger Moore mode, but rarely hits the mark. The best comes when 007 is on the phone to M and has to pause in order to deck a girl who is attacking him with a boathook: "Uh, just a little interference on my end... but it's been put to rest, sir." In all, *Serpent's Tooth* is just too science-fictional, too comic-booky, to work as a Bond adventure. And the plot owes more to the movie version of *Moonraker* than it ought.

Better is *A Silent Armageddon* by Simon Jowett and John Burns, which sees Bond assigned to protect a disabled teenaged computer hacker genius, Terri Li, who is being pursued by terrorist organisation Cerberus on account of a sophisticated 'worm' program she has created. If one can overlook some very dated 'information superhighway' virtual reality gubbins, there's a decent story here and some classy, classically-styled art from Burns. Nice, too, that the principal henchman is the son of *From Russia With Love*'s formidable SMERSH officer, Rosa Klebb (she of the sensible shoes with spring-loaded, poison-tipped blades hidden in the toecaps). It's just a shame that only two issues of a projected four ever appeared, owing to problems with late delivery of artwork.

The two-issue *Shattered Helix*, also written by Jowett, is an effective mini-epic set mostly in the Antarctic, where Cerberus – again – are up to no good, trying to get their hands on a mutagenic virus which uses the human body's own immune system to destroy a person from the inside out. Bond, accompanied by a beautiful climate change scientist and some marines, infiltrates a research lab beneath the ice and faces the almost unkillable Bullock, who has Kevlar implants under his skin.

It all ends in explosions and a page's worth of eco-preaching. The art, by David Jackson, is passable, but it would have been a real treat to see the man who provides layouts and colours, David Lloyd, illustrate the whole thing himself.

By contrast *The Quasimodo Gambit*, Dark Horse's last Bond offering, published in 1995, is unmitigated tosh. The script, from the pen of Don McGregor, lacks sure-footedness, eking out a muddled storyline that has something to do with marijuana smuggling and a plan by religious fanatics to detonate bombs in Times Square at Christmas. A minor highlight is a unique torture-by-leeches scene.

Of course, this being McGregor, the comic is hideously over-written. Narrative captions crowd every panel, striving for eloquent literary profundity and missing by a mile: "There was always an undercurrent about New York that James Bond enjoyed -- a constant conflict of impressions -- from poised artifice to gutter abandon -- he relished its staccato ability to change from block to block." Throughout, McGregor can't even make his mind up whether he's writing in the past or present tense.

And the art, by Gary Caldwell, is ghastly: stiff, unimaginative, far too reliant on airbrush colouring, with characters all but indistinguishable from one another. The script tells us that the thuggish henchman Maximilian 'Quasimodo' Steel has a hunchback; Caldwell can't be arsed to depict this.

Perhaps disheartened by the awfulness of *The Quasimodo Gambit*, the Ian Fleming literary estate has not granted any further licences to publish James Bond comics since 1995. This is a shame, because Bond still has huge potential in the medium. In the right hands – those of Warren Ellis, say, or Mark Millar – the mix of low-key heroics, quippy dialogue, glamorous women and slick weaponry could be a winner.

But one shouldn't give up hope. As the end-titles of the movies always promise, "James Bond will return..."

Addenda

1) *James Bond Jr* was a spinoff TV cartoon series of the early nineties, neither much loved nor much missed. The title character is 007's nephew – not son, as the 'Jr' might lead you to assume – who attends an English private school, Warfield Academy, along with brainbox

Horace 'IQ' Boothroyd III, grandson of Q, and mulleted über-jock Gordo Leiter, son of Felix.

Villains include kid-friendly renderings of canonical characters such as Goldfinger, Odd Job and Doctor No and of movie henchmen such as Nick Nack and Jaws (here represented with a full metal jawline and jagged teeth much in the manner of the Atlas Comics barbarian character Ironjaw), alongside bespoke baddies with punsome names like Walker D. Plank, Ms Fortune and Barbella.

Marvel produced a tie-in comic of this juvenile – in every sense – farrago which lasted twelve issues. The first five adapt episodes of the series. The remaining seven are distinguished only by being early work from future superstar comics scribe Dan Abnett.

2) There have been numerous Bond parodies and homages in comics over the years, but honourable mention must go to *L. E. G. I. O. N.* Annual #5 – for all the wrong reasons.

All of DC's 1994 annuals came under the Elseworlds banner ("heroes are taken from their usual settings...", etc.), and since there was always an espionage element to the exploits of the Licensed Extra Governmental Interstellar Operatives Network, a Bond pastiche would seem like a no-brainer.

And no brain is certainly required to enjoy this laugh-free mess in which Lobo is reimagined as a crude, tuxedo-clad secret agent, first name James, working at the behest of spymaster Vril Dox. He is assisted by Stealth, who is obliged to wear a – get this – bulletproof bikini. Thudding script from Tom Peyer, shoddy art from Mike McKone – this one's a Double-0 dud.

Doc Savage Comics (2014)

Doc Savage is the forefather of comicbook superheroes as we know them. He, more than the other members of the classic pulp fiction pantheon – more than the Shadow, the Spider, the Avenger, Zorro, any of them – established the crime-fighter template which the nascent comics industry swiftly copied and expanded on.

Doc had an Arctic-based Fortress of Solitude long before Superman did. He operated out of a New York skyscraper, much like the Fantastic Four. He fought bizarre villains, many of them with names which Stan Lee would later appropriate for his own bad guys – the Leader, the Vanisher, the Metal Master. Without the Man of Bronze, would there have been a Man of Steel? Without Clark Savage Jr., an ordinary human honed to the peak of physical and mental perfection, would there have been a Batman?

Nearly two hundred Doc Savage novels were published between 1933 and 1949, the vast majority written by Lester Dent under the 'house name' Kenneth Robeson. The series was wildly popular in its day, but Doc himself has, curiously, fared less well in the medium he did so much to shape.

Even while Doc Savage was appearing in prose form, the novels' publisher, Street & Smith, tried him out in comics. A Doc strip appeared as a back-up feature in the first three issues of *Shadow Comics* in 1940 before graduating to its own title the following year. *Doc Savage Comics* started out showcasing very abbreviated adaptations of Dent stories, but with #5 it was all change as Doc was refashioned into a standard long-underwear vigilante of the kind he had helped inspire. After his plane crashes in Tibet, he discovers a blue hood with a gem in it, the 'Sacred Ruby'. The hood gives him super-strength, hypnotic powers, and the ability to fly and hurl energy blasts.

Gone was his team of loyal sidekicks, the 'Fabulous Five': chemist Andrew Blodgett 'Monk' Mayfair, lawyer Theodore Marley 'Ham' Brooks, engineer John 'Renny' Renwick, electrical genius Thomas 'Long Tom' Roberts, and archaeologist and geologist William Harper 'Johnny' Littlejohn. The interaction between these men, in particular the bickering antagonism between apelike Monk and dapper Ham, gave added life to Doc's prose adventures and helped humanise the somewhat aloof central character. (For further 'comic' relief, Monk has a pig called Habeas Corpus and Ham a monkey called Chemistry. Even ardent Doc aficionados tend to find the japesome antics of these pets teeth-grindingly aggravating.) All this was sacrificed so that Doc could become yet another caped, cowled super do-gooder.

A second series of *Doc Savage Comics* returned Doc to his costume-less roots but didn't last long, forcing him to find a berth again in the back pages of *Shadow Comics*, where he stayed until the book's cancellation in 1949. In general, the Street & Smith Doc Savage comicbook offerings are a typical product of their times, crudely executed and occasionally downright odd, as in the tale called "X – The Unknown Quantity". Here, Monk confronts the strip's artist, Al Bare, to complain about how he is drawn. "I ain't as ugly as you make me look!" Monk fulminates, to which Bare replies, "Gad! I'll make you better-looking – but it'll be a lie!"

It wasn't until 1966 that the next Doc Savage comic appeared, a one-shot published by Gold Key in order to tie in with a proposed film adaptation of the Dent novel *The Thousand-Headed Man*. At the time, Doc was enjoying a resurgence in popularity courtesy of Bantam Books, who were reprinting his adventures in mass-market paperback form. The success of the reprints was in no small part down to the sumptuous painted covers by James Bama.

The movie never happened, but the comic, written by Leo Dorfman and drawn by Jack Sparling, isn't too bad. Doc and his aides are in a race with the villainous Sen Gat to reach the mythical City of the Thousand-Headed Man in Cambodia. This is a classic treasure-filled lost city, protected by a poisonous mist derived from cobra venom. Sparling makes Doc look peculiarly old and craggy, but the energy and vigour of the source material is all there.

Six years later, Marvel acquired the comicbook licence for Doc Savage. Its first crack at the character comprised adaptations of four of the novels – *The Man Of Bronze*, *Death In Silver*, *The Monsters* and *Brand Of The Werewolf* – devoting two issues apiece to each tale. Steve Englehart did most of the scripting, and the underrated Ross Andru provided the pencils, his work looking its best in #3-4 under Tom Palmer's delicate, lustrous inks. The emphasis in these comics is very much on action, in the Mighty Marvel manner, making them good solid fast-paced fun.

A Doc Savage movie finally become a reality in 1975, produced by

George Pal and starring TV Tarzan, Ron Ely. (It was a campy mess and a box office flop. Nonetheless it is fondly regarded by some, including the author of this piece who, aged 9, saw it at his local fleapit on a double bill with… the *Dad's Army* movie!) Marvel got in on the act by relaunching its Doc strip under its black-and-white, magazine-sized Curtis imprint. The first issue offered a painted cover by Roger Kastel based on the movie poster and promised 'A Return to Greatness! '

It was no idle boast, as this comicbook version of Doc Savage, although lasting just eight issues, is a triumph. Allegedly, writer Doug Moench read only a single Doc novel before embarking on the project. If that's true, his powers of pastiche are remarkable, because his scripts get the tone and plotting exactly right.

The story titles are evocatively spot-on: "The Doom On Thunder Isle", "Hell Reapers At The Heart Of Paradise", "The Earth Wreckers", "The Sky Stealers"… The characterisation is strong too, and Moench finds room for all the elements familiar to and cherished by Doc readers. The perpetual squabbling between Monk and Ham; Doc's feisty and troublesome female cousin Pat; the pneumatic 'flea run' transport capsule which connects Doc's headquarters on the 86th floor of the Empire State Building to his waterfront warehouse, the Hidalgo Trading Company, where he stows his fleet of incredible high-tech vehicles – all are present and correct. There are baffling puzzles, cunning gadgets, lovely but deceitful women, hidden ancient civilisations, baddies with world-conquering ambitions, and supernatural-seeming mysteries which turn out to have logical explanations.

The artwork is lush. Although there are different pencillers – John Buscema, Marie Severin, Val Mayerik – almost every story carries the mark of inker Tony DeZuniga, whose use of grey wash and stippling is exemplary. DeZuniga is no slouch in the pencilling department either, as issues #5 and #6 show, and Ernie Chan's work in #8 is similarly praiseworthy. All the Marvel Doc comics were collected in two trade paperbacks in 2010 and 2011 by, erm, DC. This is because the Distinguished Competition held the licence to the character then. If you're a hardcore Doc fan or just Doc-curious, both volumes are definitely worth your time.

While Marvel held the Doc Savage licence, it toyed with the idea of folding him firmly into the Marvel Universe. To that end, Doc made co-starring appearances with both Spider-Man and the Fantastic Four's very own super-strong grumpy rock man the Thing. In issue #3 of *Giant-Size Spider-Man*, Spidey encounters a blue-skinned alien girl at a demolition site. During the building's foundation-laying ceremony forty years earlier, Doc and his aides combat a monstrous energy entity that appears to be trying to kill the very same alien girl. The two heroes never actually meet, and the same is true of the Thing and Doc in *Marvel Two-In-One* #21, at least for the first ten pages where their storylines run in parallel as they investigate separate but linked incidents at an observatory. Then their timelines merge and together they battle Blacksun, a supervillain fused from a father and son and powered by a black hole.

DC themselves took a crack at Doc in the late 80s, testing the waters with a four-issue miniseries. It was the immediately post-*Watchmen/Dark Knight* era when realistic (read: disrespectful) deconstructions of the superhero were all the rage. Writer Dennis O'Neil's tale, "The Silver Pyramid", starts in 1945 but is soon winging forward in time to the 1960s and then the present day, all nicely illustrated by the Kubert brothers, Andy and Adam. At the end of #1 Doc is seemingly disintegrated by a mad Nazi scientist's ray, leaving his son and grandson to carry on his legacy, with diminishing returns. The son, Clark Savage III, is shot dead by police after gunning down some street hoods. The grandson, known as Chip, grows up feckless and weak-willed, while Doc's five aides continue fighting the good fight but are losing their battle with the infirmities of old age.

Doc eventually returns, looking not a day older than when he disappeared. He wasn't dead, it transpires, merely trapped on a distant planet. There followed an ongoing series which notched up 24 issues plus one annual between 1988 and 1990. Here Doc is provided with a new, younger team of sidekicks to supplement the now marginalised original Five. These include a female Israeli special forces officer, Pat's granddaughter Pam, and a bearded Russian who has patterned himself after Doc.

Throughout his run, O'Neil evinces no great love for the character, so it's a relief when he retires from the writing duties with #6. Taking over, Mike Barr swiftly undoes O'Neil's most jarring and egregious misstep: Long Tom was shown to have betrayed Doc to the Nazis out of jealousy – "I was tired of living in your shadow" – but Barr reveals that he was under the influence of a mind-controlling evildoer all along. He also jettisons the ill-fitting SF story elements O'Neil introduced, and revives Doc's only recurring villain, John Sunlight, who featured in two of the original novels, *Fortress Of Solitude* and *The Devil Genghis*. Finally, after a nice four-issue crossover with DC's other ongoing pulp-hero title *The Shadow Strikes!*, the series reverts to a period setting, where it belongs.

Rod Whigham pencils almost every issue, and there isn't much to be said for his work except that it's nowhere near as poor as the art to be found in the various Doc Savage miniseries produced by Millennium Comics in the early 90s. John Sunlight is back (again) in the first of these, a tale entitled "The Monarch Of Armageddon", while the second, "Doom Dynasty", pits Doc against Dr Nikola, the occultist criminal mastermind antihero of several late-Victorian novels by Guy Boothby. The third series, "Devil's Thoughts", is a shambolic farrago set early in Doc's career and graced with art that wouldn't look out of place in the *Beano*. A fourth series, adapting the Dent novel *Repel*, was never completed. Millennium's enthusiasm for the character cannot be faulted, but the results are uniformly amateurish.

Dark Horse was next in the round-robin of licence holders, and set out its stall by teaming Doc Savage and the Shadow in a 1995 two-issue microseries, "The Case Of The Shrieking Skeletons". This sees the two crimebusters clash over their opposing methods of dealing with crooks – the Shadow kills, while Doc does his utmost to avoid taking life – but nonetheless they manage to co-operate in thwarting a Nazi plot to create a human growth serum which turns men into super-soldiers. Steve Vance's robustly enjoyable script is accompanied by decent art from Stan Manoukian and Vince Roucher, although their Doc looks hulking and slightly inhuman rather than the perfectly proportioned giant Dent describes.

Also written by Vance, the four-issue miniseries "Curse Of The Fire God" takes Doc and the Five, plus Pat, to South America. There they encounter corrupt local politicians, a crooked oil magnate, and Mayan cultists. Again, Vance provides a well-balanced mix of pulpy elements, and all the requisite character traits are present and correct, from Johnny's love of long words – "I'll be superamalgamated!" – to Pat's tempestuous temper. Gary Gianni's covers are superb; Pat Broderick's interior artwork looks sadly pedestrian by comparison.

DC grabbed Doc Savage back as part of its 2009 First Wave initiative, in which Batman, Doc, the Spirit and other non-powered heroes were reimagined in a contemporary but noirish setting. A *Batman/Doc Savage Special* by Brian Azzarello with Phil Noto on art served as a lead-in to a six-issue *First Wave* miniseries, again by Azzarello and drawn by Rags Morales. This self-contained universe also featured versions of the Blackhawks, Black Canary and pulp character the Avenger.

Twelve issues of a Doc Savage title followed, and it's unconvincing, clunky stuff, Doc's old-school heroism awkwardly juxtaposed against modern war-on-terror story elements. Writers and artists come and go, none of them able to make the hybrid work. The Avenger-starring *Justice Inc.* back-up feature, gorgeously drawn by Scott Hampton, simply blows it out of the water.

Over the years, Doc has made cameos in various different series, usually anonymously. He has a walk-on part in Dave Stevens' *The Rocketeer*, where he is identified as the inventor of the rocket-pack which the strip's hero Cliff Secord uses to fly. Two men looking very much like Monk and Ham, although never named as such, turn up at Cliff's apartment, demanding the return of the purloined rocket-pack. Then, when he runs low on fuel in mid-air, a bronze-skinned giant in jodhpurs and flying helmet comes to his rescue in an aeroplane. Cliff's mechanic pal Peevy assumes that the stranger is multimillionaire aviator Howard Hughes – but pulp fiction fans will know better.

Doc can also be seen lurking in the shadows in the final panels of *Superman Annual* #9 (part of DC's 1997 retro-tastic Pulp Heroes event); watching a newsreel of the Sub-Mariner fighting the Human Torch in *Marvels* #1, alongside Lamont Cranston, a.k.a. the Shadow; and, thinly disguised, as Doc Brass in *Planetary* #5.

Dynamite Comics, which has lately made itself a refuge for errant pulp heroes, is currently publishing a series which rivals the Marvel Moench-written strip for the accolade of best comicbook Doc adaptation. With effortless-seeming aplomb, Chris Roberson pens adventures which are faithful to the character and his world while gradually, issue by issue, nudging him forward through time into the twenty-first century. He introduces little Easter Egg references that will delight Docolytes, for instance the plant silphium which, in the novel *Fear Cay*, turns out to be the true source of the Fountain of Youth.

Bilquis Evely's disappointingly flimsy art notwithstanding, Roberson's Doc Savage is the Man of Bronze as he ought to be: decent, noble, indomitable, eternal.

Sherlock Holmes Comics (2014)

This is the revised version of the original Comic Heroes *article, which I expanded and rewrote extensively for publication in the esteemed Sherlockians' organ, the* Baker Street Journal.

The artist who most famously illustrated the adventures of Sherlock Holmes is, of course, Sidney Paget. His intense, dramatic black-and-white watercolour images provided the perfect accompaniment to many of the tales on their first publication in *The Strand*. To Paget we owe the abiding image of the great detective in a deerstalker hat, which appears in only a handful of his depictions of Holmes. The strength and vividness of Conan Doyle's prose is not in doubt, but Paget's work unquestionably enhanced it.

In comics and graphic novels, the visual likewise complements the verbal. The medium relies on the tension between image (the sequential panels of art) and word (descriptive captions, speech balloons, thought bubbles). The difference is that the pictures do at least half of the work of storytelling, if not more. They are not there simply to adorn, as Paget's illustrations did, but to form an integral part of the reading experience, helping to convey mood and control pace and narrative flow.

How, then, have comic book narratives depicted the Great Detective? How has Holmes fared over the decades in this medium where not only are authors other than Conan Doyle chronicling his adventures but illustrators other than Paget are drawing them?

Funny-pages pastiches of Holmes started appearing even as Conan Doyle was still penning new Holmes tales. In the United States, Hearst newspapers ran daily humorous strips entitled *Padlock Bones* and *Sherlocko the Monk*, while Britain's *Punch* magazine carried cartoons about "Picklock Holes" and his friend "Potson".

Perhaps the best-known of these goofy parodies is *Sherlock Jr.* (not to be confused with the Buster Keaton movie of the same name). Making its debut in 1912, this series of repetitive comedy skits revolved around the antics of an inept, none-too-bright wannabe sleuth who invariably fails to catch the villain. It was the brainchild of Sidney Smith, who soon afterwards created the immensely successful middle-class soap opera strip *The Gumps*, but its connection to Conan Doyle's creation pretty much begins and ends with the title.

The first appearance of a recognisably conventional Sherlock Holmes in a comic book was in a 1942 issue of *Captain Marvel Jr.*, where the detective helps the eponymous youthful superhero fight a baddie with the unsubtle moniker Captain Nazi. The 40s and 50s also saw *Classics Illustrated* versions of three of the four core novels, *A Study In Scarlet*, *The Sign Of Four* and *The Hound Of The Baskervilles*, along with "The Speckled Band". These are fairly text-heavy comics, as was often the way with *Classics Illustrated*, but decently abridged and competently drawn.

It wasn't until the early 1950s that we got a proper syndicated Sherlock Holmes strip, written by Edith Meiser and drawn primarily by Frank Giacoia with occasional assistance from such luminaries of the Silver Age of comics as Mike Sekowsky and Gil Kane. Giacoia would go on to become one of the premier inkers at Marvel Comics during its nascent pomp in the sixties and seventies, where his job was tracing over the pencil layouts of other artists (such as the mighty Jack Kirby) with India ink so as to make it print-ready.

The Meiser/Giacoia strips offer straight, somewhat plodding versions of tales such as "A Scandal In Bohemia" and "The Red-Headed League", alongside an occasional bespoke story such as "The Cask Of Jamaica Rum" in which the Jamaican Governor General, Sir Aubrey Poppin, is found dead, drowned in a barrel of the titular Caribbean liquor. The tales came out in daily three-panel instalments, with a slightly longer instalment for the Sunday edition, and were later reprinted by Eternity Comics in the eighties in the standard comics format.

Giacoia's artwork is never less than competent, with here and there flashes of elegance. That said, his depiction of the London docks in the abovementioned 'rum' affair makes them look more like a New England fishing port than the bustling riverside cargo wharves of a major capital city. He also opts for the classic Holmes look of deerstalker, Inverness cape and curving meerschaum pipe, which had by then come to be the standardised image of the character and would typify many of his subsequent comics appearances.

In the mid-50s Holmes was headlining in his own full-colour comic, *All New Baffling Adventures Of Sherlock Holmes*. This was published by an outfit called Charlton Comics, who were famous, perhaps notorious, for the pedestrian quality of their product. Indeed, although the Charlton imprint survived for nearly forty years before going out of business in the eighties and did manage to turn out the occasional work of note, it has in comics circles become a byword for shoddiness and banality, the epitome of cheap-and-cheerful.

What is most baffling about *Baffling Adventures.....* which lasted for just two issues, is that the setting for the stories is contemporary America rather than Victorian England. Holmes is nonetheless dressed in deerstalker and cape and speaks in an arch, formal manner, making him highly incongruous when those around him are wearing the sharp suits of the period, driving bulky town cars with whitewall tyres and saying things like "Wow! That was sensational! What a movie it will make!"

The tales, three per issue, do not draw on Conan Doyle's plots in any way, and Holmes is paired not with loyal Dr Watson but a succession of identikit police sergeants. The mysteries, written by uncredited hands, are decent enough, but the art, also uncredited, is not. The comic, anyway, was an unauthorised adaptation, and it is said that legal pressure from the Conan Doyle estate forced it to be cancelled after only a couple of issues.

The deerstalker is also present and correct in *New Adventures Of Sherlock Holmes*, published in 1960 by Dell Comics, another cheap-and-cheerful company which specialised in adaptations of licensed material and was for a brief time, in its heyday, the largest comics publisher in the world, reportedly selling 26 million copies per month.

New Adventures Of Sherlock Holmes was actually issue #1169 of Dell's *Four Color* tryout title, and did at least bear the Conan Doyle estate's seal of approval. It contains two brand new stories, neither spectacular, although the art, by Frank Giacoia again, is respectable. "The Deadly Inheritance" sees Holmes attending a séance to settle a dispute between two brothers over their father's will, while in "The Tunnel Scheme" Professor Moriarty concocts a bank robbery plan that exploits an under-construction Channel tunnel. There's quite a bit of action and gunplay, but precious little logic or analytical deduction. Poor sales did not warrant a follow-up. (Such was the chop-and-change eclecticism of *Four Color* that the subsequent issue featured the Three Stooges!)

In the late sixties a British children's weekly magazine serialised strip adaptations of *The Sign Of Four* and *The Hound Of The Baskervilles*. *Look And Learn* was primarily a vehicle for educative, copiously illustrated articles about science, history and geography but carried regular strips as well, usually across two-page spreads. The Holmes adaptations were unusual in that they employed speech balloons when the customary format for this kind of feature was illustrations with blocks of text narrative.

They also omit certain aspects of Conan Doyle's plots: there is no romance between Dr Watson and Mary Morstan in *Four*, and in *Baskervilles* several of the supporting characters are absent, making the identity of the killer that much less opaque. However, Robert Forrest's lustrous monochrome watercolour illustration puts these among the very top tier of Holmes comics. His rendering of Victorian street scenes is evocative and richly detailed, and his mist-shrouded Dartmoor is beautifully sinister, his work rivalling that of Paget himself.

Both strips have recently been reprinted in album form by a UK imprint, Book Palace Books, collected alongside a pair of somewhat more staid adaptations of two other Conan Doyle works, *The Lost World* and *Sir Nigel*. They certainly merit investigation.

In the one-off *Sherlock Holmes* (1975) from DC Comics, the noted Batman writer Dennis O'Neil – of whom more later – adapts "The Final Problem" and "The Adventure Of The Empty House", the two stories which bookend the Great Hiatus. O'Neil crams as much fisticuffs and swordplay into eighteen pages as he can. The result is a Holmes who's more of a two-fisted pulp-fiction brawler than a cerebral detective. E. R. Cruz illustrates in a classic, fluid style. Both deerstalker and pipe are prominently featured.

A year later Marvel Comics got in on the act with an adaptation of *The Hound Of The Baskervilles*, spread across two issues (#5 and #6) of the black-and-white magazine-sized anthology title *Marvel Preview*. Doug Moench does sterling work with the script, hewing close to Conan Doyle's text, complemented by Val Mayerik's nicely gnarly line-and-wash art. The deerstalker crops up only near the end, when Holmes is out on Dartmoor, and one could argue that that is at least appropriate, since a cloth, ear-flapped travelling cap is traditionally a countryman's outdoor head apparel.

After Holmes fell into the public domain – more or less – in 1980, the floodgates were opened for a torrent of new comic book adventures. Fifteen issues of *Cases Of Sherlock Holmes* from Renegade Comics – plus a further nine from Northstar Comics, who carried on the series under various titles – came out between 1986 and 1992. These contain the full unexpurgated texts of the original stories slotted around exquisite, hyper-detailed illustrations by Dan Day. Holmes here looks very much like Basil Rathbone, and somewhat like Peter Cushing as well, an actor who in common with Rathbone portrayed the character many times onscreen. For the pictures alone, these comics are worth checking out.

The same cannot be said for a brace of miniseries published by Malibu Graphics in the early 90s. *Scarlet In Gaslight* by Martin Powell and Seppo Makinen finds Holmes facing Count Dracula, a literary mash-up that had by then already featured in prose novels by Fred Saberhagen, Loren D. Estleman and David Stuart Davies, to name but three. *A Case Of Blind Fear*, from the same two creators, sees the detective clash with H.G. Wells' mad, murderous Invisible Man, and is distinguished by some truly risible cod-Victorian dialogue. Someone refers to a 'chemist shoppe', someone else calls a telegram a 'telly', and a Hansom driver is seen muttering "Blaggart stoled me cab...". Makinen's art is similarly gauche and slapdash.

Around this time, *The Case Of The Missing Martian* saw print as a four-issue miniseries from Eternity Comics. As with *Blind Fear* it fuses works by Conan Doyle and Wells. Writer Doug Murray sets the story some years after the alien invasion in Wells' *The War Of The Worlds* and puts Holmes on the trail of the body of a dead Martian that has been stolen from the British Museum. Murray also manages to shoehorn that other great Conan Doyle character, Professor Challenger, into his fast-paced tale, which is ably illustrated by Topper Helmers. *The Missing Martian* may cover similar ground to the prose novel *Sherlock Holmes's War Of The Worlds*, but unlike that extraordinarily dull book from father-and-son duo Manly Wade Wellman and Wade Wellman, it doesn't squander the exciting opportunities presented by the concept.

The creators who gave us *Scarlet In Gaslight* and *A Case Of Blind Fear*, Powell and Makinen, reunited for a further crack at the character in *Return Of The Devil*, a two-issue series published by Adventure Comics in 1992 which pits Holmes and Watson against Aleister Crowley and Professor Moriarty's vengeful brother (the latter of whom Conan Doyle mentions in passing in "The Final Problem" and *The Valley Of Fear*). A plot involving doctored cocaine provides an excuse for countless hallucinatory dream sequences, in one of which Holmes is seen making mad passionate love to his 'wife' Irene Adler. As with *Blind Fear*, there's an uncomfortable level of female nudity and implied rape.

The Curious Case Of The Vanishing Villain by Gordon Rennie and Woodrow Phoenix (Tundra, 1993) is not another Invisible Man tale as you might expect, but instead brings various other literary characters into the mix. This elegant, metafictional tale sees Dr Jekyll engaging Holmes' services in the hunt for the monstrous Hyde, who has left the pages of his own book to rampage through other literary works, including those of Edgar Allan Poe.

Yet more literary mash-up high jinks are to be found in Caliber Comics' *The Adventure Of The Opera Ghost* (1994), an ambitious affair written by Steven P. Jones and featuring characters from Gaston Leroux's *The Phantom Of The Opera*. Aldin Baroza draws in a freeform, scratchy style that seems to be deliberately aping Eddie Campbell's work on Alan Moore's celebrated Jack the Ripper deconstruction, *From Hell*, the latter instalments of which were still being published at the time *Opera Ghost* came out. Without Campbell's skill, however, not to mention Moore's consummate narrative artistry, the results are underwhelming.

The Sussex Vampire, a 1996 one-shot also from Caliber, ought to have been more entertaining than it is. Adapting one of Conan Doyle's more Gothic Holmes yarns, acclaimed British comics scribe Warren Ellis is let down by his collaborator Craig Gilmore, whose art is sloppy and inconsistent, sometimes relying on photo reference, other times adopting a contrastingly loose, angular style. Ellis himself doesn't do too badly until the final page where, when the villain's father prescribes a year in the navy as the remedy for his young son's misdeeds, the writer inserts a jarringly inappropriate caption about "rum, sodomy and the lash" that speaks of his own authorial viewpoint rather than Conan Doyle's.

Since the turn of the century, the deerstalker has been pretty much absent from Sherlock Holmes comics and there has been a greater sophistication in creators' approaches to the character. Recently Ian Edginton has penned an excellent series of graphic novel Holmes adaptations for SelfMadeHero, in tandem with I.N.J. Culbard. These versions of the four core novels are everything a Sherlockian could ask for: dark, stately and authentic, steeped in atmosphere, utterly true to the originals. Culbard's art could be described as an acquired taste, but its deceptive simplicity carries the narrative admirably.

Edginton has also given us two miniseries of *Victorian Undead* for Wildstorm, starring Holmes. In the first, the great detective – deerstalker-free except on the cover to the collection edition – grapples with a zombie plague which is tied neatly to the infamous real-life Broad Street cholera outbreak of 1854. In the second, Jekyll and Hyde show up, as does Dracula. We may have seen Holmes meet these characters elsewhere before, but Edginton and artists Davide Fabbri and Horacio Domingues handle the crossovers with vigour and originality.

A creditable back-to-basics approach to Holmes is taken with *The Trial Of Sherlock Holmes* and *The Liverpool Demon* for Dynamite Entertainment, written by husband-and-wife team John Reppion and Leah Moore (incidentally, daughter of Alan). The former miniseries opens with Holmes accused of a murder which naturally he did not commit, while the latter delves into a seedy, supernatural world of monsters and ancient artefacts.

Both are worth a look, unlike *Sherlock Holmes: Year One*, also from Dynamite. This is partly a retelling of "The Adventure Of The *Gloria Scott*" interlaced with the kind of serial-killer-committing-murders-according-to-an-elaborate-pattern plot that was innovative when it first showed up in movies such as *Theatre Of Blood*, *The Abominable Doctor Phibes* and *Se7en* but has since been done to death. Writer Scott Beatty brings nothing new to the table. Holmes here does little detecting, and the solution to the killings more or less falls into his lap. Worse is Beatty's ham-fisted grasp of British vernacular. "Bugger all!" is not an oath, it's an abstract noun, and a line of dialogue like "Cease this violence or I shall parse my own!" may sound posh and highbrow but makes no sense whatsoever when it itself is parsed.

Sherlock Holmes And The Vampires Of London is a French *bande dessinée* (literally 'drawn strip') first published in two volumes by Toulon-based imprint Soleil and just out in a single-volume English language edition from Dark Horse Comics. Yet again Holmes is confronted by bloodsucking undead creatures, but Sylvain Cordurié's script shows respect to the canon – the action takes place just after Holmes' presumed demise at the Reichenbach Falls, so the detective himself is technically 'living dead' – and the painted artwork by the mononymous Laci is very stylish indeed.

Recent TV dramas such as *Sherlock* and *Elementary* have shown how Holmes can be successfully updated into a modern context – unlike, say, Charlton's *Baffling Adventures...* – and the current comics series *Watson And Holmes* from New Paradigm Studios puts another interesting contemporary spin on the character.

The first miniseries, *A Study In Black*, has just been collected as a trade paperback. Here both the principal characters are African-Americans: Watson an ER doctor and a veteran of the war in Afghanistan, Holmes a dreadlocked private investigator and tech genius who makes his home in an apartment in 221 Baker Street in Harlem, New York. They move through a tough world of abandoned babies, class-A drugs, and arms deals. It sounds terrible but, brought to life by writer Karl Bollers and artist Rick Leonardi, it's actually superb – an urban Holmes for the digital age. There's heart here and considerable wit. Holmes' Irregulars, for instance, are a gang of streetwise hip-hop kids, one of whom greets the detective with a cheery cry of "'Sup, Holmes?"

Wittier still is *Muppet Sherlock Holmes*, a 2010 four-issue miniseries from Boom! Studios' Boom Kids! imprint. This is, believe it or not, one of the most absurdly faithful Holmes adaptations there's been. The Great Gonzo is the great detective; Fozzie Bear is Dr Watson; Kermit is Inspector Lestrade; Miss Piggy is Irene Adler, 'Miss' Hudson, and various other female characters; and further members of the Muppet cast fill out the supporting roles. Each story riffs on a classic Holmes tale, keeping the basic plot but adding all those things Conan Doyle himself somehow neglected to include, such as jokes, slapstick, sight gags, and bathos. Not to mention, in "The Red-Headed League", bad ginger wigs.

As if to prove the international appeal of the concept of Sherlock Holmes, not to mention its malleability, we may look to a recent Japanese manga series called *Young Miss Holmes* which is written and drawn by Kaoru Shintani and so far has run to five lengthy volumes. The title character is Holmes' niece, Crystal 'Christie' Margaret Hope, a ten-year-old genius who decides to join her uncle in his crime-solving activities while her parents are away in India.

Holmes and Watson both feature (interestingly the former is known by the first name "Will" in the original Japanese editions, although he is "Sherlock" in the Anglicised version), and Christie has inherited her uncle's sharp eye, command of deduction and capacity for analytical reasoning. *Young Miss Holmes* is not essential reading for any Sherlockian, and the big-eyed, cutesy artwork may put many off. Nonetheless it contains satisfying mysteries that often riff on the originals, while introducing battily surreal elements such as a dodo bird and a dog that doubles as a steed for the heroine.

Speaking of battiness, Holmes has made a couple of appearances in comics starring a superhero character whom he at least in part inspired: Batman. In 1987, DC's flagship title *Detective Comics* reached its 572nd issue. The comic was a bumper-sized anniversary celebration commemorating fifty years of the Dark Knight, which happened to coincide with Holmes' own centennial. One segment of the story takes place in the Victorian era, where Holmes and Watson uncover a conspiracy masterminded by Professor Moriarty which has ramifications in the present day for Batman and Robin, along with fellow DC sleuths Ralph Dibny – a.k.a. the rubbery, stretchable Elongated Man – and hardboiled private eye Slam Bradley.

Right at the very end, a stooped, elderly figure in deerstalker and Inverness cape ambles out of the shadows to join the group of gathered heroes. It is none other than Holmes himself, a twinkly-eyed gent still very much alive at the ripe old age of 135, a pipe clamped firmly between his lips (although when Batman offers a match to light it for him he comments ruefully that it "is purely for show these days").

The writer of that issue, Dennis O'Neil, is evidently a Sherlock aficionado, because Holmes has an even more substantial part to play in an issue of *The Joker*, which O'Neil also wrote. This short-lived 1970s series starred Batman's giggling green-haired nemesis in mostly light-hearted capers, and issue #6, "Sherlock Stalks The Joker", has the two characters pitting their wits against each other. The twist is that it's not actually Holmes; it's a theatrical actor essaying the role onstage who, as a result of getting socked in the head twice by the "Clown Prince of Crime" during a performance, falls under the delusion that he genuinely is Holmes.

The Joker elects to recreate famous cases from the canon in his own zany style, while the ersatz Holmes pursues and eventually bests him. O'Neil lards his script with in-jokes and nudge-nudge references. The surname of the actor with the bruised noggin is Sigerson. A man who heads up a hockey league has the nickname Red. A hamburger chain proprietor called Bruce Partington has plans for a new restaurant. On a tugboat christened (somewhat improbably) *The Baskervilles*, the Joker steals the latch for a hatch, an item known in nautical parlance as a 'dog'. For those whose tolerance for terrible, convoluted puns is high, this comic is a bit of a gem.

So we have travelled a long way from Paget's refined depictions, and the road has not always been smooth. Nevertheless Sherlock Holmes has in the end proved his singular worth in comic books and graphic novels, and there is no reason to think that he won't continue to do so. The deerstalker may be gone, for which most of us will be grateful, but Holmes himself endures in the comics medium, whether it is as man, superman or Muppet.

Also from Steel Quill Books

In *Sibilant Fricative* Adam Roberts considers a broad spectrum of speculative fiction, from fantasy to science fiction, from literature to films. The book opens with insightful consideration of Philip K Dick's oeuvre followed by Ridley Scott's *Blade Runner*, and closes with a volume-by-volume analysis of Robert Jordan's *Wheel of Time* opus. One thing the author never loses sight of is the need to entertain.

"*Sibilant Fricative* is undoubtedly one of the finest collections of essays that genre criticism has ever produced."
— *Jonathan McCalmont, BSFA Vector magazine*

"...the essay on the "Two Hobbits" is worth the entry ticket alone, and there is so much more entertainment within... Erudite, entertaining, intelligent collection of essays and reviews." – *The Bristol Book Blog*

"Adam Roberts makes everything wonderful. If he wrote non-fiction about drying paint, I would still be the first in line to read it."
— *Jared Shurin of Pornokitsch.*

~

"*Titan* is one of the blandest pieces of fiction I have come across in four decades of reading novels. If the Campbell shortlist is a high-class curry restaurant of delicious, spicy and stimulating food, then *Titan* is a single slice of white bread and margarine on a white plate under the neon light of a truck drivers' café." *on Titan by Ben Bova*

"I challenge you to read 'similar to what one might find' without thinking 'the play what I wrote'... He piles stuff upon stuff, and at the end we're presented a hardback-bound big pile of stuff. And all of it rendered in dead, humourless, grey prose..." *on The Edge of the World by Kevin J Anderson*

"Let me see if I can boil down *Crossroads of Twilight*'s 700-pages for you. Drivel. There you go." *on Crossroads of Twilight by Robert Jordan.*